THINKING STRATEGIES:
ADDITION

BUILDING MASTERY OF ADDITION FACTS

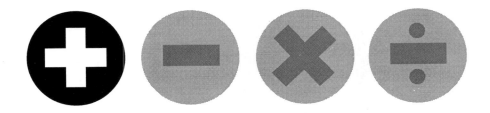

CELIA BARON

PORTAGE & MAIN PRESS

Portage & Main Press acknowledges the financial support of the Government of Canada through the Book Publishing Industry Development Program (BPIDP) for our publishing activities.

Printed and bound in Canada by The Prolific Group
Book and cover design: Relish Design Studio Ltd.
Illustrations: Jess Dixon

Library and Archives Canada Cataloguing in Publication

Baron, Celia
 Thinking strategies : addition : building mastery of addition facts / Celia Baron.

 ISBN 1-55379-016-2

 1. Addition – Study and teaching (Elementary) 2. Addition – Problems, exercises, etc. I. Title.

QA115.B375 2004   372.7'2044   C2004-903665-3

Acknowledgments

I would like to thank everyone who has helped make *Thinking Strategies: Addition* a reality. In particular, I would like to thank the many teachers and students who piloted the original manuscript. I would also like to thank Leigh Hambly and the staff at Portage & Main Press.

PORTAGE & MAIN PRESS

100-318 McDermot Avenue
Winnipeg, Manitoba
Canada R3A 0A2

Tel.: 204.987.3500
Toll free: 800.667.9673
Fax: 866.734.8477
E-mail: books@portageandmainpress.com

To my four children –
you have added so much to my life.

CONTENTS

Introduction   1

Level 1: Facts with 0, 1, 2, and 3   5

Level 2: Facts with 9 and 10   29

Level 3: Double Facts   49

Level 4: The Near-Doubles   71

Level 5: Facts with 8   91

Level 6: Remaining Facts   109

Appendix A: Teacher Resources   131

Addition Grid   132

Power Facts/
Summaries of Thinking Strategies   133

Progress Report for Students   139

Self-Assessment Progress Report for Students   140

Letter to Parents/Guardians   146

Appendix B: Partner Bingo   147

Partner Bingo   148

Appendix C: Challenge Facts   179

Challenge Facts   180

Appendix D: Playing Cards   201

Playing Cards   202

Appendix E: Templates   217

Ten-Frame Mat   218

Working Ten-Frames   219

Mini Ten-Frames   222

Ten-Frame Train   223

Number Cards   224

Dot Cards   230

Appendix F: Answer Keys   233

Student Activity Sheets   234

Partner Bingo   247

INTRODUCTION

PROGRAM GOAL

Thinking Strategies: Addition is a program designed to help students master the basic addition facts. The program accomplishes this goal by (1) introducing the facts in logical rather than numerical order and (2) using the commutative or turnaround property (teaching facts like 2 + 3 and 3 + 2 together). The program uses the mathematical processes of communication, connections, reasoning, representation, and problem solving to encourage learning. Teachers can use *Thinking Strategies: Addition* with an entire class, small groups, or individual students.

WHAT ARE THE BASIC ADDITION FACTS?

The basic addition facts are combinations, like 5 + 8 or 9 + 3, in which the addends (numbers being added) are less than 10. Because our number system is a base ten number system however, the program also includes addition facts in which the numbers being added are 10, as well as the numbers that are less than 10.

WHAT IS MASTERY OF THE BASIC FACTS?

In his book, *Elementary and Middle School Mathematics*, John Van de Walle defines mastery of a basic fact as a quick response time of less than three seconds. When a student is able to correctly respond to a fact automatically and without thinking, he/she has mastered that fact.

Building mastery of the basic facts involves the following four stages:

> Stage 1: incorrect response/an inappropriate thinking strategy
>
> Stage 2: correct response in more than three seconds using an appropriate thinking strategy
>
> Stage 3: correct response within three seconds using an appropriate thinking strategy
>
> Stage 4: correct response that is automatic and occurs without thinking

Mastery develops with practice (reviewing a variety of facts or procedures). The practice is provided in the program through student activity sheets, Power Facts, Partner Bingos, Card Games, and Challenge Facts.

Mastering the Basic Facts: The Latest Research

Van de Walle states that all students are able to master the basic facts if they follow three steps:

1. develop a strong understanding of the operations and number relationships

2. develop efficient thinking strategies for fact retrieval

3. practice the use and selection of those strategies

WHAT IS A "THINKING STRATEGY"?

A thinking strategy is a way of thinking that helps complete a fact *quickly*. For a strategy to be a thinking strategy, it must be done *mentally*, and it must be efficient.

The more senses you can involve when introducing the facts, the greater the likelihood students will remember how to complete the facts. Different strategies work for different students. By providing a variety of strategies, students can choose what works best for them. Some strategies are visual – for example, the special pictures that are used to complete the double facts. Some strategies are auditory and involve rhymes. Many of the strategies involve patterns and connecting facts that students have yet to learn with facts they already know how to complete.

PROGRAM LEVELS

Thinking Strategies: Addition is divided into six levels. Each level begins by having the students model the facts introduced in that level. These models are visual representations of the facts and help students understand why a fact is completed the way it is. Once the students have developed and understand the strategies of that level of the program, they practice the strategies. The facts are then incorporated with the facts introduced in previous levels. At the end of each level, a Level Challenge activity helps students identify and apply thinking strategies to the facts introduced to that point of the program.

Level 1: The first level examines the basic addition facts with an addend of 0, 1, 2, or 3. It introduces the concept of addition, the commutative or turnaround property, and many of the models used in the program. Four important relationships students should develop for the numbers 1 through 10 are discussed, and games and activities to practice these relationships are provided. In this level, the thinking strategies for the facts with an addend of 0, 1, 2, or 3 are introduced.

Level 2: In the second level, the basic addition facts with an addend of 9 are examined. Three important relationships students should develop for the numbers 10 through 20 are discussed, and games and activities to practice these relationships are provided. The thinking strategies for facts with an addend of 9 involve anchoring to the number 10.

Level 3: The third level examines the doubles, which are basic addition facts that have the same addends. A number of thinking strategies are introduced for completing the doubles. One strategy involves special pictures for the doubles.

Level 4: The fourth level examines the near-doubles, which are basic addition facts with addends that differ by one. Many of the near-double facts were introduced in the first three levels of the program. The near-double facts can be related to the double facts; the near-double thinking strategy based on this relationship is developed in this level.

Level 5: In the fifth level, the basic addition facts with an addend of 8 are examined. Only three facts with an addend of 8 and their turnarounds have not been introduced in the program by level 5. These facts are among the most difficult to learn. A variety of thinking strategies are developed for these facts.

Level 6: The sixth level examines the remaining basic addition facts. There are only three remaining facts and their turnarounds left to introduce. A variety of thinking strategies are developed for these facts.

PROGRAM COMPONENTS

Teacher Lessons

The lessons give clear directions for working through the program and provide instructions that teachers can use to help students master the addition facts. The lessons involve working with models and developing number relationships. Students are encouraged to find as many strategies as possible for completing the facts. With many strategies to choose from, students soon find the strategies that work best for them.

Class Discussion

Class discussions are an integral part of the program. The following are some statements and questions that can be used to encourage student participation in class discussions:

- Explain and justify your answer.
- Explain your answer in another way.
- Can someone else explain the answer in another way?
- As a group, describe a different way to find the answer.
- If you did not know how to complete this fact, what thinking strategy would you use?
- What is another fact that you can complete this way?
- How can you model this fact with a picture?
- How can you model this fact with another picture?
- How does this model explain the fact?
- Make up a story problem for this fact.
- How does your story problem illustrate the fact?

Practice for Students

The student activity sheets support understanding of number relationships and give students practice with the basic addition facts. The activity sheets, which consist mainly of secret messages, line designs, and puzzles, are intended to be fun and engaging. They have the added advantage of being mainly self-correcting.

The program makes it easy to monitor the progress of students. A level challenge activity is at the end of every level. The Level Number Challenge checks each student's ability to identify and apply the appropriate thinking strategies to the facts introduced to that point in the program. Teachers can keep track of students' progress in other ways. As the students complete each level of the program, have them make a list of the facts they have yet to master. Have the student practice these facts both at school with a classmate and at home with a parent. When the student is able to complete these facts, check them off on the student's progress report (page 139). While students are working on the activity sheet that accompanies each lesson, teachers can also check which facts students can complete.

At the completion of a level, teachers will find suggestions for more practice. Students who have not yet mastered the facts introduced in that level can still continue to the next level of the program. They will have more opportunities to practice these facts in the levels that follow.

Addition Grid

At the beginning of the program, hand out a copy of the addition grid to each student (page 132). In each level of the program, students are asked to fill in the grid for the facts they have been introduced to. Teachers may also want to keep a master grid.

Power Facts

There are six sets of Power Facts (pages 133-138) – one set for each level in the program. Each set has 20 facts. The facts consist of those that are introduced in that level plus some of the more difficult facts from previous levels. The Power Facts are asked only after the thinking strategies for those facts have been fully developed.

The Power Facts are intended to support the learning of the addition facts. Ask these facts in class each day. Allow students no more than three seconds to complete each fact on their answer sheet, and then read out the addition fact and its sum (answer). If the students have been unable to complete the fact in three seconds, or if they have completed it incorrectly, have them write the completed fact on their answer sheet. Wait 5-7 seconds between facts to give the students time to process the fact. Students can measure their improvement each day as they are able to complete more facts correctly.

Each set of Power Facts is given in rows and columns. It is important to change the order in which the facts are asked. One day ask them vertically, the next day horizontally, then from top to bottom, and another day from bottom to top. Also, change the order of the addends in the facts.

Partner Bingo

Partner Bingo (page 147) is a two-player game. Students can play it in class or at home with parents and siblings. Players have a bingo card and 16 facts that they take turns completing. As they complete each fact in order, they shade in one square on their bingo card. The same number might appear in more than one box on the bingo card, and the students must choose which to fill in. The first player to complete a row, column, or diagonal is the winner.

Partner Bingo provides practice with the basic addition facts in a fun game setting. The games are a positive way for parents to determine which addition facts their children are able to complete and which facts need more practice. There are Partner Bingo games in each level of the program.

Challenge Facts

The Challenge Facts (page 179) consist of addition facts for each level of the program. Recent research does not support using timed tests to help students master the facts. Some students become very anxious when faced with timed tests, and this can affect their sense of their ability to do mathematics.

The Challenge Facts are included in the program as a diagnostic tool. Teachers can use these sheets to find out which facts the students have mastered and which facts they have not mastered. The students can circle the facts on the Challenge Facts sheets that require more practice. There are no time limits for completing the Challenge Facts. Discourage students from guessing. Completing a fact incorrectly reinforces the incorrect answer.

There are two types of Challenge Facts, A and B, in all levels except Level 1. Type A Challenge Facts consist of the facts introduced in a particular level. Type B Challenge Facts contain all of the facts introduced in the program up to that level. Students can use the Level A Challenge Facts to practice the facts developed in that level. Students can use the Level B Challenge Facts to practice the facts introduced to that point. Students can also use the Level B Challenge Facts to practice identifying facts. To do this, students can draw shapes or use coloured pencils to identify facts that are completed with the same strategies.

Playing Cards

Playing Cards (page 201) are provided for each level of the program, with an extra deck for the first level. A "deck" of playing cards consists of forty cards, ten sets of four cards each. Each set consists of four different ways to represent a fact. The cards can be laminated. The students can play various card games with these decks, including War, Fish, Snap, and Concentration. Two extra "decks" are included: one containing dot patterns; the second with representations of the numbers 1 through 10.

Ten-Frames

The ten-frame is a powerful model for completing the addition facts. Various sizes of ten-frames are included in the program. Encourage students to use these ten-frames to model and complete addition facts. As well, a ten-frame train, together with passengers, is provided in the program (page 223).

Number Cards

Number Cards for the numbers 1 through 20 are included in the program (pages 224-229).

Teacher Assessment

The intent of the program is not only to have the students master the basic facts, but also to have them do so in a positive manner. The evaluation and assessment should reflect this. Continuous assessment and evaluation allow recognition of student achievement. When students are successful in mastering the facts, they feel good about themselves and about their ability to learn. A powerful

assessment tool is to have the students keep track of the facts that they have mastered. Doing so allows the students to see how much they are learning and to feel a sense of accomplishment.

The National Council of Teachers of Mathematics recommends the integration of assessment and instruction. The program *Thinking Strategies: Addition* supports this integration. The student activity sheet that accompanies each lesson allows teachers to assess whether or not the students are following the program. As well, many of the activities are self-correcting and allow the students to know if they have understood the lessons.

Teachers can also use the Power Facts to assess the progress of students. Students can hand in their Power Facts answer sheets each day, or they can track their own progress. With either method, the teacher can use the results to complete the students' progress reports. A student progress report for each level is included in the program (page 139).

Student Self-Assessment

In this program, students can track which facts they have mastered and which facts they have yet to master. As they complete each level of the program, have the students write about the facts they are learning in their journals. Ask them to indicate whether or not the facts in the level that they are working on are easy for them to complete. Have them explain why or why not. They may want to list both the facts they have mastered and the ones they have yet to master. Have them describe thinking strategies for the facts they have yet to master. If students need help in identifying thinking strategies, work with them to find the strategies. A student self-assessment progress report for each level is included in the program (pages 140-145).

Using Individual Response Boards

Student response boards can be either a chalkboard or a dry-erase board made of laminated sheets of cardboard. In classrooms where each student has a response board, the students can write the sums of the facts on their boards. Teachers can check off the students' progress reports as the students show the answers on their boards.

Teachers in classes with no response boards can have students mouth the answer. This method of response provides students with opportunities to answer a question, and it allows the teacher to monitor the progress of his/her students.

Parental Guidance

Teachers might want to involve parents in the learning process. Power Facts and thinking strategies can be sent home with students so that they can practice the facts with their parents as they are being taught the facts in class. Parents can also help their children by playing Partner Bingo with them.

MODELS USED IN THE PROGRAM

The following models are used in the program:

- Ten-Frames: A ten-frame is an array of 2 rows and 5 columns in which counters or dots represent numbers. The top row is filled in first, beginning on the left. Once the top row is full, the second row is filled in, again beginning on the left. For example, the fact 5 + 2 is illustrated by the following ten-frame:

- Cube Trains: A cube train consists of a row of cubes. The cube train modelling the fact 5 + 2 consists of 5 cubes of one colour and 2 cubes of another colour.

- Dominoes: The domino modelling the fact 5 + 2 consist of 5 dots on one side of the domino and 2 dots on the second side.

One or two addition buddies appear on each student activity sheet. The buddies illustrate a fact introduced in that lesson of the program. The fact is usually the first fact of the activity sheet.

LANGUAGES IN ADDITION

Van de Walle explains that it is useful to think of number sentences, models, and word problems as three separate languages. For example, the fact 5 + 2 can be expressed in the following ways:

- A number sentence would be 5 + 2 = 7.
- A model could be a ten-frame that contains 5 dots in the first row and 2 dots in the second row.
- A word problem could be a story problem involving 5 pencils and 2 pencils.

When students complete a fact, having them translate from one language to another helps them develop operation meaning. Understanding the concept of addition is the foundation for mastering and applying the addition facts. Many of the facts of each level are introduced with story problems. As well, students are encouraged to create their own story problems throughout the program.

DIFFFERENT CLASSES OF ADDITIVE STRUCTURES

Van de Walle explains that most researchers identify four categories of addition problems. Two examples of story problems from each category are given. The second set of problems involves humour. These categories, based on the kind of relationships involved, are the following: join problem, result unknown; separate problem, initial unknown; part-part-whole problem, whole unknown; compare problem, larger unknown.

- Join Problem: Result Unknown

  Leah has 5 pencils. Her friend Cathy gives her 2 more. How many pencils does Leah have altogether?

- Separate Problem: Initial Unknown

  Brian had some marbles. He gives 4 to Garrett. Now Brian has 7 marbles. How many marbles did Brian have before he gave some to Garrett?

- Part-Part-Whole Problem: Whole Unknown

  Aisha has 2 dogs and 3 turtles. How many pets does she have altogether?

- Compare Problem: Larger Unknown

  Danica has 3 more books than her sister Candace. If Candace has 8 books, how many books does Danica have?

The following story problems use humour to illustrate the different categories of additive structures.

- Join Problem: Result Unknown

  A giraffe has 5 bowties. A friend gives the giraffe 2 more bowties. How many bowties does the giraffe have altogether?

- Separate Problem: Initial Unknown

  An elephant has some watches and gives 3 to an antelope. Now the elephant has 5 watches. How many watches did the elephant have before he gave some to the antelope?

- Part-Part-Whole Problem: Whole Unknown

  A rabbit is holding 8 carrots in one paw and 5 carrots in the other paw. How many carrots is the rabbit holding altogether?

- Compare Problem: Larger Unknown

  Baby Bear is so hungry she eats 2 more bowls of porridge than Papa Bear does. If Papa Bear eats 4 bowls of porridge, how many bowls of porridge does Baby Bear eat?

LEVEL 1: FACTS WITH 0, 1, 2, AND 3

LEVEL 1 OVERVIEW

In Level 1, students are introduced to all of the basic addition facts with an addend of 0, 1, 2, or 3, and to number relationships they can and should develop with numbers 1 through 10. These number relationships are the basis of building an understanding of the operation of addition and of the thinking strategies introduced in this program. The importance of these relationships cannot be overstated.

Number Relationships 1 Through 10

In his textbook, *Elementary and Middle School Mathematics,* John Van de Walle lists the following four relationships that students can and should develop with numbers 1 through 10:

■ spatial relationships

■ one and two more, one and two less

■ anchors, or benchmarks, of 5 and 10

■ part-part-whole relationships

These relationships are very important in building an understanding of the addition facts; check that your students have developed them. If your students need more practice with these relationships, consider the activities suggested in the first level of the program.

Spatial Relationships

Spatial relationships refer to the ability to recognize sets of 1 to 10 objects in patterned arrangements and to tell how many there are without counting. To determine if your students have developed this relationship, play Dot-Pattern Flash, which uses the pattern arrangement of 1 to 10 dots (page 230): Present students with a patterned arrangement of dots for a few seconds. Have them write the number of dots they see on their response boards. This exercise allows you to check whether students can tell how many dots there are without counting. Play until students do not have to count the number of dots.

Refer to the first set of "playing cards" (pages 202-203). The students can use these cards to play games of Snap, War, Fish, and Concentration. The game of dominoes also can provide the students with practice of patterned arrangements of dots.

The One- and Two-More, One- and Two-Less Relationships

Other relationships that students should develop for the numbers 1 through 10 are one and two more, one and two less (John Van de Walle 2001). Before students are able to develop these relationships, they must be able to count up from 1 to 10 and count back from 10 to 1. To check that students can do this, start with a number less than 10. For example, start with the number 4, and have the students count up to 9. Or start with the number 8, and have the students count back to 5.

The one and two more, one and two less than relationships involve more than the ability to count on or count back one or two. They involve the understanding that, for example, the number 8 is one more than the number 7 and two more than the number 6. Completing addition facts with an addend of 1 or 2 involves the one-more-than and two-more-than relationships.

Check that your students have developed these relationships: Present 6 counters to the students. Ask the students:

■ How many counters are there? (6)

■ How many counters would there be if 2 counters were added? (6 counters and 2 counters are 8 counters)

Ask the students to explain how they found the answer 8. Their answers will provide you with important information about their number sense development. Some students will say they counted on from the number 6 ("6 → 7, 8"). Others will say they counted all ("1, 2, 3, 4, 5, 6, 7, 8"). Others will say they "just knew" that 8 is two more than the number 6. The students who say they knew that two more than the number 6 is 8 have already developed the two-more-than relationship.

It is important that all students develop the one-more-than and two-more-than relationships. Provide students who are still counting all (e.g., "1, 2, 3, 4, 5, 6, 7, 8") with more experiences with numbers until they are able to count on (e.g., "6 → 7, 8"). The following activities can help students who are counting on to develop the one-more-than and two-more-than relationships. The two examples will help students develop the one-more-than and two-more-than relationships.

(1) Distribute counters to the students. Present five to seven dot-pattern cards to them (page 230). Have them use counters to construct sets that are either one more than or two more than the set shown on the cards.

(2) Play Dot-Pattern Flash (with a twist). Instead of writing the number of dots they see on their response boards, have them write the number that is one more than or two more than the number of dots they see.

Anchoring Numbers to 5 and 10

Our number system is a base ten number system. Because two 5s make ten, the numbers 5 and 10 can serve as anchors for number relationships. For example:

■ Students can anchor the numbers 6 and 7 to the number 5. They can think of the number 6 as 5 and 1, and the number 7 as 5 and 2.

■ Students can anchor the number 4 to the number 5. They can think of 4 as 5 less 1.

■ Students can anchor the numbers 8 and 9 to the number 10. They can think of 9 as 10 less 1, and 8 as 10 less 2.

These relationships are very important and will help the students in completing their addition facts.

Introducing the Ten-Frame

The most powerful model for anchoring the numbers to 5 and 10 is the ten-frame. The ten-frame is an array of 2 rows and 5 columns in which counters or dots are placed to illustrate numbers.

Give each student a ten-frame mat and counters (page 218). Ask the students to use the counters to display the number 7 on their ten-frame. Have them fill the top row first, beginning on the left. Once the first row is full, have them place the remaining counters in the second row, again beginning on the left. Have the students note that 7 is displayed as 5 and 2.

Give the students other numbers from 1 to 10 to display on their ten-frame mats. Encourage the students to note how these numbers are anchored to 5 or 10. For example, 6 is displayed as 5 and 1, and 9 is displayed as 10 less 1.

Have the students make the connection between the ten-frame and their fingers. They have 5 fingers on each hand and 10 fingers on both their hands.

The ten-frame is a powerful model because it allows the students to visually anchor the numbers from 1 to 10 to the numbers 5 and 10 – students can picture the numbers they are adding. The more senses involved in learning, the more effective the learning will be. The ten-frame is used throughout this program.

The Ten-Frame Train

To help the students with the ten-frame, draw a train car with the ten-frame as the window. Explain to the students that this train is filled when there are 10 passengers in it. Have the passengers on the train sit in the order in which counters are placed on ten-frames.

Note: Illustrations of ten-frame trains and passengers are on page 223.

Ten-Frame Flash

Refer to the page containing ten-frames (page 220). Place one ten-frame on the overhead for a few seconds. Turn off the overhead, and ask the students how many dots they saw. Have the students write their answer on their response boards. Check whether the students are able to answer without counting the dots. Continue to do this activity with the students until they can answer without counting the dots.

Part-Part-Whole Relationships

Conceptualizing a number as being made up of two or more parts is the most important relationship a child can develop about numbers (John Van de Walle 2001). The part-part-whole relationship is fundamental to understanding addition.

Check that students understand that 4 and 1 makes 5. The models used in the program reinforce the part-part-whole relationship. This relationship can also be referred to as the part-part-all relationship.

If students need more practice with this relationship, have them create sets with two shapes of pattern blocks or two-colour counters and find the total number in each set.

Thinking Strategy: Addend of 1

The thinking strategy for an addition fact with an addend of 1 is based on the one-more-than relationship.

Consider, for example, the fact 8 + 1.

8 + 1 (addend of 1)

■ One-More-Than:
   One more than 8 is 9.
   SO, 8 + 1 = 9

Thinking Strategy: Addend of 2

The thinking strategy for an addition fact with an addend of 2 is based on the two-more-than relationship.

Consider, for example, the fact 5 + 2.

5 + 2 (addend of 2)

■ Two-More-Than:
   Two more than 5 is 7.
   SO, 5 + 2 = 7

Check that students can count on 2 correctly.

Thinking Strategy: Addend of 3

The thinking strategy for an addition fact with an addend of 3 is the following:

Consider, for example, the fact 6 + 3.

6 + 3 (addend of 3)

■ Count on 3:
   6 → 7, 8, 9
   SO, 6 + 3 = 9

Most students will need to count on 3 from 6. Check that they are able to count on 3.

The Commutative Property of Addition

The commutative, or turnaround, property of addition means that the sum of an addition fact is the same regardless of the order of the numbers being added. It is a powerful tool in mastering addition facts, and it is used throughout the program.

Students are introduced to turnaround facts, for example, 9 + 1 and 1 + 9, 5 + 2 and 2 + 5, 6 + 3 and 3 + 6 together. Since turnaround facts have the same sum, students can use the same strategy for the fact 1 + 9 as they use for 9 + 1, the same strategy for the fact 2 + 5 as they use for 5 + 2, and the same strategy for the fact 3 + 6 as they use for 6 + 3.

Consider, for example, the fact 1 + 9.

1 + 9 (addend of 1)

- One-More-Than:
  One more than 9 is 10.
  SO, 1 + 9 = 10

Thinking Strategy: Addend of 0

The thinking strategy for an addition fact with an addend of 0 is the following:

Consider, for example, the fact 6 + 0.

6 + 0 (addend of 0)

- Pattern of 0:
  The sum of a number and 0 is the number.
  SO, 6 + 0 = 6

The same strategy is used to complete the turnaround fact 0 + 6.

Level 1 consists of the following lessons:

Lesson 1A: Domino Rally with 1, 2, and 3

This lesson introduces the spatial and part-part-whole relationships for the numbers 1 through 10 as well as the operation of addition. The terms *sum* and *addend* are also introduced.

Lesson 1B: Ten-Frame Rally

This lesson introduces the ten-frame model. The ten-frame model is emphasized throughout the program.

Lesson 1C: Ten-Frame Rally with 1, 2, and 3

This lesson introduces the one-more-than and two-more-than relationships for numbers 1 through 10. Thinking strategies for facts with addends of 1, 2, and 3 are also introduced.

Lesson 1D: Match-Ups with 1, 2, and 3

This lesson introduces thinking strategies for facts with addends of 1, 2, and 3.

Lesson 1E: Cube Train Rally with 1, 2, and 3

This lesson introduces the commutative, or turnaround, property of addition.

Lesson 1F: Wacky Webs with 1, 2, and 3

In this lesson, students practice completing facts with an addend of 1, 2, or 3. They are also introduced to even and odd numbers.

Lesson 1G: Domino Rally with 0

This lesson introduces addition facts with an addend of 0.

Lesson 1H: Number Design with 0, 1, 2, and 3

In this lesson, students complete facts with addends of 0, 1, 2, and 3 by identifying and applying the appropriate thinking strategies.

Lesson 1I: Secret Message with 0, 1, 2, and 3

In this lesson, students continue to complete facts with addends of 0, 1, 2, and 3.

Lesson 1J: The Level 1 Number Challenge

This challenge assesses the students' ability to identify and apply appropriate thinking strategies to the facts introduced in Level 1. Students also review models and vocabulary introduced so far in the program.

ADDITION GRID

The addition facts considered in this level are the following:

+	0	1	2	3	4	5	6	7	8	9	10
0	0	1	2	3	4	5	6	7	8	9	10
1	1	2	3	4	5	6	7	8	9	10	
2	2	3	4	5	6	7	8	9	10		
3	3	4	5	6	7	8	9	10			
4	4	5	6	7							
5	5	6	7	8							
6	6	7	8	9							
7	7	8	9	10							
8	8	9	10								
9	9	10									
10	10										

LESSON 1A: DOMINO RALLY WITH 1, 2, AND 3

TEACHER LESSON

In this lesson, students are introduced to the operation of addition and the part-part-whole relationship. Spatial relationships that students should develop for the numbers that are less than or equal to 10 are also introduced.

Interpreting the Operation of Addition

Present the following story problem to the students:

- Amber has 4 bracelets. Her friend Tania gives her 1 more bracelet. Have many bracelets does Amber have altogether?

Have the students draw a picture showing the story problem and solve the problem.

- Amber has 5 bracelets altogether.

Note: This story problem illustrates the additive structure of joining; result unknown. Other additive structures are possible and are discussed in the Introduction to the program (page 4).

Ask the students to represent the story problem as an addition sentence.

- 4 + 1 = 5 (4 and 1 is 5)

Ask the students to describe other situations that illustrate this fact. Some examples are:

- 4 pencils and 1 pencil are 5 pencils
- 4 apples and 1 apple are 5 apples
- 4 friends and 1 friend are 5 friends

Introductory Terms

Tell the students that in an addition sentence, the parts are called *addends* and the whole is called the *sum*. For example, in the addition sentence 4 + 1 = 5, the numbers 4 and 1 are called the *addends*, and the answer, 5, is called the *sum*.

Part-Part-Whole Relationships

It is important for students to be able to conceptualize a number as being made up of two or more parts. The part-part-whole relationship is fundamental to understanding addition. The models used in the program reinforce the part-part-whole relationship. The domino model reinforces this relationship: the dots on each side of a domino indicate the parts; the total number of dots on the domino indicates the whole. If students need more practice with the development of this relationship, have them create sets with two shapes

of pattern blocks or two-colour counters and find the total number in each set.

Important! Continue to provide the students with activities that let them practice the part-part-whole relationship until they develop it.

Spatial Relationships

Spatial relationships refer to the ability to recognize sets of 1 to 10 objects in patterned arrangements and tell how many there are without counting. It is one of the important number relationships students should develop for the numbers 1 to 10. Check that your students have developed this relationship by playing games with the Dot Cards (page 230). These can include Fish, Concentration, Snap, and War. The dot cards can also be flashed on the overhead.

The Domino Model

Dominoes provide experiences with recognizing patterned arrangements of dots. The following are the arrangement of 1 to 10 dots on dominoes.

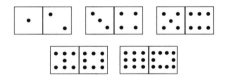

Note: Students will likely find it easier to recognize other arrangement of dots for the numbers 7, 8, and 10 (for example, 4 + 3, 4 + 4, and 5 + 5). Have the students discuss other possible arrangements of dots on dominoes.

Important! Continue to provide the students with activities that let them practice spatial relationships until they develop them.

Encouraging Class Discussion

Engaging students in whole-class discussions is an integral part of the program. Prompts for encouraging class discussions can be found on page 2 of the Introduction.

INTRODUCING THE STUDENT ACTIVITY SHEET

Distribute a copy of the sheet, Domino Rally, to each student. Read the instructions aloud as a class, and have the students complete the activity. Allow the students to draw their own arrangements of dots on the dominoes.

Domino Rally

The answer to an addition fact is called the *sum*. The sum of the addition fact 4 + 1 is 5. The addition buddy is showing the addition fact 4 + 1 with a domino.

Draw dots on the blank dominoes (below) to show the addition facts, or show what addition fact each domino represents and complete the facts.

Finally, do what the sentence at the bottom of the page asks.

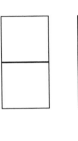

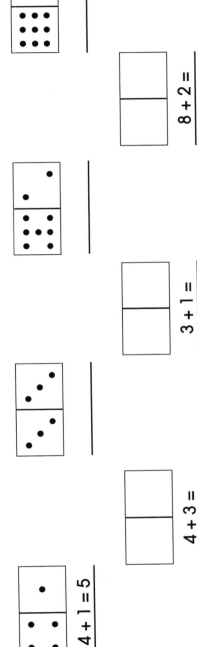

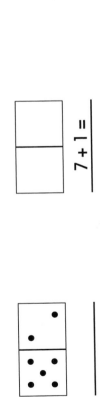

4 + 1 = 5

4 + 3 =

3 + 1 =

8 + 2 =

2 + 2 =

7 + 1 =

Draw dots that show three different dominoes with sums of 8.

LESSON 1B: TEN-FRAME RALLY

TEACHER LESSON

In this lesson, students are introduced to the ten-frame. The ten-frame is perhaps the most important model for anchoring numbers in our number system. Ten-frames are a powerful visual model that can not only help students complete their addition facts but also help students understand the base ten number system. The ten-frame model is emphasized throughout the program.

Anchoring Numbers to 5 and 10

Our number system is a base ten number system. Because two fives make ten, the numbers 5 and 10 can serve as anchors in our numeration system.

- Students can anchor the numbers 6 and 7 to 5. They can think of the number 6 as 5 and 1, and the number 7 as 5 and 2.

- Students can think of the number 4 as 5 less 1.

- Students can anchor the numbers 8 and 9 to 10 by thinking of 9 as 10 less 1, and 8 as 10 less 2.

These relationships are very important and will help the students in completing their addition facts.

Introducing the Ten-Frame

The most powerful model for anchoring the numbers to 5 and 10 is the ten-frame. The ten-frame is an array of 2 rows and 5 columns in which counters or dots are placed to illustrate numbers.

Give each student counters and a ten-frame mat. Have the students use the counters to display the number 6 on their ten-frame mat.

Explain to students that although there are many ways to place 6 counters on a ten-frame, the counters are to be placed as follows:

- Fill the top row, beginning on the left.

- When the first row is full, place the remaining 1 counter in the second row, again beginning on the left.

Have the students note that 6 is displayed as 5 and 1.

Give the students other numbers from 1 to 10, and have them display these numbers on their ten-frame mats. Encourage the students to note how these numbers are anchored to 5 and 10. For example, 7 is displayed as 5 and 2, and 9 is displayed as 10 less 1.

Point out to the students the connection between the ten-frame and the fingers on their hands. They have 5 fingers on each hand and 10 fingers on both their hands.

The Ten-Frame Train

To reinforce the ten-frame, draw a train with a ten-frame as the window. Have the students place passengers on the train in the same order as they place counters on a ten-frame.

Note: Illustrations of ten-frame trains and passengers are on page 223.

Ten-Frame Flash

Refer to the page of ten-frames (page 220). Flash a ten-frame on the overhead for a few seconds. Ask the students to write the number of dots they saw on the ten-frame on their response boards.

When the students have finished writing the number on their response boards, show them the ten-frame. Explain to the students how the number of dots compares to the number 5 or 10. For example, if there are 6 dots on the ten-frame, point out there are 5 dots in the first row and 1 dot in the second row, and that 1 more than 5 is 6. If there are 7 dots on the ten-frame, point out there are 5 dots in the first row and 2 dots in the second row.

If ten-frames are new to students, consider playing Ten-Frame Flash with ten-frames that have dots in only the first row.

Important! Continue to play Ten-Frame Flash with the students until they can recognize the number of dots on the ten-frames without counting.

Encouraging Class Discussion

Engaging students in whole-class discussions is an integral part of the program. Prompts for encouraging class discussions can be found on page 2 of the Introduction.

INTRODUCING THE STUDENT ACTIVITY SHEET

Distribute a copy of the sheet, Ten-Frame Rally, to each student. Read the instructions aloud as a class, and have the students complete the activity. (The students must show each of the numbers from 1 through 10 on the given ten-frames.)

Ten-Frame Rally

The addition buddy is showing the number 6 with a ten-frame that has 5 dots in the first row and 1 dot in the second row.

Below, use the ten-frames to show each of the numbers from 1 up to and including 10. All of the ten-frames must have a different number of dots. In some of the frames, you will have to fill in the missing dots.

6

3

___

___

5

9

___

___

___

___

LESSON 1C: TEN-FRAME RALLY WITH 1, 2, AND 3

TEACHER LESSON

In this lesson, students are introduced to the one-more-than and two-more-than relationships. They also model addition facts with addends of 1, 2, and 3 with ten-frames.

Interpreting the Operation of Addition

Present the following story problem to the students:

- Tyler has 5 goldfish and 2 neons in his fish tank. How many fish does he have altogether in his fish tank?

Have the students illustrate this story problem and solve it.

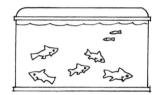

- Tyler has 7 fish altogether.

Note: This story problem illustrates the additive structure of part-part-whole; whole unknown. Other additive structures are possible and are discussed in the Introduction to the program.

Ask the students to represent the story problem as an addition sentence.

- 5 + 2 = 7

The One-More-Than and Two-More-Than Relationships

The one-more-than and two-more-than relationships are important relationships that students should develop for the numbers 1 through 10.

Present the students with the addition facts 5 + 2 and 8 + 1, and have them complete the facts.

    5 + 2 = 7
    8 + 1 = 9

Check how the students have completed these facts. It is important that all students develop the one-more-than and two-more-than relationships. Provide students who are still counting all (e.g., "1, 2, 3, 4, 5, 6, 7, 8") with more experiences with numbers until they are able to count on (e.g., "6 → 7, 8"). The following activities can help students who are counting on to develop the one-more-than and two-more-than relationships. Students who complete the facts because they, for example, "just know that 2 more than the number 5 is 7" have developed the two-more-than relationship.

See the Level 1 Overview for activities that will help students develop the one-more-than and two-more-than relationships (page 5).

Important! Continue to provide the students with experiences to practice the one-more-than and two-more-than relationships until they develop them.

Modelling Addition Facts with Ten-Frames

Give each student counters of two colours and a ten-frame mat. Present the students with the following addition facts:

    5 + 2
    8 + 1
    7 + 3

Have the students model the facts on their ten-frame, representing the two addends with different coloured counters. Have them complete the facts.

- The addition fact 5 + 2 is modelled with 5 counters in the first row and 2 counters in the second row.

Point out to the students that 5 counters in the first row and 2 counters in the second row show the number 7.

Note: The ten-frame encourages students to recognize that the number 7 is two more than the number 5.

- The addition fact 8 + 1 is modelled as follows:

Point out to the students that 8 counters and 1 counter leave one empty square in the ten-frame.

- The addition fact 7 + 3 is modelled as follows:

Point out to the students that 7 counters and 3 counters fill the ten-frame.

Ten-Frame Flash (with a twist)

When students can recognize the dots on a ten-frame, play Ten-Frame Flash (with a twist). Show them ten-frames, and ask them for the number that is one-more-than or two-more-than the number indicated on the ten-frame.

Encouraging Class Discussion

Engaging students in whole-class discussions is an integral part of the program. Prompts for encouraging class discussions can be found on page 2 of the Introduction.

INTRODUCING THE STUDENT ACTIVITY SHEET

Distribute a copy of the sheet, Ten-Frame Rally, to each student. Read the instructions aloud as a class, and have the students complete the activity.

Ten-Frame Rally

The addition buddy is showing the addition sentence 5 + 2 = 7 with a ten-frame that has 5 solid dots in the first row and 2 dots in the second row.

Name the addition sentences shown by the ten-frames or show the addition facts on the ten-frames. Complete the facts. Then do what the sentences at the bottom of the page ask.

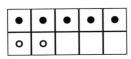

5 + 2 = 7

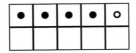

_____

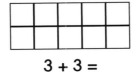

3 + 3 =

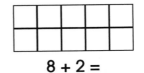

8 + 2 =

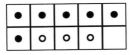

_____

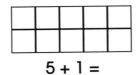

5 + 1 =

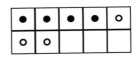

_____

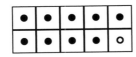

_____

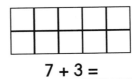

7 + 3 =

Show the thinking fact 5 + 3 on a ten-frame. Complete the fact. Explain your answer.

LESSON 1D: MATCH-UPS WITH 1, 2, AND 3

TEACHER LESSON

In this lesson, students are introduced to thinking strategies for facts with addends of 1, 2, and 3.

Introducing the Thinking Strategies: Addend of 1 or 2

The one-more-than and two-more-than relationships are the bases of the thinking strategies for facts with an addend of either 1 or 2. Present students with the following facts:

9 + 1
7 + 2

Have the students use the one-more-than and two-more-than relationships to complete the facts.

(a) 9 + 1 (addend of 1)

■ One-More-Than:
   One more than 9 is 10.
   SO, 9 + 1 = 10

(b) 7 + 2 (addend of 2)

■ Two-More-Than:
   Two more than 7 is 9.
   SO, 7 + 2 = 9

Counting on 1 or 2

If students have not yet developed the one-more-than and two-more-than relationships, encourage them to complete facts 9 + 1 and 7 + 2 as follows.

For 9 + 1, have them count on 1 from 9: "9 → 10."
To complete the fact 7 + 2, have them count on 2 from 7: "7 → 8, 9."

Note: If students have not developed the one-more-than and two-more-than relationships, provide them with experiences until they develop them. Examples of activities that will help them develop these relationships are given in the Level 1 Overview.

Introducing the Thinking Strategy: Addend of 3

Counting on 3 is the basis of the thinking strategy for facts with an addend of 3. Present the following fact to the students.

5 + 3 (addend of 3)

■ Count on 3:
   5 → 6, 7, 8
   SO, 5 + 3 = 8

Counting on 3

Encourage the students to count on 3 as follows: Have them say the number 5, pause, then say the numbers 6, 7, 8. Have them say these numbers in a rhythm.

Show them how to count on 3 a few times (e.g., for 5 + 3, say: "5 → 6, 7, 8"), then have them count on together out loud as a class. You can also clap your hands as they count on.

Next, present a number from 3 to 10, and have the students mouth the numbers as you clap your hands.

Continue to do this throughout the first level until students can successfully count on 3.

Note: Encourage students who are still using their fingers to count on without their fingers.

Encouraging Class Discussion

Engaging students in whole-class discussions is an integral part of the program. Prompts for encouraging class discussions can be found on page 2 of the Introduction.

INTRODUCING THE STUDENT ACTIVITY SHEET

Distribute a copy of the sheet, Match-Ups, to each student. Read the instructions aloud as a class, and have the students complete the activity.

Note: Students will find that the connecting lines of each set of addition facts form a pattern. They can use the patterns to check their work.

Note: If students need help completing the facts in this activity, have them model the facts on the blank ten-frames (page 219). Continue to have them do so until they are able to use the thinking strategies to complete the facts.

COMPLETING THE ADDITION GRID

Distribute a copy of the addition grid (page 132) to each student. Tell students they will be using this grid throughout the program. Explain to them that the grid will provide them with a record of their progress.

Have the students fill in the addition grid for all facts with addends of 1, 2, and 3, and with sums that are less than or equal to 10. Have students fill in both rows and columns of the grid.

Match-Ups

Complete each addition fact by connecting the dot beside the fact to the dot beside its sum.

When you have completed the "match-ups," answer the question at the bottom of the page.

6 + 2 •	• 4		5 + 3 •	• 4
7 + 3 •	• 9		2 + 2 •	• 8
8 + 1 •	• 10		9 + 1 •	• 5
2 + 2 •	• 8		5 + 2 •	• 7
4 + 3 •	• 5		4 + 1 •	• 10
1 + 1 •	• 2		6 + 3 •	• 2
2 + 3 •	• 7		2 + 1 •	• 6
4 + 2 •	• 3		3 + 3 •	• 3
1 + 2 •	• 6		1 + 1 •	• 9

What thinking strategy did you use for completing the fact 6 + 2? Explain your answer.

LESSON 1E: CUBE TRAIN RALLY WITH 1, 2, AND 3

TEACHER LESSON

In this lesson, students are introduced to pairs of facts like 6 + 2 and 2 + 6 at the same time and will examine whether or not turnaround facts have the same sum.

Turnaround Facts

Present the addition fact 6 + 2 to the students. Beside it, write the addition fact 2 + 6. Tell the students that these two facts can be called *turnaround facts*. Divide the class into cooperative working pairs. Distribute a copy of the student activity sheet to each pair of students.

Modelling Facts

Distribute two colours of interlocking cubes to each pair of students, and have them use these cubes to construct cube trains. Have them use one colour to represent one addend and the other colour to represent the other addend. Have one student in each pair model the fact 6 + 2 and the other student model its turnaround, 2 + 6. The cube trains for the facts 6 + 2 and 2 + 6 are modelled as follows:

6 + 2   2 + 6

The Commutative Property of Addition

After all students have completed the activity sheet, ask them: Do turnaround facts have the same sum?

- Turnaround facts have the same sum. The order of the addends does not affect the sum.

Have them use their cube trains to explain why turnaround facts have the same sum. If they have difficulty, offer the following explanation:

- Consider the cube train modelling the fact 6 + 2. If the cube train is turned and viewed from right to left, or turned 180°, it now looks like the cube train modelling the fact 2 + 6. Both cube trains are made up of the same number of cubes. The sum of 6 + 2 is the same as the sum of 2 + 6. This explanation is true for all turnaround facts.

Explain to students that this property is called the *turnaround* or *commutative property of addition*. The commutative property of addition means that the sum of an addition fact is the same regardless of the order of its addends. It is a powerful tool in mastering the addition facts, and it is used throughout the program.

Identifying Turnaround Facts

Present students with pairs of facts, some that are turnarounds and some that are not. Have the students indicate the pairs of facts that are turnarounds by either raising their hands or giving the thumbs-up sign.

Applying the Commutative Property of Addition

Present the addition fact 2 + 6 to the students. Have them complete the fact and explain their thinking strategy.

2 + 6 (addend of 2)

- Two-More-Than:
  Two more than 6 is 8.
  SO, 2 + 6 = 8

The commutative property of addition allows the students to use the two-more-than strategy whether or not 2 is the first or the second addend of the fact. When students are asked to complete a fact with an addend of 1, 2, or 3, have them begin with the greater number and find one, two, or three more than the larger number. For example, for the fact 2 + 6, if students have not yet developed the two-more-than relationship, have them start with the larger number, 6, then pause, and count on 7, 8. Present other facts that have a first addend of 1, 2, or 3, and have the students complete them. Ask the students which number they should begin with (the greater number). Have them complete the fact.

Encouraging Class Discussion

Engaging students in whole-class discussions is an integral part of the program. Prompts for encouraging class discussions can be found on page 2 of the Introduction.

INTRODUCING THE STUDENT ACTIVITY SHEET

Students will have completed the activity sheet and explained why the pair of turnaround facts 6 + 2 and 2 + 6 have the same sum.

Cube Train Rally

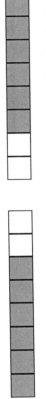

You can show the addition facts 6 + 2 and 2 + 6 with cube trains.

The numbers 6 and 2 are called *addends*, and the facts 6 + 2 and 6 + 3 are called *turnarounds*.

Below, name the addition sentences shown by the cube trains, and find the sum of each. Then, answer the question at the bottom of the page.

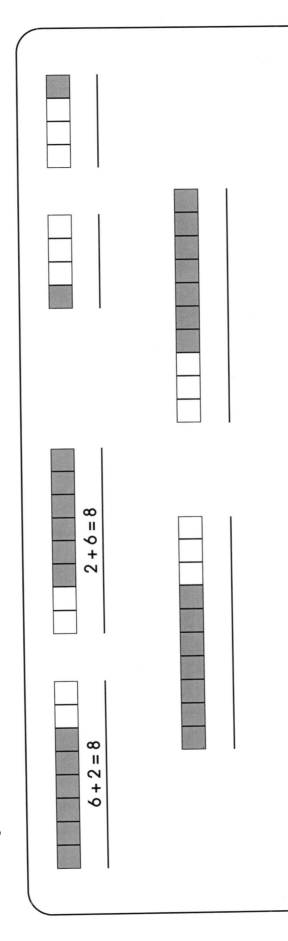

6 + 2 = 8

2 + 6 = 8

Do the addition facts 6 + 2 and 2 + 6 have the same sum? Explain your answer.

LESSON 1F: WACKY WEBS WITH 1, 2, AND 3

TEACHER LESSON

In this lesson, students practice completing addition facts with an addend of 1, 2, or 3, and they are introduced to even and odd numbers.

Identifying and Applying Thinking Strategies

Present students with the following addition facts:

3 + 6
2 + 7
1 + 9

Have students complete each fact and explain the thinking strategy they used for each. Have the students first note whether the facts have an addend of 1, 2, or 3.

(a) 3 + 6 (addend of 3)

■ Count on 3:
$6 \rightarrow 7, 8, 9$
SO, 6 + 3 = 9

Note: Make sure the students recognize that the fact has an addend of 3; they can start with 6 and count on 3.

(b) 2 + 7 (addend of 2)

■ Two-More-Than:
Two more than 7 is 9.
SO, 2 + 7 = 9

Note: Check that students recognize the fact has an addend of 2; they can start with 7 and use the two-more-than relationship.

(c) 1 + 9 (addend of 1)

■ One-More-Than:
One more than 9 is 10.
SO, 1 + 9 = 10

Note: Check that students recognize the fact has an addend of 1; they can start with 9 and use the one-more-than relationship.

Practicing One-More-Than, Two-More-Than, and Count on 3

To provide practice in completing facts with addends of 1, 2, and 3, consider the following:

Present numbers from 1 to 9, and ask the students to name the number that is one more than each number. Next, present numbers from 1 to 8, and ask the students to name the number that is two more than each number. Do the same for the numbers from 1 to 7; ask the students to name the number that is three more than each number.

Even and Odd Numbers

Distribute 10 cubes to each student. Ask the students to divide the cubes into 2 equal groups.

■ The 10 cubes can be divided into 2 groups of 5.

Explain to the students that a number such as 10 (which represents 10 objects) that can be divided into 2 equal groups is called an *even number*.

Have the students use the cubes to find other even numbers less than or equal to 10.

■ The numbers 2, 4, 6, and 8 are also even numbers because they can be divided into 2 equal groups.

Tell the students that the number 0 is also considered to be an even number.

Now ask the students if they can divide 9 cubes into 2 equal groups.

■ The 9 cubes cannot be divided into equal groups.

Tell the students that a number like 9 (which represents 9 objects) that cannot be divided into 2 equal groups is called an *odd number*.

Have the students use the cubes to find other odd numbers less than or equal to 10.

■ The numbers 1, 3, 5, 7, and 9 are also odd numbers because they cannot be divided into 2 equal groups.

Note: Further discussion of even and odd numbers, including rules for even and odd sums, is given in Lesson 6G. This lesson only introduces students to even and odd numbers.

Encouraging Class Discussion

Engaging students in whole-class discussions is an integral part of the program. Prompts for encouraging class discussions can be found on page 2 of the Introduction.

INTRODUCING THE STUDENT ACTIVITY SHEET

Distribute a copy of the sheet, Wacky Webs, to each student. Read the instructions aloud as a class, and have the students complete the activity. (In addition to completing the facts, students have to colour all cells – middle, inner, and outer – that have an even number.)

Note: The coloured cells form a pattern that students can use to check their work. The pattern provides an introduction to the rules for even and odd sums.

Wacky Webs

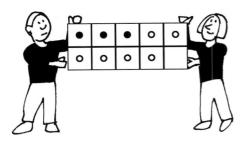

The numbers 0, 2, 4, 6, 8, and 10 are **EVEN** numbers.

The numbers 1, 3, 5, 7, and 9 are **ODD** numbers.

Below, fill in the outer cells of each web by adding the numbers in the inner cells with the number in the middle.

Colour all of the cells that have an **EVEN** number.

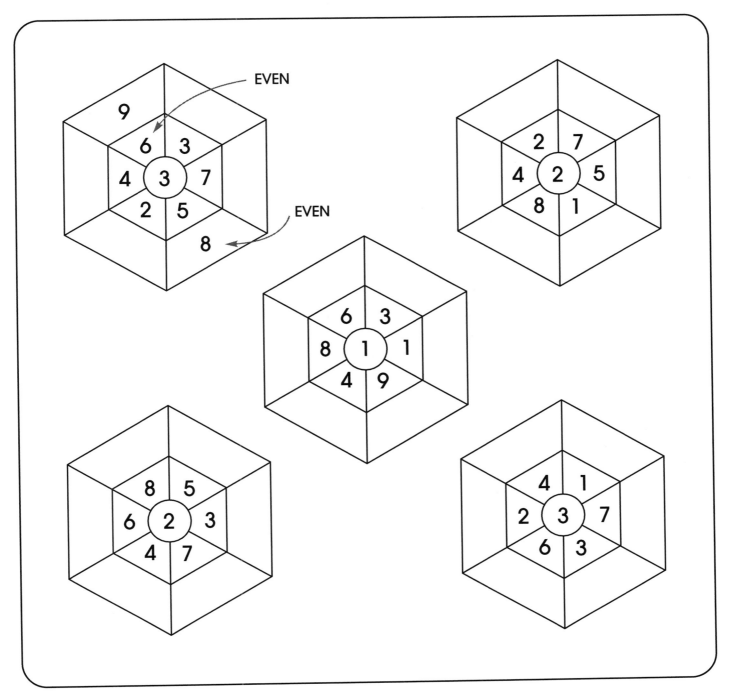

LESSON 1G: DOMINO RALLY WITH 0

TEACHER LESSON

In this lesson, the students are introduced to addition facts with an addend of 0.

The Concept of the Number 0

Ask the students what the number 0 means to them. The concept of a number 0 is not an easy one. Discussing the number 0 as a class can be helpful.

Interpreting the Operation of Addition

Present the addition fact 5 + 0 to the students. Have them illustrate the fact. Examples can include the following:

- 5 pencils and 0 pencils are 5 pencils
- 5 candies and 0 candies are 5 candies
- 5 dogs and 0 dogs are 5 dogs

Ensure students understand that when they add 0 to a number, the sum is that number. Some students may believe that when two numbers are added, the sum is always greater than the numbers being added. Have them note that when 0 is added to a number, nothing is being added to the number, and the sum is just the number.

Distribute a copy of the student activity sheet to each student. Divide the class into cooperative working pairs. Have the students model the facts on the activity sheet by drawing dots on the dominoes and/or by naming the addition sentences the dominoes show. Each domino on the activity sheet must have a different sum, and one side must remain blank. Have the students explain their thinking strategy for adding a fact with an addend of 0.

Creating Story Problems

It is important that students understand why the sum of a number and 0 is the number, not simply be told that it is a rule they must follow. One way to help the students understand what it means to add with 0 is to have them create story problems.

Ask the students to create story problems illustrating the fact 5 + 0. Suggest the story problem involve crackers. Have them solve their story problems and draw pictures illustrating them.

Introducing the Thinking Strategy: Addend of 0

When students have completed the student activity sheet, ask them what thinking strategy they used for completing a fact with an addend of 0.

- The sum of a number and 0 is the number.

Note: Check that students understand the strategy and are able to complete facts with 0. If students require practice with facts with an addend of 0, have them work with dominoes or other manipulatives until they understand the strategy. They can also model these facts on blank ten-frames (page 219).

Practicing the Thinking Strategy: Addend of 0

Present the following addition facts to the students:

$$5 + 0$$
$$0 + 7$$

Have students complete these facts with the strategy for facts with an addend of 0.

(a) **5 + 0** (addend of 0)

- Pattern of 0:
  The sum of a number and 0 is the number.
  SO, 5 + 0 = 5

(b) **0 + 7** (addend of 0)

- Pattern of 0:
  The sum of 0 and a number is the number.
  SO, 0 + 7 = 7

Note: Ensure students recognize they can use the pattern of 0 strategy regardless of whether 0 is the first addend or the second addend of the facts.

Encouraging Class Discussion

Engaging students in whole-class discussions is an integral part of the program. Prompts for encouraging class discussions can be found on page 2 of the Introduction.

INTRODUCING THE STUDENT ACTIVITY SHEET

Students will have completed the activity sheet and explained the thinking strategy for addition facts with an addend of 0.

Domino Rally

The addition buddy is standing beside a domino that shows the addition fact 5 + 0.

Below, fill in the dominoes, and complete the addition fact that each shows. All dominoes must have one side with no dots, and each must have a different sum. Then, answer the question at the bottom of the page.

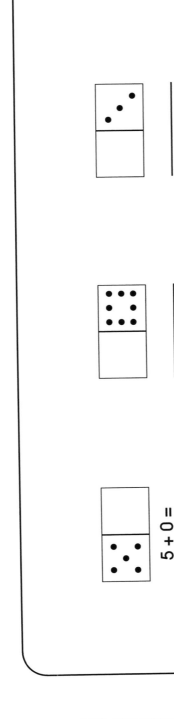

1 + 0 = _____

_____

0 + 4 = _____

5 + 0 = _____

0 + 0 = _____

What thinking strategy do you use when you add a number with 0? Explain your answer.

LESSON 1H: NUMBER DESIGN WITH 0, 1, 2, AND 3

TEACHER LESSON

In this lesson, students complete facts with addends of 0, 1, 2, and 3 by identifying and applying the appropriate thinking strategies.

Identifying and Applying Thinking Strategies

Present the students with the following addition facts, each with a missing addend:

$$
\begin{array}{cccccc}
 & 3 & 0 & & & 2 \\
+\,6 & +\,\rule{1em}{0.4pt} & +\,\rule{1em}{0.4pt} & +\,7 & +\,5 & +\,\rule{1em}{0.4pt}
\end{array}
$$

Have the students replace the missing addend with the number 0.

$$
\begin{array}{cccccc}
0 & 3 & 0 & 0 & 0 & 2 \\
+\,6 & +\,0 & +\,0 & +\,7 & +\,5 & +\,0
\end{array}
$$

Have the students complete the facts.

$$
\begin{array}{cccccc}
0 & 3 & 0 & 0 & 0 & 0 \\
+\,6 & +\,0 & +\,0 & +\,7 & +\,5 & +\,2 \\
\hline
6 & 3 & 0 & 7 & 5 & 2
\end{array}
$$

Have students explain their thinking strategy for completing the facts: The facts can all be completed using the pattern of 0. Remind the students that this strategy can be used for all facts with an addend of 0. Consider, for example, the fact 0 + 6.

0 + 6 (addend of 0)

■ Pattern of 0:
   The sum of 0 and a number is the number.
   SO, 0 + 6 = 6

Next have the students replace the missing addends with the number 1. Have them complete the facts and explain their thinking strategy.

Have students continue by replacing the missing addends by the number 2 and then the number 3.

Practicing Identifying Facts

If students need practice in identifying the facts, do the following:

1. Give each student four pieces of paper.
2. Have the students write one of the numbers "0," "1," "2," and "3" on each piece.
3. Present addition facts to the students.

Ask students to indicate if the facts are pattern of 0, one-more-than, two-more-than, or count on 3 facts by holding up the piece of paper with that number on it. If a fact does not have an addend of 0, 1, 2, or 3, tell them not to hold up any paper.

Addition Facts with Ten-Frames

For students who are having difficulty completing facts with addends of 0, 1, 2, and 3, have them model the facts on the activity sheet of this lesson on the blank ten-frames found on page 219.

Encouraging Class Discussion

Engaging students in whole-class discussions is an integral part of the program. Prompts for encouraging class discussions can be found on page 2 of the Introduction.

INTRODUCING THE STUDENT ACTIVITY SHEET

Distribute a copy of the sheet, Number Design, to each student. Read the instructions aloud as a class, and have the students complete the activity.

Note: The coloured areas form a pattern that students can use to check their work.

CHALLENGE FACTS

Use the Challenge Facts, Level 1 (pages 180-181), to help the students recognize facts with addends of 0, 1, 2, and 3. Have students place shapes around the facts with the same addends (for example, circles around all the facts with an addend of 2) and then complete them. Next, have them place triangles around the facts with an addend of 3, and so on. They can also use different coloured pencils to identify the facts.

POWER FACTS

Have students use Power Facts to practice the thinking strategies for facts with an addend of 0, 1, 2, or 3. Hand out the Power Facts, Level 1 (page 133), and have the students practice the first set of Power Facts at least once a day. Students can practice in class or at home. At this point in the program, also give students the letter for parents (page 146) to take home.

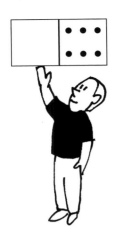

Number Design

Complete the addition facts below. When you are finished, follow the Colour Key, and colour the design.

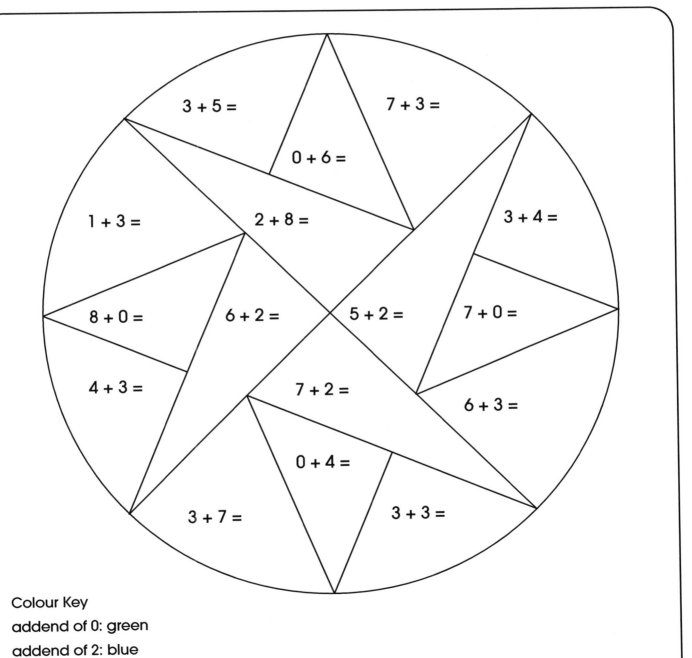

$3 + 5 =$

$7 + 3 =$

$0 + 6 =$

$1 + 3 =$

$2 + 8 =$

$3 + 4 =$

$8 + 0 =$

$6 + 2 =$

$5 + 2 =$

$7 + 0 =$

$4 + 3 =$

$7 + 2 =$

$6 + 3 =$

$0 + 4 =$

$3 + 7 =$

$3 + 3 =$

Colour Key

addend of 0: green

addend of 2: blue

addend of 3: yellow

LESSON 11: SECRET MESSAGE WITH 0, 1, 2, AND 3

TEACHER LESSON

In this lesson, students complete facts with addends of 0, 1, 2, and 3.

Practicing Thinking Strategies

Present the following addition facts to the students:

> 3 + 7
> 0 + 8
> 9 + 1
> 2 + 3

Have the students complete the facts. The students must be able to recognize and apply an appropriate thinking strategy for each fact, then explain their thinking strategy. Have the students first note whether the facts have an addend of 0, 1, 2, or 3.

(a) 3 + 7 (addend of 3)

■ Count on 3:

> $7 \rightarrow 8, 9, 10$
> SO, $3 + 7 = 10$

Note: Some students will complete this fact by picturing the ten-frame. Encourage them to do so.

(b) 0 + 8 (addend of 0)

■ Pattern of 0:

> The sum of 0 and a number is the number.
> SO, $0 + 8 = 8$

(c) 9 + 1 (addend of 1)

■ One-More-Than:

> One more than 9 is 10.
> SO, $9 + 1 = 10$

Note: Some students will complete this fact by picturing the ten-frame. Encourage them to do so.

(d) 2 + 3 (addend of 2/addend of 3)

■ Two-More-Than:

> Two more than 3 is 5.
> SO, $2 + 3 = 5$

■ Count on 3:

> $2 \rightarrow 3, 4, 5$
> SO, $2 + 3 = 5$

Note: Because the fact 2 + 3 has both an addend of 2 and an addend of 3, students can choose a strategy for either addend. Discuss with students why it is easier to start with 3 and use the two-more-than strategy.

Continue to ask the students to complete addition facts with addends of 0, 1, 2, and 3.

Ten-Frame Flash

Continue to play Ten-Frame Flash with the students. In addition to recognizing the number shown on the ten-frame, ask them for the number that is one-more-than or two-more-than the number shown.

Encouraging Class Discussion

Engaging students in whole-class discussions is an integral part of the program. Prompts for encouraging class discussions can be found on page 2 of the Introduction.

INTRODUCING THE STUDENT ACTIVITY SHEET

Distribute a copy of the sheet, Secret Message, to each student. Read the instructions aloud as a class, and have the students complete the activity.

Note: Take time to explain how the blanks are completed in this Secret Message. All the Secret Messages in the program are completed in this way. If students have difficulty in completing the code, have them write the letter that matches each sum beside each fact. Then have them place these letters in the blanks one after the other. Some students like to keep a finger on the fact; others like to check off each fact as they place its matching letter in the Secret Message.

PARTNER BINGO

Students can practice the addition facts with addends of 0, 1, 2, and 3 by playing Partner Bingo, Level 1 (pages 148-150). Have the students complete the facts in order and cross out only one square on their cards for each fact. Partner Bingo can be played in class or at home.

CARD GAMES

Card Games, Level 1, provide more practice for the facts with addends of 0, 1, 2, and 3 (pages 204-205). Card Games can be played in class or at home.

STUDENT JOURNAL

Have students choose four facts: one with an addend of 0, one with an addend of 1, one with an addend of 2, and one with an addend of 3. Have them complete the facts and explain the thinking strategies they used.

Secret Message

Complete the addition facts. The first fact is completed: 3 + 7 = 10. Check the Code Key. The letter above 10 is A. The letter A is written in the first blank. The second fact is completed: 0 + 1 = 1. Check the Code Key. The letter above 1 is T. The letter T is written in the second blank. Continue with each addition fact until you have filled in the remaining blanks with a letter from the Code Key. When you are finished, you will find the secret message.

Where do acrobats learn to walk the tightrope?

$$\frac{A}{\textcircled{1}} \quad \frac{T}{\textcircled{2}} \quad \overline{\textcircled{3}} \quad \overline{\textcircled{4}} \quad \overline{\textcircled{5}} \quad \overline{\textcircled{6}} \quad \overline{\textcircled{7}} \quad \overline{\textcircled{8}} \quad \overline{\textcircled{9}} \quad \overline{\textcircled{10}} \quad \overline{\textcircled{11}} \quad \overline{\textcircled{12}}$$

Code Key	C	T	G	L	I	S	O	H	A
	0	1	3	5	6	7	8	9	10

① 3 + 7 = 10

② 0 + 1 = 1

③ 7 + 2

④ 1 + 5

⑤ 3 + 0

⑥ 6 + 3

⑦ 5 + 2

⑧ 0 + 0

⑨ 1 + 8

⑩ 2 + 6

⑪ 5 + 3

⑫ 3 + 2

LESSON 1J: THE LEVEL 1 NUMBER CHALLENGE

The Level 1 Number Challenge involves the addition facts introduced in Level 1.

Before students take the Level 1 Number Challenge, review the terms *addend* and *sum*. Have them complete addition facts with addends of 0, 1, 2 and 3. Choose facts that the students find most challenging. The following are often difficult for students to complete:

2 + 7
1 + 9
6 + 3
9 + 0
3 + 7
0 + 1
2 + 8

Have the students discuss the thinking strategies they can use with these addition facts.

INSTRUCTIONS FOR THE LEVEL 1 CHALLENGE

Distribute a copy of the challenge sheet to each student. Explain the challenge: There are nine facts at the top of the page. Below the facts, there are nine boxes with a clue in each box. Complete the facts, then match each completed fact with one of the clues and place it in that box. Cross out each fact after it has been placed in its box. For students who would like an extra challenge, have them add the sums of the three facts in each row, then add the sums of the three facts in each column. (See answer key for the mystery number.)

SUGGESTIONS FOR MORE PRACTICE

Students will have many more opportunities to practice the addition facts of this level as they work through the program. However, if they need more practice, consider the following suggestions:

- Check that students have developed the relationships for the numbers 1 through 10 explained in the overview of Level 1 (pages 5-7). These relationships are prerequisites to building mastery of the addition facts. They are the following:

  1. Spatial Relationships

  2. One-More and Two-More, One-Less and Two-Less

  3. Anchors or benchmarks of 5 and 10

  4. Part-Part-Whole

  Continue to provide the students with experiences that develop these relationships. Activities that provide experiences with these relationships are provided in the Overview of Level 1 (pages 5-7).

- Check that students can identify addition facts with an addend of 0, 1, 2, or 3. The addend can either be the first addend or the second.

- Check that students can count on 1, 2, and 3 when they are given a number that is less than 10. Have students practice counting on until they can do so confidently.

- Check that students understand the thinking strategy for addition facts with an addend of 0.

- Identify the facts that students find difficult. Help them develop thinking strategies for these facts. Have them list the facts they find difficult, and encourage them to practice these facts both with a classmate in school and a parent at home.

- Have students continue to practice the first set of Power Facts.

- Have students play Partner Bingo in class or at home. There are 3 Partner Bingos for this level of the program (pages 148-150).

Level 1 Number Challenge

Complete the addition facts below. Then, read the clue in each box, and find the fact that matches it. Place each completed fact into the box with its matching clue.

$$\begin{array}{r} 2 \\ +3 \\ \hline \end{array} \qquad \begin{array}{r} 1 \\ +0 \\ \hline \end{array} \qquad \begin{array}{r} 2 \\ +2 \\ \hline \end{array} \qquad \begin{array}{r} 5 \\ +2 \\ \hline \end{array} \qquad \begin{array}{r} 3 \\ +6 \\ \hline \end{array} \qquad \begin{array}{r} 0 \\ +2 \\ \hline \end{array} \qquad \begin{array}{r} 5 \\ +1 \\ \hline \end{array} \qquad \begin{array}{r} 1 \\ +2 \\ \hline \end{array} \qquad \begin{array}{r} 3 \\ +5 \\ \hline \end{array}$$

This fact is shown with the following picture: 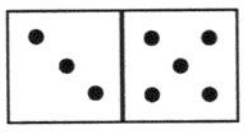	This fact joins 1 and 2.	This fact has the same addends.
This fact has the least sum.	This fact is shown with the following picture: 	The sum of this fact is three more than 6.
This fact is shown with the following picture: 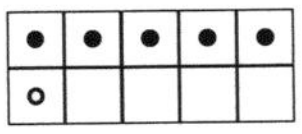	The sum of this fact is two more than 5.	This fact is shown with the following picture: 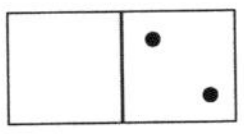

LEVEL 2: FACTS WITH 9 AND 10

LEVEL 2 OVERVIEW

Level 2 introduces the basic addition facts with an addend of either 9 or 10, as well as three important relationships that students can and should develop with numbers 10 to 20.

Number Relationships 10 to 20

John Van de Walle (2001) lists three types of relationships students can and should develop with numbers 10 to 20.

1. A Pre-Place-Value Relationship with 10
2. Extending More and Less Relationships
3. Double and Near-Double Relationships

A Pre-Place-Value Relationship with 10

The position of a numeral in the base-ten numeration system affects its value. For example, the numeral 1 in the number 15 represents the number 10. A set of 10 should play a major role in students' initial understanding of numbers between 10 and 20 (John Van de Walle 2001). Although students may not yet have a complete development of place-value concepts, when they see a set of 10 and a set of 5, they should know without counting that the total is 15.

The names of numbers between 10 and 20 are not helpful in developing this relationship. Consider these numbers. The numbers between 11 and 20 are named *eleven, twelve, thirteen, fourteen, fifteen,* and so on. The names *eleven* and *twelve* are derived from the German *einlif* and *twelf*, which mean "one left" and "two left." The names of the numbers after twelve are *thirteen* (three and ten), *fourteen* (four and ten), and so on. The names of the numbers after the "teens" are more helpful. For example, the number 25 is *twenty-five* (two tens and five), while the number 35 is *thirty-five* (three tens and five).

The ten-frame is an excellent model for developing the pre-place-value relationship with 10, and it is used throughout this level.

Modelling with Ten-Frames

To check that students have developed the pre-place value relationship, present the addition fact 10 + 5 to the students. Have them model this fact with two ten-frames. Have the students place 10 counters in the first ten-frame and 5 counters in the second ten-frame. Ask the students to name the sum represented by these ten-frames.

Check that the students are able to answer 15 without counting. Now have the students turn the mats around. Ask the students to name the sum represented by these ten-frames (5 and 10 is 15). Repeating the words *five, ten,* and *fifteen* can help students make connections with this relationship.

Continue this activity for other numbers between 10 and 20 until students no longer have to count.

Ten-Frame Flash

Practice the pre-place-value relationship with 10 by playing Ten-Frame Flash for the numbers from 10 to 20. Show the students two ten-frames for a few seconds. (Make sure one of the ten-frames has ten dots.) The ten-frame with ten dots can be the first or the second ten-frame shown. Ask the students how many dots they see. Have the students use their response boards to answer the question.

The Ten-Frame Train

To help the student with the pre-place-value relationship with 10, draw two train cars with the ten-frames as the windows. Have the passengers on the train sit in the order in which counters are placed on ten-frames. Place ten passengers in the first train and ten or less passengers in the second train. Have the students name the number of passengers in the two trains.

Number Cards

To reinforce that 15 is the total of a set of 10 and 5, refer to the Number Cards (pages 224-229). Hold up a card showing the number 10, and place a 5 in front of the 0. Ask the students what the numeral 1 represents. Remove the 5 from the 0, and show the students that the numeral 1 represents 10.

Extending One-More-Than and Two-More-Than and One-Less-Than and Two-Less-Than Relationships

Another important relationship students should develop for the numbers 10 to 20 is an extension of one-more-than and two-more-than relationships to these numbers. *First, check that students are able to count up from 1 to 20 and count back from 20 to 1.* Do this by starting with a number like 8 and having the students count up to 16, or starting with a number like 15 and having the students count back to 9. Have the students count up and down until they can do so confidently.

The following two-player game provides practice of the one-more-than and two-more-than and one-less-than and two-less-than relationships for the numbers less than or equal to 20.

The Game: The game is played with a pile of 40 counters and a die with numbers +1, +2, +3, −1, −2, and −3. Each student takes 10 counters from the middle pile and the two players take turns rolling the die. If a player rolls a +1, +2, or +3, he/she takes that many counters from the pile. If a player rolls a −1, −2, or −3, he/she puts back that many counters into the pile. The first player to have 20 counters wins the game. If a player loses all his/her counters, the other player automatically wins the game.

During the game, have the players name the number of counters they have after every turn. Also note how they keep track of the number of counters they have. Some students will group the counters in 5s, others in 10s, still others will group the counters as if on a ten-frame mat.

Double and Near-Double Relationships

The double and near-double relationships are considered in the next two levels of the program.

Thinking Strategy: Addend of 10

The thinking strategy for facts with an addend of 10 is based on the place value relationship with 10.

Consider, for example, the fact 8 + 10.

8 + 10 (addend of 10)

- Pattern of 10:
  A set of 8 and a set of 10 is 18.
  SO, 8 + 10 = 18

Thinking Strategies: Addend of 9

The primary thinking strategies for facts with an addend of 9 are (1) the build-10 strategy and (2) the helping fact strategy. These strategies are based on the place value relationship with 10.

Thinking Strategy: Build-10

Consider, for example, the fact 9 + 4.

Model this fact with ten-frames as follows:

Note that one counter from the second ten-frame can be moved to the first ten-frame. The first ten-frame now has ten counters. The second ten-frame has 3 counters left. A ten-frame with ten counters and a ten-frame with 3 counters represent the number 13.

9 + 4 (addend of 9)

- Build-10:
  Build 10 by taking 1 from 4 and giving it to 9.
  9 + 1 = 10 and 4 − 1 = 3
  10 + 3 = 13
  SO, 9 + 4 = 13

Thinking Strategy: Helping Fact

All facts that students have mastered can be used as a helping fact for facts they have yet to master. For example, a fact with an addend of 9 can be completed using a corresponding fact with an addend of 10 as a helping fact.

Consider, for example, the fact 9 + 4.

- Helping Fact:
  10 + 4 = 14
  9 = 10 − 1
  14 − 1 = 13
  SO, 9 + 4 = 13

Level 2 consists of the following lessons:

Lesson 2A: Ten-Frame Rally with 10

This lesson introduces the pre-place-value relationship with 10. The ten-frame model is used to develop a thinking strategy for addition facts with an addend of 10.

Lesson 2B: Ten-Frame Rally with 9

This lesson uses the ten-frame model to develop the build-10 thinking strategy for addition facts with an addend of 9.

Lesson 2C: Secret Message with 9 and 10

This lesson introduces the helping fact thinking strategy for addition facts with an addend of 9.

Lesson 2D: Match-Ups with 9

This lesson provides practice with the thinking strategies for facts with an addend of 9.

Lesson 2E: Number Design with 3, 9, and 10

This lesson incorporates facts having an addend of either 9 or 10 with facts having an addend of 3. Students identify and apply appropriate thinking strategies for these facts.

Lesson 2F: Jellybean Jumble with 0, 1, 2, 3, 9, and 10

The addition facts in this level have been developed and practiced. This lesson incorporates facts having an addend of either 9 or 10 with the facts introduced in Level 1. Students identify and apply appropriate thinking strategies for these facts.

Lesson 2G: Secret Message with 0, 1, 2, 3, 9, and 10

In this lesson, students continue to complete facts from the first two levels.

Lesson 2H: The Level 2 Number Challenge

This challenge assesses the students' ability to identify and apply appropriate thinking strategies to the facts introduced in Level 1 and Level 2. Students also review models and vocabulary introduced so far in the program.

ADDITION GRID

The addition facts considered in this level are the following:

+	0	1	2	3	4	5	6	7	8	9	10
0	0	1	2	3	4	5	6	7	8	9	10
1	1	2	3	4	5	6	7	8	9	10	11
2	2	3	4	5	6	7	8	9	10	11	12
3	3	4	5	6	7	8	9	10		12	13
4	4	5	6	7						13	14
5	5	6	7	8						14	15
6	6	7	8	9						15	16
7	7	8	9	10						16	17
8	8	9	10							17	18
9	9	10	11	12	13	14	15	16	17	18	19
10	10	11	12	13	14	15	16	17	18	19	20

THINKING STRATEGIES: ADDITION

LESSON 2A: TEN-FRAME RALLY WITH 10

TEACHER LESSON

In this lesson, students model and develop a thinking strategy for addition facts with an addend of 10.

Important! Check that students are able to count up from 1 to 20 and count back from 20 to 1.

A Pre-Place-Value Relationship with 10

Although students may not yet have a complete understanding of the concept of place value, when they see a set of 10 and a set of 5, they should know without counting that the total is 15.

The Ten-Frame Train

To check whether students have developed the pre-place value relationship with 10, draw 2 ten-frame train cars with 10 passengers in the first train and 5 passengers in the second train.

Ask the students how many passengers are in both trains (15 passengers). Check to find out if students are able to answer 15 without counting.

Modelling with Ten-Frames

Now have each student model the fact 10 + 5 with counters and two ten-frame mats. Have the students place 10 counters in the first ten-frame and 5 counters in the second ten-frame. Ask the students to name the sum represented by these ten-frames (10 and 5 is 15).

Check that the students are able to answer 15 without counting. Have students turn the mats around. Ask the students to name the sum represented by these ten-frames (5 and 10 is 15).

Repeating the words *five, ten,* and *fifteen* can help students develop the pre-place value relationship with 10. Continue this activity with them for other numbers between 10 and 20 until they no longer have to count on.

Ten-Frame Flash

Play Ten-Frame Flash for the numbers from 10 to 20. Show the students two ten-frames for a few seconds (make sure one of the ten-frames has 10 dots). The ten-frame with 10 dots can be either the first or second ten-frame. Ask the students how many dots they see. Have the students answer the questions on their response boards.

Important! Provide students with activities that practice the pre-place-value relationship with 10 until they develop these relationships.

Number Cards

To reinforce that 15 is a set of 10 and a set of 5, refer to the Number Cards (pages 224-229). Hold up a card showing the number 10 and place a 5 in front of the 0. Ask the students what the numeral 1 represents. Remove the 5 from the 0, and show them that the numeral 1 represents 10.

Addend of 10

Divide the class into cooperative working pairs. Distribute counters and ten-frame mats as well as a copy of the activity sheet to each student. Explain to students that they will use ten-frames to complete addition facts with an addend of 10. They will also have to explain their thinking strategy for completing facts with an addend of 10.

When students have completed the activity sheet, ask them their thinking strategy for adding a number with 10. They can justify their strategy by modelling the fact with ten-frames.

Thinking Strategy: Addend of 10

The addend of 10 thinking strategy for the fact 10 + 5 can be written as follows:

10 + 5 (addend of 10)

■ Pattern of 10:
A set of 10 and a set of 5 is 15.
SO, 10 + 5 = 15

Encouraging Class Discussion

Engaging students in whole-class discussions is an integral part of the program. Prompts for encouraging class discussions can be found on page 2 of the Introduction.

INTRODUCING THE STUDENT ACTIVITY SHEET

Students will have completed the activity sheet during the lesson.

COMPLETING THE ADDITION GRID

Have the students fill in their addition grid for facts with an addend of 10. They can fill in both a row and a column.

Ten-Frame Rally

This addition buddy is holding two ten-frames to show an addition fact with an addend of 10.

Below, fill in the ten-frames and the addition facts they show. Then, answer the question at the bottom of the page.

10 + 5 = 15

10 ___ 5

___

5 + 10 = 15

5 ___ 10

___

10 ___ 10

___

10 ___ 6

___

What is your thinking strategy when you add a number with 10? Explain your answer.

LESSON 2B: TEN-FRAME RALLY WITH 9

TEACHER LESSON

In this lesson, students model and develop the build-10 thinking strategy for addition facts with an addend of 9.

Interpreting the Operation of Addition

Present the following story problem to the students:

- There are 9 passengers in one ten-frame train and 6 passengers in another ten-frame train. How many passengers are in the two trains altogether?

Have the students draw a picture illustrating this problem. Have them represent it as a number sentence.

- 9 + 6 = 15
  There are 15 passengers altogether.

Note: This story problem illustrates the additive structure part-part-whole. Other additive structures are possible and are discussed in the Introduction to the program.

Ask the students to explain how they found the sum of 15. Some students will count on from 9 ("9" → "10, 11, 12, 13, 14, 15"). Others may note that they can move the passenger from the second row of the second train to the first train. There would then be 10 passengers in the first train and 5 passengers in the second train. A ten-frame with 10 and a ten-frame with 5 represent the number 15.

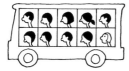 

Explain to the students that they can complete a fact with an addend of 9 by taking 1 from the other addend and adding it to 9 to "build 10."

Introducing the Thinking Strategy: Build-10

Divide the class into cooperative working groups. Distribute counters and ten-frame mats as well as a copy of the activity sheet, Ten-Frame Rally, to each student. Explain to students that they will use ten-frames to complete addition facts with an addend of 9. They will also have to explain their thinking strategy for completing facts with an addend of 9.

When the students have completed the activity sheet, ask them how they can use the build-10 thinking strategy to complete facts with an addend of 9.

The build-10 thinking strategy is particularly effective for facts with an addend of 9. It is also effective for other facts, including those with an addend of 8. The build-10 strategy for facts with an addend of 8 is considered in Level 5.

The build-10 strategy for the fact 9 + 6 is the following:

9 + 6 (addend of 9)

- Build-10:
  Build 10 by taking 1 from 6 and giving it to 9.
  9 + 1 = 10 and 6 – 1 = 5
  10 + 5 = 15
  SO, 9 + 6 = 15

Practicing the Strategy: Build-10

Have the students use the build-10 strategy to complete the fact 4 + 9.

4 + 9 (addend of 9)

- Build-10:
  Build 10 by taking 1 from 4 and giving it to 9.
  9 + 1 = 10 and 4 – 1 = 3
  10 + 3 = 13
  SO, 4 + 9 = 13

Have the students justify this strategy by modelling the fact with ten-frames.

Note: The students can build-10 whenever they have an addend of 9. The 9 can be the first addend or the second. Remind the students that the order of the addends does not affect the sum.

Ten-Frame Flash

To apply the build-10 strategy, students have to take 1 from the number added with 9 and add it to 9. To provide more practice with finding one less than a number, play Ten-Frame Flash with the students. Show the students a ten-frame, and ask them for the number that is one less than the number indicated on the ten-frame. Have them answer with their response cards.

Encouraging Class Discussion

Engaging students in whole-class discussions is an integral part of the program. Prompts for encouraging class discussions can be found on page 2 of the Introduction.

INTRODUCING THE STUDENT ACTIVITY SHEET

Students will have completed the activity sheet during the lesson.

Ten-Frame Rally

Complete the following addition facts with addends of 9 by building 10. In some places, you will also have to fill in the blanks. Then, answer the question at the bottom of the page.

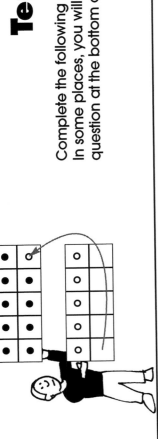

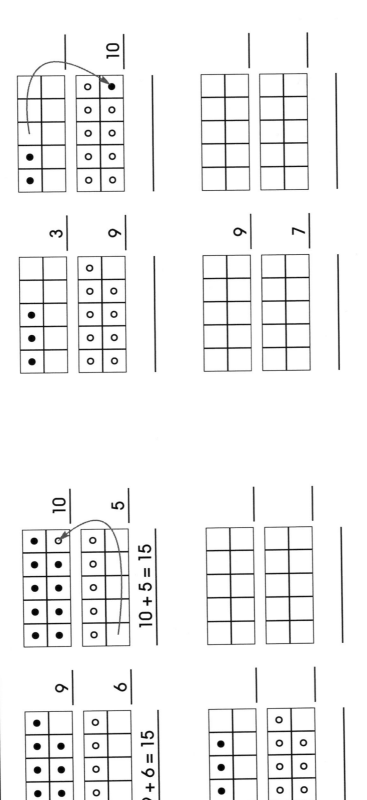

9 + 6 = 15

10 + 5 = 15

What is your thinking strategy for completing a fact with an addend of 9? Explain your answer.

LESSON 2C: SECRET MESSAGE WITH 9 AND 10

TEACHER LESSON

In this lesson, students practice the strategy for facts with an addend of 10 and the build-10 strategy for facts with an addend of 9. The students are also introduced to the helping fact thinking strategy.

Practicing the Thinking Strategy: Addend of 10

Present the addition fact 10 + 7 to the students. Have the students note that the fact has an addend of 10. Ask them to complete this fact and explain their thinking strategy.

10 + 7 (addend of 10)

■ Pattern of 10:
  A set of 10 and a set of 7 is 17.
  SO, 10 + 7 = 17

Practicing the Thinking Strategy: Build-10

Present the addition fact 9 + 7 to the students. Have the students note that the fact has an addend of 9. Ask them to complete this fact using the build-10 thinking strategy.

9 + 7 (addend of 9)

■ Build-10:
  Build 10 by taking 1 from 7 and giving it to 9.
  9 + 1 = 10 and 7 − 1 = 6
  10 + 6 = 16
  SO, 9 + 7 = 16

Comparing Facts with an Addend of 10 and an Addend of 9

Present students with the following addition sentences having addends of 10 and addends of 9.

10 + 1 = 11	9 + 1 = 10
10 + 2 = 12	9 + 2 = 11
10 + 3 = 13	9 + 3 = 12
10 + 4 = 14	9 + 4 = 13
10 + 5 = 15	9 + 5 = 14
10 + 6 = 16	9 + 6 = 15
10 + 7 = 17	9 + 7 = 16
10 + 8 = 18	9 + 8 = 17
10 + 9 = 19	9 + 9 = 18

Ask the students to look for patterns. Introduce the following if the students do not suggest them:

■ The sum of a fact with an addend of 10 has a 1 in the tens position, and the numeral in the ones position is the same as the number being added with 10.

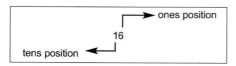

■ The sum of a fact with an addend of 9 has a 1 in the tens position, and the numeral in the ones position is one less than the number being added with 9.

■ The sum of a fact with an addend of 9 is one less than its corresponding fact with an addend of 10.

Introducing the Thinking Strategy: Helping Fact

Any fact that a student has mastered can be used to help complete a fact not yet mastered. Students can complete facts with an addend of 9 by using corresponding facts with an addend of 10 as helping facts.

Consider the fact 9 + 7. Have the students compare the addition fact 9 + 7 to the addition fact 10 + 7. The number 9 is one less than the 10, and the sum of 9 + 7 is one less than the sum of 10 + 7.

9 + 7 (addend of 9)

■ Helping Fact:
  10 + 7 = 17
  9 = 10 − 1
  17 − 1 = 16
  SO, 9 + 7 = 16

Ten-Frame Flash

To provide students with more practice with finding one less than a number between 10 and 20, play Ten-Frame Flash. Show students two ten-frames (make sure one ten-frame has 10 dots). Ask the students for the number that is one less than the number shown on the ten-frames. Have them answer with their response cards.

Important! Continue to provide students with activities that extend the one-less-than relationship to the numbers 10 to 20.

Encouraging Class Discussion

Engaging students in whole-class discussions is an integral part of the program. Prompts for encouraging class discussions can be found on page 2 of the Introduction.

INTRODUCING THE STUDENT ACTIVITY SHEET

Distribute a copy of the sheet, Secret Message, to each student. Read the instructions aloud as a class, and have the students complete the activity.

Note: Remind students to fill in each blank with the letter that matches the sum, not the letter that matches the question number. (See page 24 for more detail, if necessary.)

COMPLETING THE ADDITION GRID

Have the students fill in their addition grid for facts with an addend of 9. They can fill in both a row and a column.

Secret Message

Complete the addition facts. The first fact is completed: 10 + 7 = 17. Check the Code Key. The letter above 17 is T. Write the letter T in the first blank. The second fact is completed: 9 + 7 = 16. Check the Code Key. The letter above 16 is H. Write the letter H in the second blank. Continue with each addition fact until you have filled in the remaining blanks with a letter from the Code Key. When you are finished, you will find the secret message.

‾(1) ‾(2) ‾(3) ‾(4) ‾(5) ‾(6) ‾(7) ‾(8) ‾(9) ‾(10) ‾(11) ‾(12) ‾(13) ‾(14) ‾(15) ‾(16) ‾(17) ‾(18)

Where does a horse eat its morning cereal?

Code Key	S	L	B	E	R	K	H	T	A	F
	9	10	12	13	14	15	16	17	18	19

(1)
$$10$$
$$\underline{+7}$$
$$17$$

(2)
$$9$$
$$\underline{+7}$$
$$16$$

(3)
$$3$$
$$\underline{+10}$$

(4)
$$3$$
$$\underline{+9}$$

(5)
$$10$$
$$\underline{+4}$$

(6)
$$9$$
$$\underline{+4}$$

(7)
$$8$$
$$\underline{+10}$$

(8)
$$6$$
$$\underline{+9}$$

(9)
$$10$$
$$\underline{+9}$$

(10)
$$9$$
$$\underline{+9}$$

(11)
$$9$$
$$\underline{+0}$$

(12)
$$8$$
$$\underline{+9}$$

(13)
$$0$$
$$\underline{+9}$$

(14)
$$9$$
$$\underline{+8}$$

(15)
$$9$$
$$\underline{+9}$$

(16)
$$3$$
$$\underline{+9}$$

(17)
$$9$$
$$\underline{+1}$$

(18)
$$4$$
$$\underline{+9}$$

LESSON 2D: MATCH-UPS WITH 9

TEACHER LESSON

In this lesson, the students practice the thinking strategies for facts with an addend of 9.

Identifying and Applying Thinking Strategies

Tell students there is often more than one strategy for completing a fact. When they know more than one strategy, they can choose the one that works best for them.

Present the students with the following addition facts:

5 + 9
9 + 9
3 + 9

Ask the students to complete these facts and explain their thinking strategies.

Have students note that each fact has an addend of 9; they can apply thinking strategies for facts with an addend of 9.

(a) 5 + 9 (addend of 9)

■ Build-10:
   Build 10 by taking 1 from 5.
   9 + 1 = 10 and 5 − 1 = 4
   10 + 4 = 14
   SO, 5 + 9 = 14

■ Helping Fact:
   5 + 10 = 15
   9 = 10 − 1
   15 − 1 = 14
   SO, 5 + 9 = 14

Note: The ten-frame model is very effective for modelling facts with an addend of 5. For example:

(b) 9 + 9 (addend of 9)

■ Build-10:
   Build 10 by taking 1 from 9.
   9 + 1 = 10 and 9 − 1 = 8
   10 + 8 = 18
   SO, 9 + 9 = 18

■ Helping Fact:
   10 + 9 = 19
   9 = 10 − 1
   19 − 1 = 18
   SO, 9 + 9 = 18

Note: The fact 9 + 9 is a double fact. An additional thinking strategy for this double fact is given in Level 3. Level 3 considers the double facts.

(c) 3 + 9 (addend of 3/addend of 9)

■ Count on 3:
   9 → 10, 11, 12
   SO, 3 + 9 = 12

■ Build-10:
   Build 10 by taking 1 from 3.
   9 + 1 = 10 and 3 − 1 = 2
   10 + 2 = 12
   SO, 3 + 9 = 12

■ Helping Fact:
   3 + 10 = 13
   9 = 10 − 1
   13 − 1 = 12
   SO, 3 + 9 = 12

Note: Because the fact 3 + 9 has an addend of 3 and an addend of 9, students can use thinking strategies for either addend. Discuss with students which strategy they prefer, and have them justify their choice.

Encouraging Class Discussion

Engaging students in whole-class discussions is an integral part of the program. Prompts for encouraging class discussions can be found on page 2 of the Introduction.

INTRODUCING THE STUDENT ACTIVITY SHEET

Distribute a copy of the sheet, Match-Ups, to each student. Read the instructions aloud as a class, and have the students complete the activity.

POWER FACTS

Have students practice the second set of Power Facts (page 134) at least once a day. They can also continue to practice the first set of Power Facts. Students can practice in class and at home.

PARTNER BINGO

Partner Bingo, Level 2A, provides students more practice for the addition facts with an addend of 9 (pages 151-152). Have the students complete the facts in order and cross out only one square on their card for each fact. Partner Bingo can be played in class or at home.

CARD GAMES

Card Games, Level 2, provide more practice for facts with an addend of 9 (pages 206-207). Students can play in class or at home.

STUDENT JOURNAL

Have students choose a fact with an addend of 9 and explain their thinking strategy for completing it.

Match-Ups

Complete each addition fact by connecting the dot beside the fact to the dot beside its sum.

When you have completed the "match-ups," answer the question at the bottom of the page.

5 + 9 •	• 17	9 + 7 •	• 12
7 + 9 •	• 12	4 + 9 •	• 17
9 + 4 •	• 15	9 + 8 •	• 13
9 + 8 •	• 14	9 + 3 •	• 16
3 + 9 •	• 16	6 + 9 •	• 9
9 + 6 •	• 13	9 + 9 •	• 19
9 + 10 •	• 19	1 + 9 •	• 11
2 + 9 •	• 18	9 + 5 •	• 14
9 + 0 •	• 10	9 + 2 •	• 10
9 + 9 •	• 11	10 + 9 •	• 18
9 + 1 •	• 9	0 + 9 •	• 15

What thinking strategy did you use for completing the fact 5 + 9? Explain your answer.

LESSON 2E: NUMBER DESIGN WITH 3, 9, AND 10

TEACHER LESSON

In this lesson, students incorporate facts having addends of 9 and 10 with facts having addends of 3.

Identifying Thinking Strategies

Now that the thinking strategies for facts with addends of 9 and 10 have been developed, have the students complete addition facts with addends of either 9 or 10 together with facts with addends of 3.

Have them consider, for example, the following six facts. There are two facts with an addend of 9, two with an addend of 10, and two with an addend of 3. Have the students identify these facts.

```
  9      7      3     10      6      5
+ 8    + 10   + 6    + 4    + 9    + 3
```

addend of 9

```
  9      6
+ 8    + 9
```

addend of 10

```
  7     10
+10    + 4
```

addend of 3

```
  3      5
+ 6    + 3
```

Applying Thinking Strategies

Ask the students how they would apply thinking strategies for the facts they identified.

(a) 9 + 8 (addend of 9)

- Build-10:
  Build 10 by taking 1 from 8.
  9 + 1 = 10 and 8 − 1 = 7
  10 + 7 = 17
  SO, 9 + 8 = 17

- Helping Fact:
  10 + 8 = 18
  9 = 10 − 1
  18 − 1 = 17
  SO, 9 + 8 = 17

Have the students use similar thinking strategies to complete the fact 6 + 9.

(b) 7 + 10 (addend of 10)

- Pattern of 10:
  A set of 7 and a set of 10 is 17.
  SO, 7 + 10 = 17

Have the students use a similar thinking strategy to complete the fact 10 + 4.

(c) 3 + 6 (addend of 3)

- Count on 3:
  6 → 7, 8, 9
  SO, 3 + 6 = 9

Have the students use a similar thinking strategy to complete the fact 5 + 3.

Addition Facts with Ten-Frames

Students who have difficulty completing facts with an addend of 9 or 10 can model the facts on the blank ten-frames found on pages 218-219.

Encouraging Class Discussion

Engaging students in whole-class discussions is an integral part of the program. Prompts for encouraging class discussions can be found on page 2 of the Introduction.

INTRODUCING THE STUDENT ACTIVITY SHEET

Distribute a copy of the sheet, Number Design, to each student. Read the instructions aloud as a class, and have the students complete the activity.

CHALLENGE FACTS

Use the Challenge Facts, Level 2B (page 184), to help the students identify facts that have addends of 0, 1, 2, 3, 9, and 10. Have the students place shapes around the facts. For example, have them place circles around all the facts with an addend of 9 and then complete them. Next, have them place rectangles around the facts with an addend of 10, and so on. They can also use different coloured pencils to identify the facts.

Number Design

Complete the addition facts below. When you are finished, follow the Colour Key, and colour the design.

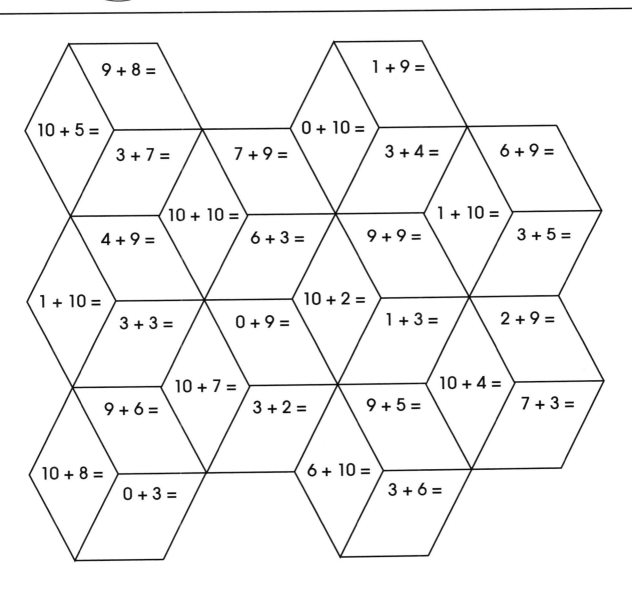

9 + 8 =

10 + 5 =

3 + 7 =

7 + 9 =

1 + 9 =

0 + 10 =

3 + 4 =

6 + 9 =

10 + 10 =

4 + 9 =

6 + 3 =

9 + 9 =

1 + 10 =

3 + 5 =

1 + 10 =

3 + 3 =

0 + 9 =

10 + 2 =

1 + 3 =

2 + 9 =

10 + 7 =

9 + 6 =

3 + 2 =

9 + 5 =

10 + 4 =

7 + 3 =

10 + 8 =

0 + 3 =

6 + 10 =

3 + 6 =

Colour Key

addend of 10: purple

addend of 9: blue

addend of 3: green

LESSON 2F: JELLYBEAN JUMBLE WITH 0, 1, 2, 3, 9, AND 10

TEACHER LESSON

In this lesson, students complete facts introduced so far in the program by identifying and applying the appropriate thinking strategies.

Identifying and Applying Thinking Strategies

Present the students with the following addition facts:

7 + 9
3 + 7
2 + 0
10 + 6
9 + 2
1 + 6

Have the students complete the facts. The students must be able to recognize and apply an appropriate thinking strategy for each fact, then explain their thinking strategies. Have the students first note whether the facts have an addend of 0, 1, 2, 3, 9, or 10.

(a) 7 + 9 (addend of 9)

■ Build-10:
Build 10 by taking 1 from 7.
9 + 1 = 10 and 7 − 1 = 6
10 + 6 = 16
SO, 7 + 9 = 16

■ Helping Fact:
7 + 10 = 17
9 = 10 − 1
17 − 1 = 16
SO, 7 + 9 = 16

(b) 3 + 7 (addend of 3)

■ Count on 3:
7 → 8, 9, 10
SO, 3 + 7 = 10

Note: Some students will complete this fact by picturing the ten-frame. Encourage them to do so.

(c) 2 + 0 (addend of 0/addend of 2)

■ Pattern of 0:
The sum of a number and 0 is the number.
SO, 2 + 0 = 2

■ Two-More-Than:
Two more than 0 is 2.
SO, 2 + 0 = 2

Note: Because the fact 2 + 0 has an addend of 0 and an addend of 2, students can choose a strategy for either addend. Discuss with students which strategy they prefer, and have them justify their choice.

(d) 10 + 6 (addend of 10)

■ Pattern of 10:
A set of 10 and a set of 6 is 16.
SO, 10 + 6 = 16

(e) 9 + 2 (addend of 2/addend of 9)

■ Two-More-Than:
Two more than 9 is 11.
SO, 9 + 2 = 11

■ Build-10:
Build 10 by taking 1 from 2.
9 + 1 = 10 and 2 − 1 = 1
10 + 1 = 11
SO, 9 + 2 = 11

■ Helping Fact:
10 + 2 = 12
9 = 10 − 1
12 − 1 = 11
SO, 9 + 2 = 11

Note: Because the fact 9 + 2 has both an addend of 9 and an addend of 2, students can choose a strategy for either addend. Discuss with students which strategy they prefer, and have them justify their choice.

(f) 1 + 6 (addend of 1)

■ One-More-Than:
One more than 6 is 7.
SO, 1 + 6 = 7

Encouraging Class Discussion

Engaging students in whole-class discussions is an integral part of the program. Prompts for encouraging class discussions can be found on page 2 of the Introduction.

INTRODUCING THE STUDENT ACTIVITY SHEET

Distribute a copy of the sheet, Jellybean Jumble, to each student. Read the instructions aloud as a class, and have the students complete the activity.

Note: The coloured jellybeans form a pattern that students can use to check their work.

Jellybean Jumble

Complete the addition facts below. You will find that the sum of one of the three facts in each group is different from the sums of the other two facts. Colour the jellybean in each group that has the different sum.

7 + 9 =

10 + 7 =   10 + 6 =

3 + 7 =

2 + 8 =   10 + 1 =

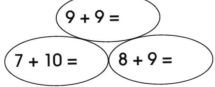

9 + 9 =

7 + 10 =   8 + 9 =

9 + 3 =

10 + 1 =   2 + 10 =

5 + 10 =

9 + 6 =   10 + 6 =

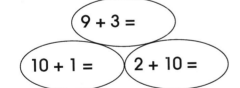

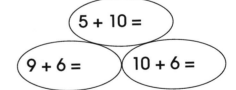

3 + 4 =   1 + 6 =

0 + 8 =

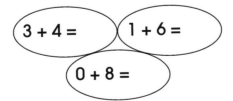

9 + 4 =

2 + 9 =   3 + 10 =

2 + 4 =

3 + 3 =   3 + 5 =

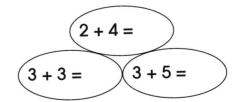

LESSON 2G: SECRET MESSAGE WITH 0, 1, 2, 3, 9, AND 10

TEACHER LESSON

In this lesson, students complete facts introduced so far in the program by identifying and applying the appropriate thinking strategies.

Preparing for the Level 2 Number Challenge

Encourage students to practice the second set of Power Facts (page 134). Students can also play Partner Bingo, Level 2 (pages 151-154), either in class or at home, to prepare for the Level 2 Challenge.

Identifying and Applying Thinking Strategies

Present the students with the following addition facts:

9 + 4
6 + 3
2 + 8
10 + 1
0 + 3

Have the students complete the facts and explain their thinking strategies.

(a) 9 + 4 (addend of 9)

- Build-10:

  Build 10 by taking 1 from 4.
  9 + 1 = 10 and 4 − 1 = 3
  10 + 3 = 13
  SO, 9 + 4 = 13

- Helping Fact:

  10 + 4 = 14
  9 = 10 − 1
  14 − 1 = 13
  SO, 9 + 4 = 13

(b) 6 + 3 (addend of 3)

- Count on 3:

  6 → 7, 8, 9
  SO, 6 + 3 = 9

(c) 2 + 8 (addend of 2)

- Two-More-Than:

  Two more than 8 is 10.
  SO, 2 + 8 = 10

Note: Some students will complete this fact by picturing the ten-frame. Encourage them to do so.

(d) 10 + 1 (addend of 1/addend of 10)

- One-More-Than:

  One more than 10 is 11.
  SO, 10 + 1 = 11

- Pattern of 10:

  A set of 10 and a set of 1 is 11.
  SO, 10 + 1 = 11

Note: Because the fact 10 + 1 has both an addend of 1 and an addend of 10, students can choose strategies for either addend. Discuss with students which strategy they prefer, and have them justify their choice.

(e) 0 + 3 (addend of 0/addend of 3)

- Pattern of 0:

  The sum of 0 and a number is the number.
  SO, 0 + 3 = 3

- Count on 3:

  0 → 1, 2, 3
  SO, 0 + 3 = 3

Note: Because the fact 0 + 3 has both an addend of 0 and an addend of 3, students can choose strategies for either addend. Discuss with students which strategy they prefer, and have them justify their choice.

Encouraging Class Discussion

Engaging students in whole-class discussions is an integral part of the program. Prompts for encouraging class discussions can be found on page 2 of the Introduction.

INTRODUCING THE STUDENT ACTIVITY SHEET

Distribute a copy of the sheet, Secret Message, to each student. Read the instructions aloud as a class, and have the students complete the activity.

PARTNER BINGO

Students can practice all facts introduced in the program so far by playing Partner Bingo, Level 2B (pages 153-154). Have the students complete the facts in order and cross out one square on their card for each fact. Partner Bingo can be played in class or at home.

Secret Message

Complete the addition facts. In the Code Key, find the number that matches the sum of the first fact. Write the letter that is above that number in the first blank. Now, find the number in the Code Key that matches the sum of the second fact. Write the letter that is above it in the second blank. Continue with each addition fact until you have filled in the remaining blanks with a letter from the Code Key. When you are finished, you will find the secret message.

How can bees go to school?

$\overline{①}\ \overline{②}\ \overline{③}\ \overline{④}\quad \overline{⑤}\ \overline{⑥}\ \overline{⑦}\quad \overline{⑧}\ \overline{⑨}\ \overline{⑩}\ \overline{⑪}$

$\overline{⑫}\ \overline{⑬}\ \overline{⑭}\quad \overline{⑮}\ \overline{⑯}\ \overline{⑰}\ \overline{⑱}\ \overline{⑲}\ \overline{⑳}\quad \overline{㉑}\ \overline{㉒}\ \overline{㉓}\ \overline{㉔}$

Code Key	Y	N	U	C	O	E	Z	B	T	A	L	H	S	K
	5	6	7	8	9	10	11	12	13	14	15	16	17	18

① 9 +4   ② 7 +9   ③ 2 +8   ④ 3 +2   ⑤ 7 +1   ⑥ 10 +4

⑦ 0 +6   ⑧ 3 +10   ⑨ 9 +5   ⑩ 9 +9   ⑪ 3 +7   ⑫ 4 +9

⑬ 10 +6   ⑭ 1 +9   ⑮ 9 +8   ⑯ 3 +5   ⑰ 9 +7   ⑱ 6 +3

⑲ 2 +7   ⑳ 6 +9   ㉑ 9 +3   ㉒ 1 +6   ㉓ 10 +1   ㉔ 9 +2

LESSON 2H: THE LEVEL 2 NUMBER CHALLENGE

The Level 2 Number Challenge includes the addition facts introduced in Level 2, as well as those introduced in Level 1.

Before students take the Level 2 Number Challenge, review the terms *addend* and *sum*. Have them complete addition facts with addends of 0, 1, 2, 3, 9, and 10. Choose facts that the students find most challenging. The following are often difficult for students to complete:

9 + 7
6 + 3
8 + 9
10 + 2
1 + 8
2 + 7
4 + 9

Have the students discuss the different thinking strategies they can use with these addition facts.

INSTRUCTIONS FOR THE LEVEL 2 CHALLENGE

Distribute a copy of the challenge sheet to each student. Explain the challenge: There are nine facts at the top of the page. Below the facts, there are nine boxes with a clue in each box. Complete the facts, then match each completed fact with one of the clues, and place it in that box. Cross out each fact after it has been placed in its box. For students who would like an extra challenge, have them add the sums of the three facts in each row, then add the sums of the three facts in each column. (See answer key for the mystery number.)

SUGGESTIONS FOR MORE PRACTICE

Students will have many more opportunities to practice the addition facts of this level as they work through the program. However, if students need more practice, consider the following suggestions:

- Check that students can count forwards and backwards from 1 to 20.

- Check that students have developed the pre-place-value relationship for the numbers from 10 to 20.

- Check that students have developed the one-more-than, two-more-than, one-less-than, and two-less-than relationships for the numbers from 1 to 20.

- Check that students can model numbers between 10 and 20 with ten-frames.

- Check that students can complete facts with an addend of 10.

- Check that students understand and can apply either the build-10 or the helping fact strategy for facts with an addend of 9.

- Write seven addition facts in a row, each with a missing addend. Have the students place a 0 for each of the missing addends. Have the students complete the facts, then repeat for 1, 2, 3, 9, and 10. For example, consider the following:

6			4	8		10
+	+ 3	+ 9	+	+	+ 5	+

6	9	9	4	8	9	10
+ 9	+ 3	+ 9	+ 9	+ 9	+ 5	+ 9

- Identify the facts that students find difficult. Help them develop thinking strategies for these facts. Have them list the facts they find difficult, and encourage them to practice these facts both with a classmate in school and a parent at home.

- Have students continue to practice the first two levels of Power Facts.

- Have students play Partner Bingo in class or at home. There are 4 Partner Bingos (pages 151-154) for this level of the program.

- Have students make up humorous story problems for the facts.

Level 2 Number Challenge

Complete the addition facts below. Then, read the clue in each box, and find the fact that matches it. Place each completed fact into the box with its matching clue.

$$\begin{array}{c} 7 \\ +9 \\ \hline \end{array} \qquad \begin{array}{c} 1 \\ +3 \\ \hline \end{array} \qquad \begin{array}{c} 2 \\ +6 \\ \hline \end{array} \qquad \begin{array}{c} 9 \\ +5 \\ \hline \end{array} \qquad \begin{array}{c} 1 \\ +1 \\ \hline \end{array} \qquad \begin{array}{c} 7 \\ +3 \\ \hline \end{array} \qquad \begin{array}{c} 0 \\ +0 \\ \hline \end{array} \qquad \begin{array}{c} 10 \\ +2 \\ \hline \end{array} \qquad \begin{array}{c} 4 \\ +2 \\ \hline \end{array}$$

This fact is shown with the following picture: 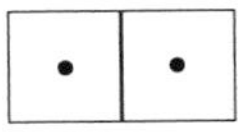	This fact joins 10 and 2.	This fact is shown with the following picture: 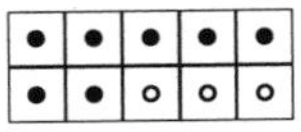
This fact has the greatest sum.	The sum of this fact is two more than 6.	This fact has the least sum.
This fact is shown with the following picture: 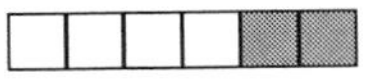	The sum of this fact is one more than 3.	This fact is shown with the following picture: 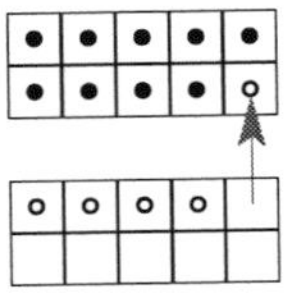

LEVEL 3: DOUBLE FACTS

LEVEL 3 OVERVIEW

Level 3 considers the double facts, which are addition facts with the same addends. The following double facts have been introduced in Level 1 and in Level 2:

$$0 + 0$$
$$1 + 1$$
$$2 + 2$$
$$3 + 3$$
$$9 + 9$$
$$10 + 10$$

The double facts introduced in this level are the following:

$$4 + 4$$
$$5 + 5$$
$$6 + 6$$
$$7 + 7$$
$$8 + 8$$

Number Relationships 10 to 20

In the overview to Level 2, the following relationships were introduced for the numbers 1 through 20:

1. A Pre-Place-Value Relationship with 10
2. Extending More and Less Relationships
3. Double and Near-Double Relationships

The double relationships are considered in this level of the program. The near-double relationships are considered in Level 4 of the program.

Introducing the Thinking Strategy: Double Facts

Three thinking strategies are introduced for double facts (1) the special picture strategy, (2) the build-10 strategy, and (3) the helping fact strategy.

Introducing the Thinking Strategy: Special Picture

The double facts can be related to special pictures. The special pictures provide visual cues for the doubles. The special pictures for the doubles are the following:

$3 + 3 = 6$ – a bug with 3 legs on each side

$4 + 4 = 8$ – a spider with 4 legs on each side

$5 + 5 = 10$ – a person with 5 fingers on each hand

$6 + 6 = 12$ – an egg carton with 2 rows of 6 eggs

$7 + 7 = 14$ – a calendar with 2 weeks of 7 days

$8 + 8 = 16$ – a box of crayons with 2 rows of 8 crayons

$9 + 9 = 18$ – an 18-wheeler double with 9 wheels
 on each side

Rap Song

The following song can help the students use these special pictures to complete the double facts:

$3 + 3$ – Don't YOU bug me!
$4 + 4$ – There's a spider on my door!
$5 + 5$ – Ten fingers are ALIVE!
$6 + 6$ – Twelve eggs – let's mix!
$7 + 7$ – Fourteen days in heaven!
$8 + 8$ – Sixteen crayons are great!
$9 + 9$ – 18-wheelers drive fine!
$10 + 10$ – Twenty and we can start again!

Build-10 Strategy

The build-10 strategy was introduced in Level 2 as one of the primary thinking strategies for completing facts with an addend of 9. It can also be used for facts with an addend of 8 and will be considered in more detail in Level 5. In this level, the build-10 strategy is used for the fact $9 + 9$ and also introduced for the fact $8 + 8$.

Helping Fact Strategy

The helping fact strategy was also introduced in Level 2. Any fact that a student has mastered can be used to help complete a fact that a student has yet to master. Because our number system is a base ten number system, facts with an addend of 5 or 10 are often used as helping facts. Students often find the facts $5 + 5$ and $10 + 10$ easy to master, and they can use them as helping facts for other doubles.

Consider, for example, the fact $6 + 6$.

■ Helping Fact:
 $5 + 5 = 10$
 $6 = 5 + 1$
 $10 + 1 + 1 = 12$
 SO, $6 + 6 = 12$

Level 3 consists of the following lessons:

Lesson 3A: Cube Train Rally with the Doubles

This lesson introduces the double facts, as well as special pictures for three of them.

Lesson 3B: Secret Message with the Doubles

This lesson examines thinking strategies for the double facts $8 + 8$ and $9 + 9$, and introduces their special pictures.

Lesson 3C: Picture Rally with the Doubles

This lesson introduces special pictures for the remaining double facts.

Lesson 3D: Match-Ups with the Doubles

This lesson provides practice with the thinking strategies for the doubles.

Lesson 3E: Number Design with 3, 9, and the Doubles

This lesson incorporates the double facts with facts having an addend of either 3 or 9. Students identify and apply appropriate thinking strategies for these facts.

Lesson 3F: Jellybean Jumble with 0, 1, 2, 3, 9, 10, and the Doubles

In this lesson, students practice completing facts of Levels 1-3. Students identify and apply appropriate thinking strategies for these facts.

Lesson 3G: Wacky Webs with 0, 1, 2, 3, 9, 10, and the Doubles

The addition facts in this level have been developed and practiced. This lesson incorporates the double facts with facts introduced in the first two levels of the program. Even numbers are also considered in this lesson.

Lesson 3H: Secret Message with 0, 1, 2, 3, 9, 10, and the Doubles

In this lesson, students continue to complete facts introduced so far in the program.

Lesson 3I: The Level 3 Number Challenge

This challenge assesses the students' ability to identify and apply appropriate thinking strategies to the facts introduced in Levels 1-3. Students also review models and vocabulary introduced so far in the program.

ADDITION GRID

The addition facts considered in this level are the following:

+	0	1	2	3	4	5	6	7	8	9	10
0	0	1	2	3	4	5	6	7	8	9	10
1	1	2	3	4	5	6	7	8	9	10	11
2	2	3	4	5	6	7	8	9	10	11	12
3	3	4	5	6	7	8	9	10		12	13
4	4	5	6	7	8					13	14
5	5	6	7	8		10				14	15
6	6	7	8	9			12			15	16
7	7	8	9	10				14		16	17
8	8	9	10						16	17	18
9	9	10	11	12	13	14	15	16	17	18	19
10	10	11	12	13	14	15	16	17	18	19	20

LESSON 3A: CUBE TRAIN RALLY WITH THE DOUBLES

TEACHER LESSON

In this lesson, students are introduced to the double facts and model them with cube trains. As well, they are introduced to special pictures for three of the double facts.

Interpreting the Operation of Addition

Present the following story problem to the students:

■ When Garrett went grocery shopping with his dad, they bought a carton of eggs. Garrett noticed there were 6 eggs on one side of the egg carton and six eggs on the other side. How many eggs were in the egg carton altogether?

Have the students draw a picture illustrating this problem. Have them represent the story problem as a number sentence.

■ 6 + 6 = 12
There were 12 eggs in the egg carton.

Note: This story problem illustrates the additive structure, part-part-whole; whole unknown. Other additive structures are possible and are discussed in the Introduction to the program.

Introducing the Doubles

Point out to the students that the fact 6 + 6 has the same addends. Tell students that facts with the same addends are called *double facts* or *doubles*.

Note: If students have been introduced to the operation of multiplication, explain to them that the above story problem also illustrates the multiplication fact 2 x 6.

Modelling the Doubles

Explain to students they are going to model the doubles with cube trains.

Have the students model the fact 6 + 6 with two cube trains of different colours. Have them place one cube train under the other and connect them.

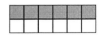

Ask them to complete the fact 6 + 6.

■ 6 + 6 = 12

Ask the students: How many ten-frames are required to model the fact 6 + 6?

■ Two ten-frames are required.

Ask: Why are two ten-frames required?

■ The sum 12 is greater than 10.

Have the students note that they can break the cube trains into 2 cube trains of length 5 and 2 cube trains of length 1. The 2 cube trains of length 5 consist of 10 cubes. Have the students note the similarity between 2 cube trains of length 5 and a ten-frame.

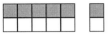

Have the students do the same for the fact 7 + 7.

Applying the Helping Fact Strategy

Ask the students how they can use the fact 5 + 5 as a helping fact to complete the fact 6 + 6.

6 + 6 (double fact)

■ Helping Fact:
5 + 5 = 10
6 = 5 + 1
10 + 1 + 1 = 12
SO, 6 + 6 = 12

The students can also use the fact 5 + 5 as a helping fact to complete the fact 7 + 7.

Introducing the Thinking Strategy: Special Picture

There are special pictures that can help the students complete doubles. Introduce these pictures to the students over a period of a few days: three special pictures are given in this lesson, and the pictures for the other doubles are given in the next two lessons.

3 + 3 = 6 – a bug with 3 legs on each side
5 + 5 = 10 – a person with 5 fingers on each hand
6 + 6 = 12 – an egg carton with 2 rows of 6 eggs

To reinforce these pictures, bring a plastic bug and an egg carton to class.

Encouraging Class Discussion

Engaging students in whole-class discussions is an integral part of the program. Prompts for encouraging class discussions can be found on page 2 of the Introduction.

INTRODUCING THE STUDENT ACTIVITY SHEET

Distribute a copy of the sheet, Cube Train Rally, to each student. Read the instructions aloud as a class, and have the students complete the activity.

Cube Train Rally

The fact 6 + 6 has the same addends and is called a *double fact*. All double facts have two addends that are the same. You can show double facts with cube trains.

Below, you will find several questions. In some, use the cube trains to find the double fact. In some, use the double fact to draw the cube trains it is showing. In others, you have to show both the cube trains and the double fact the addends represent. Just remember that each set of cube trains must show a different sum. When you are finished, answer the question at the bottom of the page.

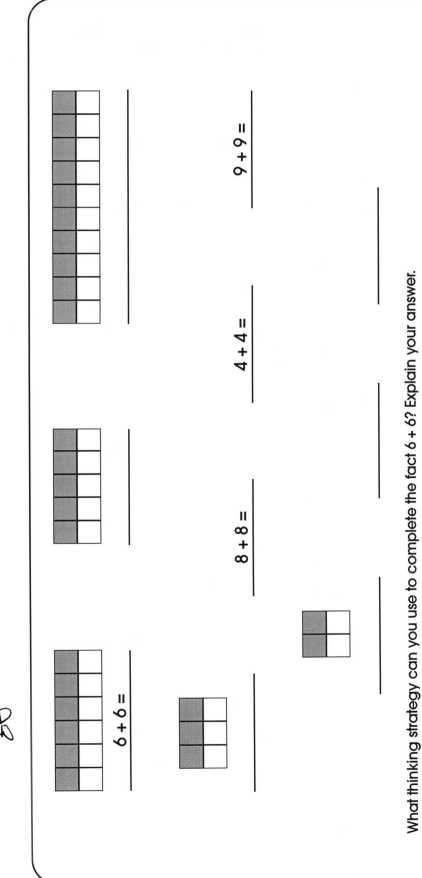

6 + 6 =

8 + 8 =

4 + 4 =

9 + 9 =

What thinking strategy can you use to complete the fact 6 + 6? Explain your answer.

LESSON 3B: SECRET MESSAGE WITH THE DOUBLES

TEACHER LESSON

In this lesson, students skip-count by 2s. They apply the build-10 and helping fact strategies for the double facts 9 + 9 and 8 + 8. Special pictures for these double facts are introduced.

Skip Counting

Have students skip count by 2s from 2 to 20. Point out that these numbers are the sums of the double facts. Have the students note that 5 counts are 10, and they can use the addition sentence 5 + 5 = 10 to help them complete the facts 6 + 6 and 7 + 7. Have them also note that 10 counts are 20, and they can use the addition sentence 10 + 10 = 20 to help them complete the facts 9 + 9 and 8 + 8.

Applying the Build-10 and Helping Fact Thinking Strategies

Present the double fact 9 + 9 to the students. Have them complete the fact and then explain their thinking strategies.

9 + 9 (addend of 9)

■ Build-10:
   Build 10 by taking 1 from 9.
   9 + 1 = 10 and 9 − 1 = 8
   10 + 8 = 18
   SO, 9 + 9 = 18

■ Helping Fact:
   10 + 9 = 19
   9 = 10 − 1
   19 − 1 = 18
   SO, 9 + 9 = 18

Explain to the students that the double fact 8 + 8 can also be completed with these strategies.

8 + 8 (addend of 8)

■ Build-10:
   Build 10 by taking 2 from 8.
   8 + 2 = 10 and 8 − 2 = 6
   10 + 6 = 16
   SO, 8 + 8 = 16

■ Helping Fact:
   8 + 10 = 18
   8 = 10 − 2
   18 − 2 = 16
   SO, 8 + 8 = 16

Note: The students can model the build-10 strategy with ten-frames. Students often find the build-10 and helping fact strategies for facts with an addend of 8 more difficult than for facts with an addend of 9. These strategies for facts with an addend of 8 are developed more fully in Level 5.

The Special Picture Strategy

There are special pictures for the double facts 8 + 8 and 9 + 9 that the students may find helpful.

> The special picture for 8 + 8 is a box of 16 crayons with 2 rows of 8 crayons.

> The special picture for 9 + 9 is an 18-wheeler double with 9 wheels on each side.

To reinforce these special pictures, bring a box of 16 crayons and a picture of an 18-wheeler double to class.

Creating Story Problems

Ask the students to create a story problem involving a double fact. Suggest the story problems involve twins. Have the students solve their story problem and draw pictures illustrating the problem. When students interpret addition facts as story problems, it reinforces their concept of the operation of addition.

Encouraging Class Discussion

Engaging students in whole-class discussions is an integral part of the program. Prompts for encouraging class discussions can be found on page 2 of the Introduction.

INTRODUCING THE STUDENT ACTIVITY SHEET

Distribute a copy of the sheet, Secret Message, to each student. Read the instructions aloud as a class, and have the students complete the activity.

Secret Message

Complete the addition facts. In the Code Key, find the number that matches the sum of the first fact. Write the letter that is above that number in the first blank. Now, find the number in the Code Key that matches the sum of the second fact. Write the letter that is above it in the second blank. Continue with each addition fact until you have filled in the remaining blanks with a letter from the Code Key. When you are finished, you will find the secret message.

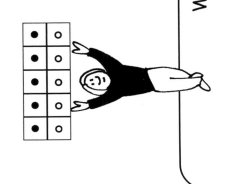

Why is the dinosaur wearing purple pyjamas?

$\overline{1}$ $\overline{2}$ $\overline{3}$ $\overline{4}$ $\overline{5}$ $\overline{6}$ $\overline{7}$ $\overline{8}$ $\overline{9}$ $\overline{10}$ $\overline{11}$ $\overline{12}$

$\overline{13}$ $\overline{14}$ $\overline{15}$ $\overline{16}$ $\overline{17}$ $\overline{18}$ $\overline{19}$ $\overline{20}$ $\overline{21}$ $\overline{22}$ $\overline{23}$ $\overline{24}$

Code Key	R	N	A	E	I	T	S	W	H	O
	2	4	6	8	10	12	14	16	18	20

① $\begin{array}{r} 5 \\ +5 \\ \hline \end{array}$

② $\begin{array}{r} 6 \\ +6 \\ \hline \end{array}$

③ $\begin{array}{r} 7 \\ +7 \\ \hline \end{array}$

④ $\begin{array}{r} 8 \\ +8 \\ \hline \end{array}$

⑤ $\begin{array}{r} 9 \\ +9 \\ \hline \end{array}$

⑥ $\begin{array}{r} 5 \\ +5 \\ \hline \end{array}$

⑦ $\begin{array}{r} 6 \\ +6 \\ \hline \end{array}$

⑧ $\begin{array}{r} 4 \\ +4 \\ \hline \end{array}$

⑨ $\begin{array}{r} 10 \\ +10 \\ \hline \end{array}$

⑩ $\begin{array}{r} 2 \\ +2 \\ \hline \end{array}$

⑪ $\begin{array}{r} 4 \\ +4 \\ \hline \end{array}$

⑫ $\begin{array}{r} 7 \\ +7 \\ \hline \end{array}$

⑬ $\begin{array}{r} 3 \\ +3 \\ \hline \end{array}$

⑭ $\begin{array}{r} 1 \\ +1 \\ \hline \end{array}$

⑮ $\begin{array}{r} 4 \\ +4 \\ \hline \end{array}$

⑯ $\begin{array}{r} 5 \\ +5 \\ \hline \end{array}$

⑰ $\begin{array}{r} 2 \\ +2 \\ \hline \end{array}$

⑱ $\begin{array}{r} 6 \\ +6 \\ \hline \end{array}$

⑲ $\begin{array}{r} 9 \\ +9 \\ \hline \end{array}$

⑳ $\begin{array}{r} 4 \\ +4 \\ \hline \end{array}$

㉑ $\begin{array}{r} 8 \\ +8 \\ \hline \end{array}$

㉒ $\begin{array}{r} 3 \\ +3 \\ \hline \end{array}$

㉓ $\begin{array}{r} 7 \\ +7 \\ \hline \end{array}$

㉔ $\begin{array}{r} 9 \\ +9 \\ \hline \end{array}$

LESSON 3C: PICTURE RALLY WITH THE DOUBLES

TEACHER LESSON

In this lesson. student are introduced to special pictures for the remaining doubles.

Checking the Addition Grid

Have the students check their addition grids for the doubles they have already completed. They are the following:

$$0 + 0 = 0$$
$$1 + 1 = 2$$
$$2 + 2 = 4$$
$$3 + 3 = 6$$
$$9 + 9 = 18$$
$$10 + 10 = 20$$

Ask the students to explain their thinking strategies for these doubles.

Thinking Strategies for the Remaining Doubles

In the two previous lessons, students were introduced to special pictures to help them complete the remaining doubles. They have been introduced to all but the special pictures for the facts 4 + 4 and 7 + 7.

The special picture for the fact 4 + 4 is a spider with 4 legs on each side.

The special picture for the fact 7 + 7 is a calendar with 2 weeks of 7 days.

The Special Picture Strategy

The following is a list of the special pictures for the doubles:

3 + 3 = 6 – a bug with 3 legs on each side
4 + 4 = 8 – a spider with 4 legs on each side
5 + 5 = 10 – a person with 5 fingers on each hand
6 + 6 = 12 – an egg carton with 2 rows of 6 eggs
7 + 7 = 14 – a calendar with 2 weeks of 7 days
8 + 8 = 16 – a box of crayons with 2 rows of 8 crayons
9 + 9 = 18 – an 18-wheeler double with 9 wheels on each side

Have the students make a poster to illustrate these special pictures.

Note: Encourage the students to think of other special pictures for the double facts, and have them share these with their classmates

Rap Song

The following song might help the students remember the special pictures.

3 + 3 – Don't YOU bug me!
4 + 4 – There's a spider on my door!
5 + 5 – Ten fingers are ALIVE!
6 + 6 – Twelve eggs – let's mix!
7 + 7 – Fourteen days in heaven!
8 + 8 – Sixteen crayons are great!
9 + 9 – 18-wheelers drive fine!
10 + 10 – Twenty and we can start again!

Patterns with Doubles

Have students complete the following facts:

1 + 1 = 2	6 + 6 = 12
2 + 2 = 4	7 + 7 = 14
3 + 3 = 6	8 + 8 = 16
4 + 4 = 8	9 + 9 = 18
5 + 5 = 10	10 + 10 = 20

Ask the students to look for patterns. Introduce the following if the students do not suggest them:

- The facts have the same addends and are double facts.
- The numeral in the ones position of the sum of the double 6 + 6 is the same as the numeral of the sum of the double 1 + 1, the numeral in the ones position of the sum of the double 7 + 7 is the same as the numeral of the sum of the double 2 + 2, and so on.
- The sums increase by 2.
- The sums are even numbers. (Even numbers are considered in more detail in Lesson 3G.)

Encouraging Class Discussion

Engaging students in whole-class discussions is an integral part of the program. Prompts for encouraging class discussions can be found on page 2 of the Introduction.

INTRODUCING THE STUDENT ACTIVITY SHEET

Distribute a copy of the sheet, Picture Rally, to each student. Read the instructions aloud as a class, and have the students complete the activity.

Note: Encourage students to draw as best as they can. When they draw the special pictures, they are reinforcing the images of the doubles.

COMPLETING THE ADDITION GRID

Have the students fill in their addition grid for the doubles.

Note: Make sure the students note that the sums of the double facts are on the diagonal of the grid.

Picture Rally

The special picture of the double fact 4 + 4 is a spider with 4 legs on each side of its body.

Below, draw the special pictures of the following doubles, and find the sum for each fact.

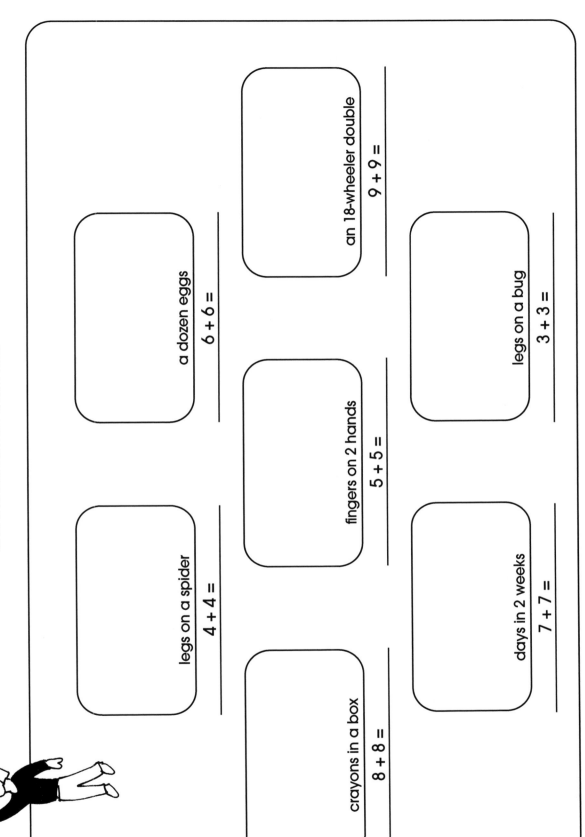

legs on a spider

4 + 4 =

a dozen eggs

6 + 6 =

an 18-wheeler double

9 + 9 =

crayons in a box

8 + 8 =

fingers on 2 hands

5 + 5 =

days in 2 weeks

7 + 7 =

legs on a bug

3 + 3 =

LESSON 3D: MATCH-UPS WITH THE DOUBLES

TEACHER LESSON

In this lesson, the students practice the thinking strategies for the doubles.

Practicing the Thinking Strategies: Doubles

Present students with the following double facts:

8 + 8
5 + 5
3 + 3
2 + 2
10 + 10
0 + 0

Ask the students to explain what these facts mean to them and to complete them. Ask the students to explain what thinking strategies they used.

(a) 8 + 8 (double fact)

■ Special Picture:
Picture a box of crayons with 2 rows of 8 crayons.
SO, 8 + 8 = 16

Note: The build-10 strategy and helping fact strategy can be used for this fact. The build-10 and helping fact strategy for this fact were introduced in Lesson 3B and are considered in more detail in Level 5.

(b) 5 + 5 (double fact)

■ Special Picture:
Picture a person with 5 fingers on each hand.
SO, 5 + 5 = 10

Note: Some students will complete this fact by picturing the ten-frame. Encourage them to do so.

(c) 3 + 3 (addend of 3/double fact)

■ Count on 3:
3 → 4, 5, 6
SO, 3 + 3 = 6

■ Special Picture:
Picture a bug with 3 legs on each side.
SO, 3 + 3 = 6

Note: Because the fact 3 + 3 has two addends of 3 and is a double fact, students can choose a strategy for either. Discuss with students which strategy they prefer, and have them justify their choice.

(d) 2 + 2 (addend of 2/double fact)

■ Two-More-Than:
Two more than 2 is 4.
SO, 2 + 2 = 4

Note: The double fact 2 + 2 does not have a special picture. If students like, they can choose a special picture.

(e) 10 + 10 (addend of 10)

■ Pattern of 10:
A set of 10 and a set of 10 is 20.
SO, 10 + 10 = 20

(f) 0 + 0 (addend of 0)

■ Pattern of 0:
The sum of 0 and a number is the number.
SO, 0 + 0 = 0

Encouraging Class Discussion

Engaging students in whole-class discussions is an integral part of the program. Prompts for encouraging class discussions can be found on page 2 of the Introduction.

INTRODUCING THE STUDENT ACTIVITY SHEET

Distribute a copy of the sheet, Match-Ups, to each student. Read the instructions aloud as a class, and have the students complete the activity.

Note: The connecting lines of each set of facts form a pattern that students can use to self-correct their work.

POWER FACTS

Have students practice the third set of Power Facts (page 135) at least once a day. They can also continue practicing the first two sets of facts. Students can practice in school and at home.

PARTNER BINGO

Partner Bingo, Level 3A, provides more practice for the doubles (pages 155-156). Have the students complete the facts in order and cross out only one square on their card for each fact. Partner Bingo can be played in class or at home.

CARD GAMES

Card Games, Level 3, provide more practice for the doubles (pages 208-209). Students can play in class or at home.

STUDENT JOURNAL

Have students choose three double facts and explain their thinking strategies for completing them.

Match-Ups

Complete each addition fact by connecting the dot beside the fact to the dot beside its sum.

When you have completed the "match-ups," answer the question at the bottom of the page.

8 + 8 •	• 12	4 + 4 •	• 14
6 + 6 •	• 16	8 + 8 •	• 16
9 + 9 •	• 8	7 + 7 •	• 8
4 + 4 •	• 18	9 + 9 •	• 6
7 + 7 •	• 2	6 + 6 •	• 0
0 + 0 •	• 6	10 + 10 •	• 20
2 + 2 •	• 10	0 + 0 •	• 12
10 + 10 •	• 20	3 + 3 •	• 18
5 + 5 •	• 4	1 + 1 •	• 4
3 + 3 •	• 0	5 + 5 •	• 10
1 + 1 •	• 14	2 + 2 •	• 2

What thinking strategy did you use for completing the fact 8 + 8? Explain your answer.

LESSON 3E: NUMBER DESIGN WITH 3, 9, AND THE DOUBLES

TEACHER LESSON

In this lesson, students incorporate the double facts with facts having addends of 3 and 9.

Identifying Thinking Strategies

With the thinking strategies for the double facts now developed, have the students complete the addition facts below, together with facts having addends of 3 and 9.

In the six facts below, two facts are doubles, two facts have an addend of 3, and two facts have an addend of 9. Have the students identify these facts.

$$\begin{array}{cccccc} 7 & 3 & 8 & 6 & 9 & 7 \\ +\,7 & +\,4 & +\,9 & +\,6 & +\,5 & +\,3 \end{array}$$

double fact

$$\begin{array}{cc} 7 & 6 \\ +\,7 & +\,6 \end{array}$$

addend of 3

$$\begin{array}{cc} 3 & 7 \\ +\,4 & +\,3 \end{array}$$

addend of 9

$$\begin{array}{cc} 8 & 9 \\ +\,9 & +\,5 \end{array}$$

Applying Thinking Strategies

Ask the students how they would apply thinking strategies for the facts they identified.

(a) 7 + 7 (double fact)

- Special Picture:
  Picture a calendar with 2 weeks of 7 days.
  SO, 7 + 7 = 14

- Helping Fact:
  5 + 5 = 10
  7 = 5 + 2
  10 + 2 + 2 = 14
  SO, 7 + 7 = 14

Have the students use the special picture strategy to complete the fact 6 + 6.

(b) 3 + 4 (addend of 3)

- Count on 3:
  4 → 5, 6, 7
  SO, 3 + 4 = 7

Have the students use a similar thinking strategy to complete the fact 7 + 3.

(c) 8 + 9 (addend of 9)

- Build-10:
  Build 10 by taking 1 from 8.
  9 + 1 = 10 and 8 − 1 = 7
  10 + 7 = 17
  SO, 8 + 9 = 17

- Helping Fact:
  8 + 10 = 18
  9 = 10 − 1
  18 − 1 = 17
  SO, 8 + 9 = 17

Have the students use a similar thinking strategy to complete the fact 9 + 5.

Note: The addition facts 3 + 4 and 8 + 9 are called *near-doubles.* Thinking strategies for these facts are introduced in the next level of the program. Encourage students who complete these facts with the help of their corresponding double facts to do so.

Encouraging Class Discussion

Engaging students in whole-class discussions is an integral part of the program. Prompts for encouraging class discussions can be found on page 2 of the Introduction.

INTRODUCING THE STUDENT ACTIVITY SHEET

Distribute a copy of the sheet, Number Design, to each student. Read the instructions aloud as a class, and have the students complete the activity.

Note: The coloured areas form a pattern that students can use to check their work.

CHALLENGE FACTS

Use the Challenge Facts, Level 3B (page 186), to help the students identify facts that have addends of 0, 1, 2, 3, 9, and 10, or are doubles. Have students place shapes around the facts. For example, have them place circles around all the double facts and then complete them. Next, have them place triangles around the facts with an addend of 9, and so on. They can also use different coloured pencils to identify the facts.

Number Design

Complete the addition facts below. When you are finished, follow the Colour Key, and colour the design.

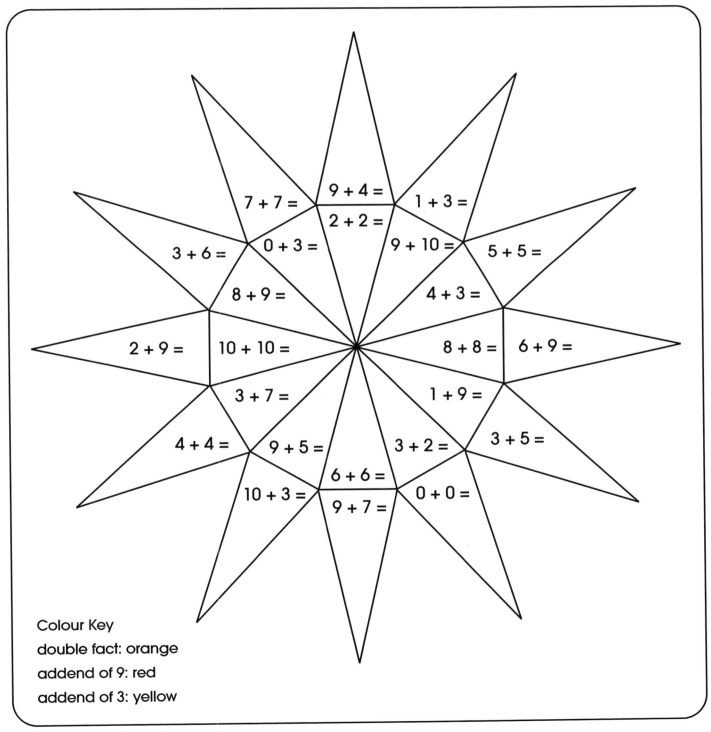

7 + 7 =

9 + 4 =

1 + 3 =

2 + 2 =

3 + 6 =

0 + 3 =

9 + 10 =

5 + 5 =

8 + 9 =

4 + 3 =

2 + 9 =

10 + 10 =

8 + 8 =

6 + 9 =

3 + 7 =

1 + 9 =

4 + 4 =

9 + 5 =

3 + 2 =

3 + 5 =

10 + 3 =

6 + 6 =

0 + 0 =

9 + 7 =

Colour Key

double fact: orange

addend of 9: red

addend of 3: yellow

LESSON 3F: JELLYBEAN JUMBLE WITH 0, 1, 2, 3, 9, 10, AND THE DOUBLES

TEACHER LESSON

In this lesson, students practice completing facts with an addend of 0, 1, 2, 3, 9, or 10, and facts that are doubles.

Identifying and Applying Thinking Strategies

Present the students with the following addition facts:

9 + 9
3 + 6
5 + 2
6 + 6
4 + 9
6 + 1
10 + 8

Have the students complete the facts. The students must be able to recognize and apply an appropriate thinking strategy for each fact, then explain their thinking strategies. Have the students first note whether the facts have an addend of 0, 1, 2, 3, 9, or 10, or are doubles.

(a) 9 + 9 (addend of 9/double fact)

■ Build-10:
Build 10 by taking 1 from 9.
$9 + 1 = 10$ and $9 - 1 = 8$
$10 + 8 = 18$
SO, $9 + 9 = 18$

■ Helping Fact:
$9 + 10 = 19$
$9 = 10 - 1$
$19 - 1 = 18$
SO, $9 + 9 = 18$

■ Special Picture:
Picture an 18-wheeler double.
SO, $9 + 9 = 18$

Note: Because the fact 9 + 9 has both an addend of 9 and is a double fact, students can consider thinking strategies for either. Discuss with students which strategy they prefer, and have them justify their choice.

(b) 3 + 6 (addend of 3)

■ Count on 3:
$6 \rightarrow 7, 8, 9$
SO, $3 + 6 = 9$

(c) 5 + 2 (addend of 2)

■ Two-More-Than:
Two more than 5 is 7.
SO, $5 + 2 = 7$

(d) 6 + 6 (double fact)

■ Special Picture:
Picture an egg carton with 2 rows of 6 eggs.
SO, $6 + 6 = 12$

■ Helping Fact:
$5 + 5 = 10$
$6 = 5 + 1$
$10 + 1 + 1 = 12$
SO, $6 + 6 = 12$

(e) 4 + 9 (addend of 9)

■ Build-10:
Build 10 by taking 1 from 4
$9 + 1 = 10$ and $4 - 1 = 3$
$10 + 3 = 13$
SO, $4 + 9 = 13$

■ Helping Fact:
$4 + 10 = 14$
$9 = 10 - 1$
$14 - 1 = 13$
SO, $4 + 9 = 13$

(f) 6 + 1 (addend of 3)

■ One-More-Than:
One more than 6 is 7
SO, $6 + 1 = 7$

(g) 10 + 8 (addend of 10)

■ Pattern of 10:
A set of 10 and a set of 8 is 18.
SO, $10 + 8 = 18$

Encouraging Class Discussion

Engaging students in whole-class discussions is an integral part of the program. Prompts for encouraging class discussions can be found on page 2 of the Introduction.

INTRODUCING THE STUDENT ACTIVITY SHEET

Distribute a copy of the sheet, Jellybean Jumble, to each student. Read the instructions aloud as a class, and have the students complete the activity.

Jellybean Jumble

Complete the addition facts below. You will find that the sum of one of the three facts in each group is different from the sums of the other two facts. Colour the jellybean in each group that has the different sum.

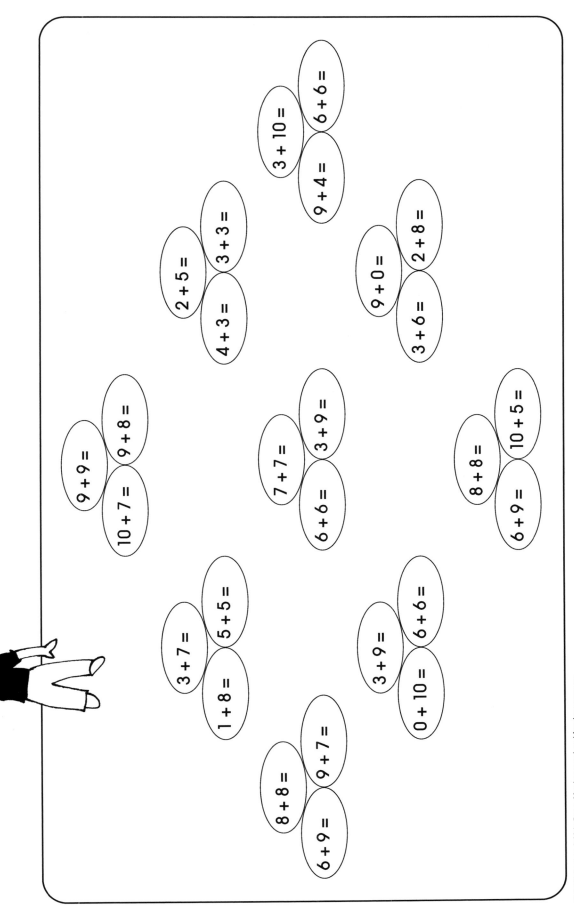

9 + 9 =
9 + 8 =
10 + 7 =

2 + 5 =
3 + 3 =
4 + 3 =

3 + 10 =
6 + 6 =
9 + 4 =

9 + 0 =
2 + 8 =
3 + 6 =

7 + 7 =
3 + 9 =
6 + 6 =

8 + 8 =
10 + 5 =
6 + 9 =

3 + 7 =
5 + 5 =
1 + 8 =

3 + 9 =
6 + 6 =
0 + 10 =

8 + 8 =
9 + 7 =
6 + 9 =

LESSON 3G: WACKY WEBS WITH 0, 1, 2, 3, 9, 10, AND THE DOUBLES

TEACHER LESSON

In this lesson, students incorporate the double facts with facts from Level 1 and Level 2. They also identify even and odd numbers.

Identifying and Applying Thinking Strategies

Continue to present addition facts with an addend of 0, 1, 2, 3, 9, or 10, and the doubles to the students. Have the students complete the facts. The students must be able to recognize and apply an appropriate thinking strategy for each fact, then explain their thinking strategies. Have the students first note whether the facts have an addend of 0, 1, 2, 3, 9, or 10, are double facts.

Even Numbers

Have the students consider the number 6. Ask: Is the number 6 even?

■ The number 6 is even.

Ask the students: Why is the number 6 even?

■ 3 + 3 = 6, and 6 can be divided into 2 groups of 3.

Have the students model this explanation with cube trains.

Now, have the students consider the number 14. Ask: Is the number 14 even?

■ The number 14 is even.

Ask the students: Why is the number 14 even?

■ 7 + 7 = 14, and 14 can be divided into 2 groups of 7.

Have the students model this explanation with cube trains.

Ask the students: Is the sum of any double fact even?

■ The sum of any double fact is even.

Ask the students: Why is the sum of any double fact even?

■ A double fact consists of 2 equal addends; therefore, the sum of any double fact can be divided into two equal groups.

Have the students name the sums of the double facts.

■ 0, 2, 4, 6, 8, 10, 12, 14, 16, 18, 20

Odd Numbers

Have the students consider the number 3. Ask: Why is the number 3 not even?

■ 2 + 1 = 3; 3 cannot be divided into 2 equal groups.

Have the students model this explanation with cube trains. Tell the students that a number that cannot be divided into 2 equal groups is called *odd*.

Now, have the students consider the number 13. Ask: Is the number 13 odd?

■ The number 13 is odd.

Ask the students: Why is the number 13 odd?

■ 7 + 6 = 13; 13 cannot be divided into 2 equal groups.

Have the students model this explanation with cube trains.

Have the students name the odd numbers that are less than 20.

■ 1, 3, 5, 7, 9, 11, 13, 15, 17, 19

Have the students note that odd numbers are not the sums of the double facts.

Encouraging Class Discussion

Engaging students in whole-class discussions is an integral part of the program. Prompts for encouraging class discussions can be found on page 2 of the Introduction.

INTRODUCING THE STUDENT ACTIVITY SHEET

Distribute a copy of the sheet, Wacky Webs, to each student. Read the instructions aloud as a class, and have the students complete the activity.

Note: The coloured cells form a pattern that students can use to check their work. The pattern will help them become aware of the rules for even and odd sums.

Note: Even and odd sums, including rules, are further considered in Lesson 6G. Lesson 3G is an introduction to even and odd numbers.

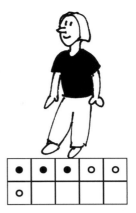

Wacky Webs

The sums of the double facts (0, 2, 4, 6, 8, 10, 12, 14, 16, 18, and 20) are **EVEN** numbers.

The numbers 1, 3, 5, 7, 9, 11, 13, 15, 17, and 19 are **ODD** numbers.

Below, fill in the outer cells of each web by adding the numbers in the inner cells with the number in the middle.

Colour all of the cells that have an **EVEN** number.

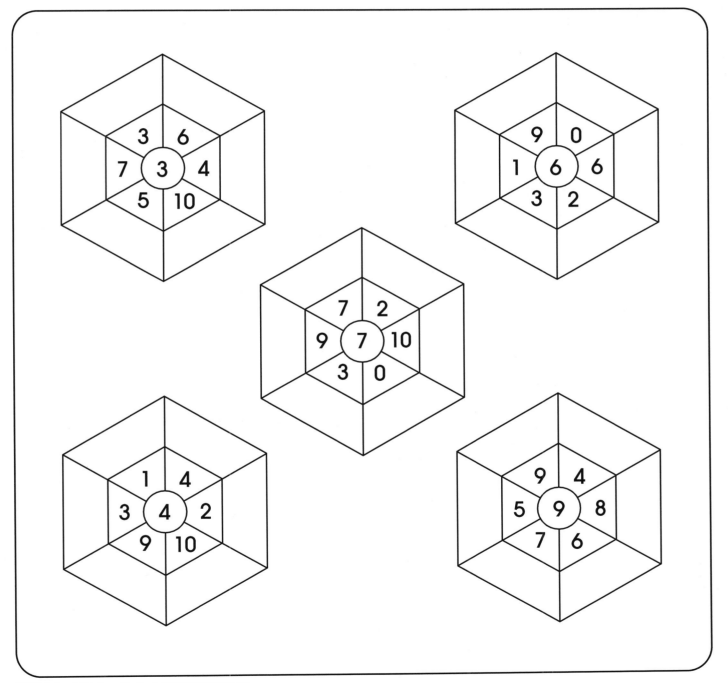

LESSON 3H: SECRET MESSAGE WITH 0, 1, 2, 3, 9, 10, AND THE DOUBLES

TEACHER LESSON

In this lesson, students practice completing facts with addends of 0, 1, 2, 3, 9, 10, and facts that are doubles.

Preparing for the Level 3 Number Challenge

Encourage students to practice the third set of Power Facts (page 135). Students can also play Partner Bingo, Level 3 (pages 155-158), either in class or at home, to prepare for the Level 3 Challenge.

Identifying and Applying Thinking Strategies

Present the students with the following addition facts:

2 + 2
5 + 3
1 + 0
8 + 8
2 + 9

Have the students complete the facts and explain their thinking strategies.

(a) 2 + 2 (addend of 2/double fact)

- Two-More-Than:
  Two more than 2 is 4.
  SO, 2 + 2 = 4

Note: The double fact 2 + 2 does not have a special picture. If students like, they can choose a special picture.

(b) 5 + 3 (addend of 3)

- Count on 3:
  5 → 6, 7, 8
  SO, 5 + 3 = 8

(c) 1 + 0 (addend of 0/addend of 1)

- Pattern of 0:
  The sum of a number and 0 is the number.
  SO, 1 + 0 = 1

- One-More-Than:
  One more than 0 is 1.
  SO, 1 + 0 = 1

Note: Because the fact 1 + 0 has both an addend of 1 and an addend of 0, students can consider thinking strategies for either addend. Discuss with students which strategy they prefer, and have them justify their choice.

(d) 8 + 8 (double fact)

- Special Picture:
  Picture a box of crayons with 2 rows of 8 crayons.
  SO, 8 + 8 = 16

Note: The build-10 strategy and helping fact strategy can be used for this fact. The build-10 strategy and helping fact strategy for this fact were introduced in Lesson 3B and are considered in more detail in Level 5.

(e) 2 + 9 (addend of 2/addend of 9)

- Two-More-Than:
  Two more than 9 is 11.
  SO, 2 + 9 = 11

- Build-10:
  Build 10 by taking 1 from 2.
  9 + 1 = 10 and 2 − 1 = 1
  10 + 1 = 11
  SO, 2 + 9 = 11

- Helping Fact:
  2 + 10 = 12
  9 = 10 − 1
  12 − 1 = 11
  SO, 2 + 9 = 11

Note: Because the fact 2 + 9 has both an addend of 2 and an addend of 9, students can consider thinking strategies for either addend. Discuss with students which strategy they prefer, and have them justify their choice.

Encouraging Class Discussion

Engaging students in whole-class discussions is an integral part of the program. Prompts for encouraging class discussions can be found on page 2 of the Introduction.

INTRODUCING THE STUDENT ACTIVITY SHEET

Distribute a copy of the sheet, Secret Message, to each student. Read the instructions aloud as a class, and have the students complete the activity.

PARTNER BINGO

Students can practice all facts introduced in the program so far by playing Partner Bingo, Level 3B (pages 157-158). Have the students complete the facts in order and cross out only one square on their card for each fact. Partner Bingo can be played in class or at home.

Secret Message

Complete the addition facts. In the Code Key, find the number that matches the sum of the first fact. Write the letter that is above that number in the first blank. Now, find the number in the Code Key that matches the sum of the second fact. Write the letter that is above it in the second blank. Continue with each addition fact until you have filled in all of the remaining blanks with a letter from the Code Key. When you are finished, you will find the secret message.

Why do spiders make good baseball players?

$\overline{1}$ $\overline{2}$ $\overline{3}$ $\overline{4}$ $\overline{5}$ $\overline{6}$ $\overline{7}$ $\overline{8}$ $\overline{9}$ $\overline{10}$ $\overline{11}$ $\overline{12}$ $\overline{13}$ $\overline{14}$

$\overline{15}$ $\overline{16}$ $\overline{17}$ $\overline{18}$ $\overline{19}$ $\overline{20}$ $\overline{21}$ $\overline{22}$ $\overline{23}$ $\overline{24}$ $\overline{25}$ $\overline{26}$ $\overline{27}$ $\overline{28}$

Code Key	L	B	Y	U	T	I	A	R	E	F	S	N	C	H
	0	4	6	7	8	9	10	11	12	13	14	15	16	18

① 2 + 2   ② 6 + 6   ③ 7 + 9   ④ 2 + 8   ⑤ 3 + 4   ⑥ 7 + 7   ⑦ 3 + 9

⑧ 4 + 4   ⑨ 9 + 9   ⑩ 10 + 2   ⑪ 3 + 3   ⑫ 8 + 8   ⑬ 3 + 7   ⑭ 9 + 6

⑮ 5 + 9   ⑯ 0 + 7   ⑰ 2 + 9   ⑱ 6 + 6   ⑲ 9 + 7   ⑳ 5 + 5   ㉑ 3 + 5

㉒ 8 + 8   ㉓ 8 + 10   ㉔ 4 + 9   ㉕ 0 + 0   ㉖ 7 + 2   ㉗ 9 + 3   ㉘ 7 + 7

LESSON 31: THE LEVEL 3 NUMBER CHALLENGE

The Level 3 Number Challenge includes the addition facts introduced in Level 3, as well as those introduced in Level 1 and Level 2.

Before students take the Level 3 Number Challenge, review the terms *addend* and *sum*. Have them complete addition facts with addends of 0, 1, 2, 3, 9, 10, and the doubles. Choose facts that the students find most challenging. The following are often difficult for students to complete:

8 + 8
9 + 5
1 + 0
6 + 6
3 + 5
2 + 8
7 + 7

Have the student discuss the different thinking strategies they can use with these addition facts.

INSTRUCTIONS FOR THE LEVEL 3 CHALLENGE

Distribute a copy of the challenge sheet to each student. Explain the challenge: There are nine facts at the top of the page. Below, there are nine boxes with a clue in each box. Complete the facts, then match each completed fact with one of the clues, and place it in that box. Cross out each fact after it has been placed in its box. For students who would like an extra challenge, have them add the sums of the three facts in each row, then add the sums of the three facts in each column. (See answer key for the mystery number.)

SUGGESTIONS FOR MORE PRACTICE

Students will have many more opportunities to practice the addition facts of this level as they work through the program. However, if the students need more practice, consider the following suggestions:

- Check that students can model the doubles.

- Check that students know the special pictures for the doubles.

- Write seven addition facts in a row, each with a missing addend. Have the students place a 9 for each of the missing addends, then repeat. Have the students complete the facts. Have them do the same for 1, 2, 3, 9, 10, and the same addend. For example, consider the following.

```
        8                 4         6
  + 7   +      + 0   + 9   +    + 3  +


    9     8     9     9     4     9     6
  + 7   + 9   + 0   + 9   + 9   + 3   + 9
```

- Identify the facts that students find difficult. Help them develop thinking strategies for these facts. Have them list the facts they find difficult, and encourage them to practice these facts both with a classmate in school and a parent at home.

- Have students continue to practice the first three levels of Power Facts.

- Have students play Partner Bingo in class or at home. There are 4 Partner Bingos for this level of the program (pages 155-158).

Level 3 Number Challenge

Complete the addition facts below. Then, read the clue in each box, and find the fact that matches it. Place each completed fact into the box with its matching clue.

6	9	4	0	9	2	3	2	7
+ 6	+ 7	+ 4	+ 2	+ 9	+ 2	+ 7	+ 4	+ 7

This fact is shown with the following picture: [dot picture]	This double fact has addends of 7.	This fact is shown with the following picture: [ten-frame picture]
The sum of this fact is two less than 20.	This fact is shown with the following picture: [dot picture]	This fact has the least sum.
The sum of this fact is the number of legs on a spider.	The sum of this fact is 2 more than 4.	This fact is shown with the following picture: [dot picture]

LEVEL 4: THE NEAR-DOUBLES

LEVEL 4 OVERVIEW

In Level 4, students are introduced to the near-doubles. The near-doubles are facts with addends that differ by one. These facts can also be called *next door number neighbour facts*. Students are introduced to the near-double thinking strategy. Many near-double facts have been introduced in previous levels of the program. For these facts, the near-double strategy offers an additional choice in how to complete them.

Prerequisites for the Near-Double Thinking Strategy

The near-double thinking strategy involves the following three steps:

Step 1: Identify the smaller addend.
Step 2: Double the smaller addend.
Step 3: Add 1 to the sum of the double.

Note: Students can also complete near-doubles by doubling the larger addend and subtracting one. Choosing the smaller addend is recommended as most students find it easier to add one to the sum of the double fact than to subtract one from the sum. However, if students prefer to double the larger addend and subtract one, allow them do so. If they choose the larger addend, ensure that they subtract one rather than add one.

Before introducing the near-double thinking strategy, make sure the students can do the following:

- identify near-doubles
- identify the smaller addend
- understand the doubles
- understand the one-more-than relationship

Identifying Near-Doubles

Present a number of facts to the students, including near-doubles. Read the facts aloud, and have the students identify the near-double facts by raising their hand or giving the thumbs-up sign.

Identifying the Smaller Addend

Write near-double facts on the chalkboard. Check that the students can identify the smaller addend in each fact.

Reviewing Thinking Strategies for the Doubles

In order to complete the near-doubles, students have to complete the double facts. Check that the students can use special pictures, the build-10 strategy, or the helping fact strategy to complete the doubles.

Practicing the One-More-Than Relationship for Numbers Less Than 20

Present students with a number less than 20. Check that they can name the number that is one more than the number.

Ten-Frame Flash

Practice the one-more-than relationship by playing Ten-Frame Flash with numbers less than or equal to 20. For example, show students two ten-frames, one containing 10 dots and one containing 8 dots. Have students name the number that is one more than the number of dots shown on the two ten-frames.

Introducing Thinking Strategies: Near-Double Facts

Consider the fact 7 + 6:

7 + 6 (near-double)

Step 1: Identify the smaller addend.

- The smaller addend is 6.

Step 2: Double the smaller addend.

- 6 + 6 = 12

Step 3: Add 1 to the sum of the double.

- 12 + 1 = 13
  SO, 7 + 6 = 13

Note: The double fact 6 + 6 can be completed with the special picture of a dozen eggs or with the helping fact 5 + 5.

Level 4 consists of the following lessons:

Lesson 4A: Cube Train Rally with the Near-Doubles

This lesson introduces the near-double facts.

Lesson 4B: Secret Message with the Near-Doubles

This lesson introduces the three-step thinking strategy for completing the near-double facts.

Lesson 4C: Match-Ups with the Near-Doubles

This lesson provides practice with the thinking strategies for the near-double facts.

Lesson 4D: Number Design with 3, 9, 10, the Doubles, and the Near-Doubles

This lesson incorporates the near-double facts with the double facts and with facts having an addend of 10. Students identify and apply appropriate thinking strategies for these facts.

Lesson 4E: Jellybean Jumble with 0, 1, 2, 3, 9, 10, the Doubles, and the Near-Doubles

In this lesson, students complete facts introduced in the first four levels of the program by identifying and applying the appropriate thinking strategies.

Lesson 4F: Wacky Webs with 0, 1, 2, 3, 9, 10, the Doubles, and the Near-Doubles

This lesson incorporates the near-double facts with the facts introduced in Levels 1-3. Students identify and apply appropriate thinking strategies for these facts. Even and odd numbers are also considered in this lesson.

Lesson 4G: Secret Message with 0, 1, 2, 3, 9, 10, the Doubles, and the Near-Doubles

In this lesson, students continue to complete facts introduced so far in the program.

Lesson 4H: The Level 4 Number Challenge

This challenge assesses the students' ability to identify and apply appropriate thinking strategies to the facts introduced in Levels 1-4. Students also review models and vocabulary introduced so far in the program.

ADDITION GRID

The addition facts considered in this level are the following:

+	0	1	2	3	4	5	6	7	8	9	10
0	0	1	2	3	4	5	6	7	8	9	10
1	1	2	3	4	5	6	7	8	9	10	11
2	2	3	4	5	6	7	8	9	10	11	12
3	3	4	5	6	7	8	9	10		12	13
4	4	5	6	7	8	9				13	14
5	5	6	7	8	9	10	11			14	15
6	6	7	8	9		11	12	13		15	16
7	7	8	9	10			13	14	15	16	17
8	8	9	10				15	16	17	18
9	9	10	11	12	13	14	15	16	17	18	19
10	10	11	12	13	14	15	16	17	18	19	20

LESSON 4A: CUBE TRAIN RALLY WITH THE NEAR-DOUBLES

TEACHER LESSON

In this lesson, students are introduced to the near-double facts and model these facts with cube trains.

Interpreting the Operation of Addition

Present the following story problem to the students:

■ Jason completed 1 more math problem than his friend Serge. If Serge completed 6 math problems, how many math problems did Jason complete? How many math problems did they complete altogether?

Have the students represent this story problem as a number sentence.

■ 6 + 1 = 7

■ Jason completed 7 math problems.
6 + 7 = 13
Altogether they completed 13 math problems.

Note: This story problem illustrates the additive structures of comparison, larger unknown and part-part-whole, whole unknown. Other additive structures are possible and are discussed in the Introduction to the program.

Introducing the Near-Doubles

Ask the students to compare the addends of the fact 6 + 7.

■ The addends differ by 1. The addend 7 is one more than the addend 6.

Explain to the students that facts with addends that differ by 1 are called *near-doubles*. Some students may prefer to call them *next door number neighbours*. Ask the students to name the near-double facts with addends less than or equal to 10.

Identifying Near-Doubles

Present the students with facts, some of which are near-doubles and some of which are not near-doubles. Have the students identify the facts that are near-doubles by either raising their hands or giving the thumbs-up sign.

Modelling Near-Doubles

Have the student model the fact 6 + 7 with cube trains.

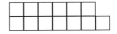

Have them note the following:

■ The cube train showing 7 has one more cube than the cube train showing 6.

Have the students compare the length of the cube trains.

■ The cube train showing 7 is one cube longer than the cube train showing 6.

Have the students model other near-double facts with cube trains.

Prerequisites for the Near-Double Thinking Strategy

The near-double thinking strategy involves the following three steps:

Step 1: Identify the smaller addend.

Step 2: Double the smaller addend.

Step 3: Add 1 to the sum of the double.

Before introducing the near-double thinking strategy, make sure the students can identify the smaller addend.

Identifying the Smaller Addend

Write the following near-double facts on the chalkboard. Check that the students can identify the smaller addend in each fact.

Near-doubles

3	7	5	8	6
+ 2	+ 8	+ 4	+ 9	+ 5

Smaller addend

2	7	4	8	5

Note: Have the students note the smaller addend can be either the first or the second addend in the fact.

Reviewing the Thinking Strategies for the Doubles

Check that the students can complete the doubles. Completing the doubles is a prerequisite for completing the near-doubles.

Practicing the One-More-Than Relationship for Numbers Less Than 20

Present students with a number that is less than 20. Ensure that they can name the number that is one more than it. Practice by playing Ten-Frame Flash with numbers less than 20. Have one of the ten-frames contain 10 dots. Have students name the number that is one more than the number of dots shown on the two ten-frames.

Encouraging Class Discussion

Engaging students in whole-class discussions is an integral part of the program. Prompts for encouraging class discussions can be found on page 2 of the Introduction.

INTRODUCING THE STUDENT ACTIVITY SHEET

Distribute a copy of the sheet, Cube Train Rally, to each student. Read the instructions aloud as a class, and have the students complete the activity.

Cube Train Rally

The addends of the fact 6 + 7 differ by one. The fact 6 + 7 is called a *near-double* or *next door number neighbour*.

You can show near-double facts with cube trains. In the first row below, complete the near-double fact that the cube trains show. In the second row, draw cube trains and complete the near-double fact the cube trains show. In the third row, draw cube trains and show and complete the near-double fact for each. Every cube train picture on this sheet must show a different sum.

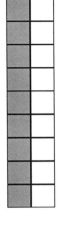

6 + 7 = _____

4 + 5 = _____

8 + 7 = _____

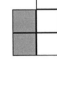

1 + 2 = _____

_____

What thinking strategy can you use to complete the fact 6 + 7? Explain your answer.

_____

LESSON 4B: SECRET MESSAGE WITH THE NEAR-DOUBLES

TEACHER LESSON

In this lesson, students are introduced to the thinking strategy for the near-doubles.

Identifying Near-Doubles

Present the addition fact 5 + 6 to the students. Ask them to identify the fact.

- Since the addends differ by 1, the fact 5 + 6 is a near-double.

Introducing the Thinking Strategy: Near-Doubles

Have the students consider the fact 5 + 6. Ask them which double facts they can use to help them complete the near-double 5 + 6.

- 5 + 5 or 6 + 6

If the students use the double 5 + 5, they have to add 1 to the sum to complete the fact 5 + 6. If the students use the double 6 + 6, they have to subtract 1 from the sum to complete the fact 5 + 6. Since it is easier to add 1 than to subtract 1, suggest the students use the double 5 + 5 to help them complete the near-double 5 + 6.

Encourage the students to complete a near-double fact by doubling the smaller addend and then adding one. However, if students prefer to double the larger addend, and subtract one, allow them to do so. Make sure that if they choose the larger addend, they subtract one rather than add one.

Applying the Thinking Strategy: Near-Doubles

Ask the students to use the following three step near-double thinking strategy to complete the fact 5 + 6.

5 + 6 (near-double)

- Three-Step Strategy:
  Step 1: Identify the smaller addend.
  The smaller addend is 5.
  Step 2: Double the smaller addend.
  5 + 5 = 10
  Step 3: Add 1 to the sum of the double.
  10 + 1 = 11
  SO, 5 + 6 = 11

Note: The students can complete the double fact 5 + 5 with the special picture of a person with 5 fingers on each hand.

Note: The fact 5 + 6 has an addend of 5. The ten-frame model is particularly helpful for completing facts with an addend of 5. The fact can be pictured with 2 rows of 5 dots and one more dot. Encourage students to picture the ten-frames for facts with an addend of 5.

Practicing the Thinking Strategy: Near-Doubles

Present the following facts to the students.

$$
\begin{array}{ccccc}
7 & 5 & 7 & 8 & 6 \\
+8 & +4 & +6 & +9 & +5 \\
\end{array}
$$

- Have the students identify the smaller addend of each fact.
- Next, have students double the smaller addend of each fact.
- Finally, have students add 1 to the sum of the doubles of each fact.

Creating Story Problems

Ask each student to choose a near-double fact and create a story problem that illustrates the fact. Suggest students use socks, shoes, or mittens. Have them model their story problems with pictures, then solve their story problems.

Encouraging Class Discussion

Engaging students in whole-class discussions is an integral part of the program. Prompts for encouraging class discussions can be found on page 2 of the Introduction.

INTRODUCING THE STUDENT ACTIVITY SHEET

Distribute a copy of the sheet, Secret Message, to each student. Read the instructions aloud as a class, and have the students complete the activity.

Note: Suggest that students first circle the smaller addend of each near-double fact in the activity.

STUDENT JOURNAL

Have students choose a near-double fact and explain their thinking strategies for completing it.

COMPLETING THE ADDITION GRID

Have the students fill in their addition grid for the near-doubles. Many of the near-double facts have already been filled in.

Note: Make sure the students note that the sums of the near-double facts lie on either side of the diagonal of the grid.

Secret Message

Complete the addition facts. In the Code Key, find the number that matches the sum of the first fact. Write the letter that is above that number in the first blank. Now, find the number in the Code Key that matches the sum of the second fact. Write the letter that is above it in the second blank. Continue with each addition fact until you have filled in the remaining blanks with a letter from the Code Key. When you are finished, you will find the secret message.

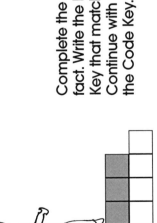

$\overline{①}$ $\overline{②}$ $\overline{③}$ $\overline{④}$ $\overline{⑤}$ $\overline{⑥}$ $\overline{⑦}$ $\overline{⑧}$ $\overline{⑨}$ $\overline{⑩}$ $\overline{⑪}$ $\overline{⑫}$

$\overline{⑬}$ $\overline{⑭}$ $\overline{⑮}$ $\overline{⑯}$ $\overline{⑰}$ $\overline{⑱}$ $\overline{⑲}$ $\overline{⑳}$ $\overline{㉑}$ $\overline{㉒}$ $\overline{㉓}$ $\overline{㉔}$

What would you have if you read a story on the back of a car?

Code Key	E	L	O	N	A	H	T	I	G
	6	7	10	11	13	14	15	16	17

① 5 +5

② 5 +6

③ 3 +3

④ 4 +3

⑤ 8 +8

⑥ 8 +9

⑦ 7 +7

⑧ 7 +8

⑨ 8 +7

⑩ 6 +7

⑪ 3 +4

⑫ 3 +3

⑬ 5 +5

⑭ 6 +5

⑮ 3 +3

⑯ 8 +7

⑰ 7 +6

⑱ 8 +8

⑲ 4 +3

⑳ 3 +4

㉑ 8 +8

㉒ 9 +8

㉓ 7 +7

㉔ 7 +8

LESSON 4C: MATCH-UPS WITH THE NEAR-DOUBLES

TEACHER LESSON

In this lesson, the students practice the thinking strategies for the near-doubles.

Practicing the Thinking Strategy: Near-Doubles

Present students with the following near-double facts:

$$8 + 7$$
$$4 + 3$$
$$9 + 8$$

Ask students to identify these facts and complete them. Have students explain what thinking strategies they used.

(a) 8 + 7 (near-double fact)

- Three-Step Strategy:

    Step 1: Identify the smaller addend.
    The smaller addend is 7.

    Step 2: Double the smaller addend.
    $7 + 7 = 14$

    Step 3: Add 1 to the sum of the double.
    $14 + 1 = 15$
    SO, $8 + 7 = 15$

Note: The students can complete the double fact $7 + 7$ with the special picture of a calendar or with the helping fact $5 + 5$.

Note: The build-10 strategy and helping fact strategy can also be used for this fact and are considered in more detail in Level 5.

(b) 4 + 3 (addend of 3/near-double fact)

- Count on 3:

    $4 \rightarrow 5, 6, 7$
    SO, $4 + 3 = 7$

- Three-Step Strategy:

    Step 1: Identify the smaller addend.
    The smaller addend is 3.

    Step 2: Double the smaller addend.
    $3 + 3 = 6$

    Step 3: Add 1 to the sum of the double.
    $6 + 1 = 7$
    SO, $4 + 3 = 7$

Note: Because the fact $4 + 3$ has an addend of 3 and is a near-double fact, students can choose a strategy for either. Discuss with students which strategy they prefer, and have them justify their choice.

(c) 9 + 8 (addend of 9/near-double fact)

- Three-Step Strategy:

    Step 1: Identify the smaller addend.
    The smaller addend is 8.

    Step 2: Double the smaller addend.
    $8 + 8 = 16$

    Step 3: Add 1 to the sum of the double.
    $16 + 1 = 17$
    SO, $9 + 8 = 17$

- Build-10:

    Build 10 by taking 1 from 8.
    $9 + 1 = 10$ and $8 - 1 = 7$
    $10 + 7 = 17$
    SO, $9 + 8 = 17$

- Helping Fact:

    $10 + 8 = 18$
    $9 = 10 - 1$
    $18 - 1 = 17$
    SO, $9 + 8 = 17$

Note: The students can complete the double fact $8 + 8$ with the special picture of crayons or with the helping fact $10 + 10$.

Note: Because the fact $9 + 8$ has both an addend of 9 and is a near-double fact, students can choose a strategy for either. Discuss with students which strategy they prefer, and have them justify their choice.

Encouraging Class Discussion

Engaging students in whole-class discussions is an integral part of the program. Prompts for encouraging class discussions can be found on page 2 of the Introduction.

INTRODUCING THE STUDENT ACTIVITY SHEET

Distribute a copy of the sheet, Match-Ups, to each student. Read the instructions aloud as a class, and have the students complete the activity.

POWER FACTS

Have students practice the fourth set of Power Facts (page 136) at least once a day. They can also continue to practice the first three sets of facts. Students can practice in class and at home.

PARTNER BINGO

Partner Bingo, Level 4A, provides more practice for the near-doubles (pages 159-160). Have the students complete the facts in order and cross out only one square on their card for each fact. Partner Bingo can be played in class or at home.

CARD GAMES

Card Games, Level 4, provide more practice for the near-doubles (pages 210-211). Students can play in class or at home.

Match-Ups

Complete each addition fact by connecting the dot beside the fact to the dot beside its sum.

When you have completed the "match-ups," answer the question at the bottom of the page.

8 + 7 •	• 1	7 + 6 •	• 13
3 + 4 •	• 13	4 + 5 •	• 1
6 + 7 •	• 7	7 + 8 •	• 5
1 + 0 •	• 15	6 + 5 •	• 3
5 + 6 •	• 11	9 + 8 •	• 7
8 + 9 •	• 17	4 + 3 •	• 17
4 + 5 •	• 3	1 + 2 •	• 11
3 + 2 •	• 19	3 + 2 •	• 15
9 + 10 •	• 5	0 + 1 •	• 9
2 + 1 •	• 9	10 + 9 •	• 19

What thinking strategy did you use for completing the fact 8 + 7? Explain your answer.

LESSON 4D: NUMBER DESIGN WITH 3, 9, 10, THE DOUBLES, AND THE NEAR-DOUBLES

TEACHER LESSON

In this lesson, students incorporate the near-double facts with the double facts and facts with an addend of 10.

Identifying Thinking Strategies

Now that the thinking strategies for the near-double facts have been developed, have the students complete the following addition facts together with the double facts and facts with an addend of 10.

The following facts include two facts that are near-doubles, two facts that are doubles, and two facts with an addend of 10. Have the students identify these facts.

```
  5      6     10      7      5      7
+ 4    + 6    + 4    + 7    + 10    + 8
```

near-doubles

```
  5      7
+ 4    + 8
```

doubles

```
  6      7
+ 6    + 7
```

addend of 10

```
 10      5
+ 4    + 10
```

Applying Thinking Strategies

Ask the students how they would apply thinking strategies for the facts they identified.

(a) 5 + 4 (near-double)

- Three-Step Strategy:
    Step 1: 4 is the smaller addend
    Step 2: 4 + 4 = 8
    Step 3: 8 + 1 = 9
            SO, 5 + 4 = 9

Note: Students can use the special picture of a spider to complete the double fact 4 + 4.

Note: Since the fact has an addend of 5, it can be pictured with a ten-frame having 5 dots in the first row and 4 dots in the second. This ten-frame shows the number 9. Encourage students to picture ten-frames for facts with an addend of 5.

Using the three-step strategy, have the students complete the fact 7 + 8.

(b) 6 + 6 (double fact)

- Special Picture:
    Picture an egg carton with 2 rows of 6 eggs.
    SO, 6 + 6 = 12

Note: Students can also complete the double fact 6 + 6 with the helping fact 5 + 5.

Have students use a similar thinking strategy to complete the fact 7 + 7.

(c) 10 + 4 (addend of 10)

- Pattern of 10:
    A set of 10 and a set of 4 is 14.
    SO, 10 + 4 = 14

Have students use a similar thinking strategy to complete the fact 5 + 10.

Encouraging Class Discussion

Engaging students in whole-class discussions is an integral part of the program. Prompts for encouraging class discussions can be found on page 2 of the Introduction.

INTRODUCING THE STUDENT ACTIVITY SHEET

Distribute a copy of the sheet, Number Design, to each student. Read the instructions aloud as a class, and have the students complete the activity.

Note: The coloured areas form a pattern that students can use to check their work.

CHALLENGE FACTS

Use the Challenge Facts, Level 4B (page 188), to help the students identify facts that have addends of 0, 1, 2, 3, 9, 10, are doubles, and are near-doubles. Have the students place shapes around the facts. For example, have them place circles around all the near-double facts and then complete them. Next, have them place rectangles around all double facts, and so on. They can also use different coloured pencils to identify the facts.

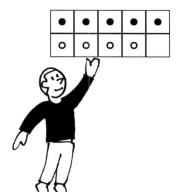

Number Design

Complete the addition facts. Choose your own colours for the Colour Key, then colour the design.

5 + 4 =

9 + 7 =

10 + 3 =

6 + 5 =

3 + 7 =

5 + 5 =

3 + 1 =

10 + 10 =

2 + 2 =

6 + 9 =

9 + 6 =

9 + 4 =

6 + 6 =

7 + 8 =

0 + 1 =

3 + 0 =

3 + 6 =

1 + 2 =

8 + 7 =

9 + 2 =

1 + 9 =

7 + 7 =

9 + 5 =

0 + 0 =

8 + 8 =

2 + 3 =

5 + 3 =

4 + 4 =

5 + 6 =

6 + 3 =

4 + 9 =

6 + 7 =

Colour Key

near doubles: _____

doubles: _____

addend of 3: _____

addend of 9: _____

LESSON 4E: JELLYBEAN JUMBLE WITH 0, 1, 2, 3, 9, 10, THE DOUBLES, AND THE NEAR-DOUBLES

TEACHER LESSON

In this lesson, students complete facts with addends of 0, 1, 2, 3, 9, 10, doubles, and near-doubles by identifying and applying the appropriate thinking strategies.

Identifying and Applying Thinking Strategies

Present the students with the following addition facts:

$1 + 2$
$6 + 9$
$8 + 7$
$3 + 6$
$4 + 4$
$10 + 2$

Have the students complete the facts. The students must be able to recognize and apply an appropriate thinking strategy for each fact, then explain their thinking strategies. Have the students first note whether the facts have an addend of 0, 1, 2, 3, 9, 10, are doubles, or are near-doubles.

(a) 1 + 2 (addend of 1/addend of 2/near-double fact)

■ One-More-Than:
  One more than 2 is 3.
  SO, $1 + 2 = 3$

■ Two-More-Than:
  Two more than 1 is 3.
  SO, $1 + 2 = 3$

■ Three-Step Strategy:
  Step 1: The smaller addend is 1.
  Step 2: $1 + 1 = 2$
  Step 3: $1 + 2 = 3$
       SO, $1 + 2 = 3$

Note: Discuss with students why the one-more-than strategy is more efficient for this fact than the other strategies.

(b) 6 + 9 (addend of 9)

■ Build-10:
  Build 10 by taking 1 from 6.
  $9 + 1 = 10$ and $6 - 1 = 5$
  $10 + 5 = 15$
  SO, $6 + 9 = 15$

■ Helping Fact:
  $6 + 10 = 16$
  $9 = 10 - 1$
  $16 - 1 = 15$
  SO, $6 + 9 = 15$

(c) 8 + 7 (near-double)

■ Three-Step Strategy:
  Step 1: The smaller addend is 7.
  Step 2: $7 + 7 = 14$
  Step 3: $14 + 1 = 15$
       SO, $8 + 7 = 15$

Note: The students can complete the double fact $7 + 7$ with the special picture of a calendar or with the helping fact $5 + 5$.

Note: The build-10 strategy and helping fact strategy can be used for this fact. They are considered in more detail in Level 5.

(d) 3 + 6 (addend of 3)

■ Count on 3:
  $6 \rightarrow 7, 8, 9$
  SO, $3 + 6 = 9$

(e) 4 + 4 (double fact)

■ Special Picture:
  Picture a spider with 4 legs on each side.
  SO, $4 + 4 = 8$

(f) 10 + 2 (addend of 2/addend of 10)

■ Two-More-Than:
  Two more than 10 is 12.
  SO, $10 + 2 = 12$

■ Pattern of 10:
  A set of 10 and a set of 2 is 12.
  SO, $10 + 2 = 12$

Note: Because this fact has an addend of 10 and an addend of 2, students can choose a strategy for either addend. Discuss with students which strategy they prefer, and have them justify their choice.

Encouraging Class Discussion

Engaging students in whole-class discussions is an integral part of the program. Prompts for encouraging class discussions can be found on page 2 of the Introduction.

INTRODUCING THE STUDENT ACTIVITY SHEET

Distribute a copy of the sheet, Jellybean Jumble, to each student. Read the instructions aloud as a class, and have the students complete the activity.

Jellybean Jumble

Complete the addition facts below. You will find that the sum of one of the four facts in each group is different from the sums of the other three facts. Colour the jellybean in each group that has the different sum.

1 + 2 =   0 + 5 =

4 + 1 =   2 + 3 =

4 + 5 =   3 + 7 =

3 + 6 =   7 + 2 =

6 + 7 =

4 + 9 =   3 + 10 =

3 + 9 =

4 + 3 =

0 + 7 =   3 + 3 =

1 + 6 =

3 + 7 =

6 + 5 =   8 + 2 =

5 + 5 =

8 + 9 =

8 + 8 =   10 + 6 =

9 + 7 =

5 + 6 =   2 + 9 =

6 + 7 =   1 + 10 =

7 + 7 =   9 + 5 =

4 + 10 =   8 + 7 =

LESSON 4F: WACKY WEBS WITH 0, 1, 2, 3, 9, 10, THE DOUBLES, AND THE NEAR-DOUBLES

TEACHER LESSON

In this lesson, students complete facts with an addend of 0, 1, 2, 3, 9, 10, doubles, or near-doubles by identifying and applying the appropriate thinking strategies. They also identify even and odd numbers.

Identifying and Applying Thinking Strategies

Present students with the following facts:

3 + 4
9 + 4
5 + 5

Have the students complete the facts. The students must be able to recognize and apply an appropriate thinking strategy for each fact, then explain their thinking strategies. Have the students first note if the facts have an addend of 3, 9, are doubles, or near-doubles.

(a) 3 + 4 (addend of 3/near-double fact)

■ Count on 3:
4 → 5, 6, 7
SO, 3 + 4 = 7

■ Three-Step Strategy:
Step 1: The smaller addend is 3.
Step 2: 3 + 3 = 6
Step 3: 6 + 1 = 7
SO, 3 + 4 = 7

Note: Discuss with students which strategy they prefer, and ask them to justify their choice.

(b) 9 + 4 (addend of 3/addend of 9)

■ Build-10:
Build 10 by taking 1 from 4.
9 + 1 = 10 and 4 − 1 = 3
10 + 3 = 13
SO, 9 + 4 = 13

■ Helping Fact:
10 + 4 = 14
9 = 10 − 1
14 − 1 = 13
SO, 9 + 4 = 13

(c) 5 + 5 (double fact)

■ Special Picture:
Picture a person with 5 fingers on each hand.
SO, 5 + 5 = 10

Note: Some students will complete the fact 5 + 5 by picturing a ten-frame with 5 counters in the first row and 5 counters in the second row. Encourage them to do so.

Even and Odd Numbers

Have the students name the even numbers that are less than or equal to 20.

■ 0, 2, 4, 6, 8, 10, 12, 14, 16, 18, 20

Have the students name the odd numbers that are less than or equal to 20.

■ 1, 3, 5, 7, 9, 11, 13, 15, 17, 19

Have the students consider the addition sentence 3 + 4 = 7. Ask the students: Is the sum of this fact even or odd? (odd)

Ask the students: Why is the number 7 odd?

■ It is not possible to divide 7 into two equal groups.

Have the students model this explanation with cube trains.

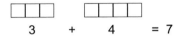

3   +   4   = 7

Ask the students: Is the sum of any near-double fact odd? (yes)

Ask the students: Why is the sum of a near-double fact always odd?

■ Since a near-double fact consists of addends that differ by 1, it is not possible to divide its sum into two equal groups.

Encouraging Class Discussion

Engaging students in whole-class discussions is an integral part of the program. Prompts for encouraging class discussions can be found on page 2 of the Introduction.

INTRODUCING THE STUDENT ACTIVITY SHEET

Distribute a copy of the sheet, Wacky Webs, to each student. Read the instructions aloud as a class, and have the students complete the activity.

Note: The coloured cells form a pattern that students can use to check their work. The pattern will help them become aware of the rules for even and odd sums. Further explanation of even and odd sums, including rules, is given in Lesson 6G.

Wacky Webs

The numbers 0, 2, 4, 6, 8, 10, 12, 14, 16, 18, and 20 are **EVEN** numbers.

The numbers 1, 3, 5, 7, 9, 11, 13, 15, 17, and 19 are **ODD** numbers.

Below, fill in the outer cells of each web by adding the numbers in the inner cells with the number in the middle.

Colour all of the cells that have an **EVEN** number.

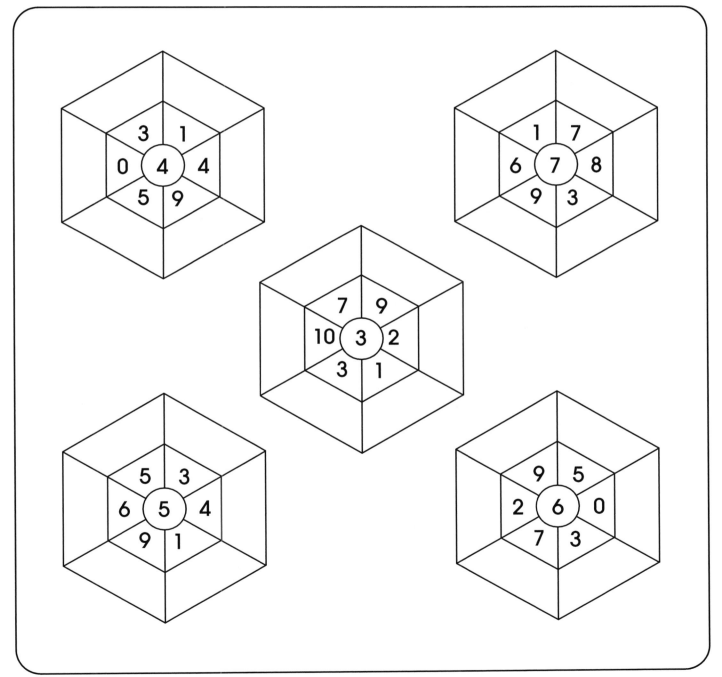

LESSON 4G: SECRET MESSAGE WITH 0, 1, 2, 3, 9, 10, THE DOUBLES, AND THE NEAR-DOUBLES

TEACHER LESSON

In this lesson, students practice completing facts with addends of 0, 1, 2, 3, 9, 10, doubles, and near-doubles.

Preparing for the Level 4 Number Challenge

Encourage students to practice the fourth set of Power Facts (page 136). Students can also play Partner Bingo, Level 4 (pages 159-162), either in class or at home, to prepare for the Level 4 Challenge.

Identifying and Applying Thinking Strategies

Present the students with the following addition facts:

10 + 9
3 + 7
9 + 0
7 + 6
8 + 2
1 + 4
7 + 7

Have the students complete the facts and explain their thinking strategies.

(a) 10 + 9 (addend of 10/addend of 9/near-double)

- Pattern of 10:

    A set of 10 and a set of 9 is 19.
    SO, 10 + 9 = 19

Note: Discuss with students why it is more efficient to consider the strategy for the addend of 10 than it is to use strategies for the addend of 9 and near-double facts.

(b) 3 + 7 (addend of 3)

- Count on 3:

    7 → 8, 9, 10
    SO, 3 + 7 = 10

Note: Some students will complete this fact by picturing a ten-frame. Encourage them to do so.

(c) 9 + 0 (addend of 0/addend of 9)

- Pattern of 0:

    The sum of a number and 0 is the number.
    SO, 9 + 0 = 9

Note: Discuss with students why it is not possible to complete the fact with the build-10 strategy, and why the pattern of 0 strategy is more efficient than the helping fact strategy for an addend of 9.

(d) 7 + 6 (near-double)

- Three-Step Strategy:

    Step 1: The smaller addend is 6.
    Step 2: 6 + 6 = 12
    Step 3: 12 + 1 = 13
        SO, 7 + 6 =13

Note: The students can complete the double fact 6 + 6 with the special picture of a dozen eggs or with the helping fact 5 + 5.

(e) 8 + 2 (addend of 2)

- Two-More-Than:

    Two more than 8 is 10.
    SO, 8 + 2 = 10

Note: Some students will complete this fact by picturing a ten-frame. Encourage them to do so.

(f) 1 + 4 (addend of 1)

- One-More-Than:

    One more than 4 is 5.
    SO, 1 + 4 = 5

(g) 7 + 7 (double fact)

- Special Picture:

    Picture a calendar with 2 weeks of 14 days.
    SO, 7 + 7 = 14

- Helping Fact:

    5 + 5 = 10
    7 = 5 + 2
    10 + 2 + 2 = 14
    SO, 7 + 7 = 14

Encouraging Class Discussion

Engaging students in whole-class discussions is an integral part of the program. Prompts for encouraging class discussions can be found on page 2 of the Introduction.

INTRODUCING THE STUDENT ACTIVITY SHEET

Distribute a copy of the sheet, Secret Message, to each student. Read the instructions aloud as a class, and have the students complete the activity.

PARTNER BINGO

Students can practice all facts introduced in the program so far by playing Partner Bingo, Level 4B (pages 161-162). Have the students complete the facts in order and cross out only one square on their card for each fact. Partner Bingo can be played in class or at home.

Secret Message

Complete the addition facts below. In the Code Key, find the number that matches the sum of the first fact. Write the letter that is above that number in the first blank. Now, find the number in the Code Key that matches the sum of the second fact. Write the letter that is above it in the second blank. Continue with each addition fact until you have filled in all of the remaining blanks with a letter from the Code Key. When you are finished, you will find the secret message.

How can you tell that the train was happy?

$\overline{1}$ $\overline{2}$ $\overline{3}$ $\overline{4}$ $\overline{5}$ $\overline{6}$ $\overline{7}$ $\overline{8}$ $\overline{9}$ $\overline{10}$ $\overline{11}$ $\overline{12}$

$\overline{13}$ $\overline{14}$ $\overline{15}$ $\overline{16}$ $\overline{17}$ $\overline{18}$ $\overline{19}$ $\overline{20}$ $\overline{21}$ $\overline{22}$ $\overline{23}$ $\overline{24}$ $\overline{25}$ $\overline{26}$ $\overline{27}$ $\overline{28}$

Code Key	S	N	R	H	D	I	E	K	T	A	O	L	W
	7	8	9	10	11	12	13	14	15	16	17	18	19

1) $10 + 9$
2) $5 + 5$
3) $6 + 7$
4) $3 + 5$
5) $7 + 8$
6) $8 + 2$
7) $9 + 4$

8) $5 + 10$
9) $6 + 3$
10) $8 + 8$
11) $3 + 9$
12) $4 + 4$
13) $10 + 9$
14) $9 + 8$

15) $5 + 4$
16) $7 + 7$
17) $3 + 10$
18) $6 + 5$
19) $9 + 3$
20) $8 + 7$
21) $9 + 10$

22) $3 + 7$
23) $6 + 6$
24) $4 + 3$
25) $9 + 6$
26) $9 + 9$
27) $7 + 6$
28) $10 + 1$

LESSON 4H: THE LEVEL 4 NUMBER CHALLENGE

The Level 4 Number Challenge includes the addition facts introduced in Level 4, as well as those introduced in Levels 1, 2, and 3.

Before students take the Level 4 Number Challenge review the terms *addend* and *sum*. Have them complete addition facts with an addend of 0, 1, 2, 3, 9, 10, doubles, and near-doubles. Choose facts that the students find most challenging. The following are often difficult for students to complete:

8 + 7
9 + 6
0 + 10
3 + 7
8 + 8
3 + 6
6 + 7

Have the student discuss the different thinking strategies they can use with these addition facts.

INSTRUCTIONS FOR THE LEVEL 4 CHALLENGE

Distribute a copy of the challenge sheet to each student. Explain the challenge: There are nine facts at the top of the page. Below, there are nine boxes with a clue in each box. Complete the facts, then match each completed fact with one of the clues, and place it in that box. Cross out each fact after it has been placed in its box. For students who would like an extra challenge, have them add the sums of the three facts in each row, then add the sums of the three facts in each column. (See answer key for the mystery number.)

SUGGESTIONS FOR MORE PRACTICE

Students will have many more opportunities to practice the addition facts of this level as they work through the program. However, if the students need more practice, consider the following suggestions.

■ Check that students can identify near-double facts.

■ Check that students can identify the smaller of the two addends in near-double facts.

■ Check that students can complete the doubles.

■ Check that students can name the number that is one more than a number less than 20.

■ Check that students can follow the three-step procedure for completing the near-doubles.

■ Write seven addition facts in a row, each with a missing addend. Have the students place a 0, 1, 2, 3, 9, 10, the same addend, or an addend that differs by 1 for each of the missing addends. Have the students complete the facts. For example, consider the following:

7		0	9		8	
+	+ 4	+	+	+ 6	+	+ 5

7	5	0	9	7	8	4
+ 8	+ 4	+ 1	+ 10	+ 6	+ 9	+ 5

■ Identify the facts that students find difficult. Help them develop thinking strategies for these facts. Have the students list the facts they find difficult, and encourage them to practice these facts both with a classmate in school and a parent at home.

■ Have students continue to practice the first four levels of Power Facts.

■ Have students play Partner Bingo in class or at home. There are 4 Partner Bingos for this level of the program (pages 159-162).

■ Have the students make up rap songs or adopt familiar songs for the facts.

Level 4 Number Challenge

Complete the addition facts below. Then, read the clue in each box, and find the fact that matches it. Place each completed fact into the box with its matching clue.

5	7	3	2	9	8	10	7	5
+ 6	+ 7	+ 5	+ 8	+ 4	+ 7	+ 2	+ 9	+ 4

The sum of this fact is one more than the number of days in two weeks.	This fact is shown with the following picture: 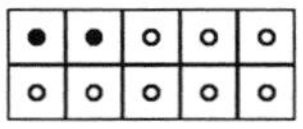	This is the near-double fact with addends of 5 and 6.
This fact is shown with the following picture: 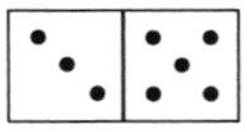	The sum of this fact is 2 more than 10.	This is the fact with the greatest sum.
This fact is shown with the following picture: 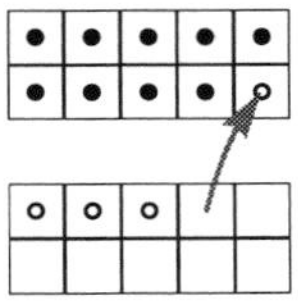	This fact is a double fact. It has the same addends.	This fact is shown with the following picture: 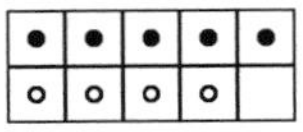

LEVEL 5: FACTS WITH 8

LEVEL 5 OVERVIEW

Level 5 examines the basic addition facts with an addend of 8. Many of the facts with an addend of 8 have already been introduced in previous levels of the program.

There are four basic facts with an addend of 8, and their turnarounds, that have not been introduced. They are:

3 + 8 and 8 + 3
4 + 8 and 8 + 4
5 + 8 and 8 + 5
6 + 8 and 8 + 6

The build-10 and helping fact strategies are the main thinking strategies for completing these facts. These strategies are based on the place value relationship with 10.

Build-10 Strategy

The build-10 thinking strategy can not only be used for facts with an addend of 9 but also for other facts. The build-10 thinking strategy for facts with an addend of 8 is to build-10 by taking 2 from the number added with 8 and adding it to 8.

The build-10 strategy can be modelled with ten-frames. For example, consider the fact 8 + 4.

Helping Fact Strategy

The helping fact thinking strategy for facts with an addend of 8 is similar to the helping fact strategy for facts with an addend of 9. When using a helping fact with an addend of 10 to complete a fact with an addend of 8, subtract 2 from the sum of the helping fact.

Ten-Frame Flash

To apply the build-10 strategy, students have to take away 2 from the addend that is being added with 8. To provide more practice with finding two less than a number from 2 to 10, play Ten-Frame Flash with the students. Show the students a ten-frame, and ask them for the number that is two less than the number indicated on the ten-frame. Have them answer with their response cards.

To apply the helping fact strategy, students have to take away 2 from the sum of the corresponding helping fact. To provide more practice with finding two less than a number from 10 to 20, play Ten-Frame Flash with two ten-frames. Show the students two ten-frames, with one containing ten counters. Ask them for the number that is two less than the number indicated on the ten-frames. Have them answer with their response cards.

The Ten-Frame Train

The ten-frame train can help the students with the build-10 strategy. If one ten-frame train has 8 passengers and the other train has 4 passengers, two of the passengers from the second train must move to the first train to fill the first train, leaving 2 passengers in the second train.

Introducing the Thinking Strategies: Addend of 8

The primary thinking strategies for facts with an addend of 8 are the build-10 and helping fact strategies. Consider, for example, the fact 8 + 4.

8 + 4 (addend of 8)

- Build-10:
  Build 10 by taking 2 from 4 and giving it to 8.
  8 + 2 = 10 and 4 − 2 = 2
  10 + 2 = 12
  SO, 8 + 4 = 12

- Helping Fact:
  10 + 4 = 14
  8 = 10 − 2
  14 − 2 = 12
  SO, 8 + 4 = 12

Level 5 consists of the following lessons:

Lesson 5A: Ten-Frame Rally with 8

This lesson introduces the build-10 thinking strategy for facts with an addend of 8.

Lesson 5B: Wacky Webs with 8, 9, and 10

In this lesson, students compare the thinking strategies for facts with an addend of 8, 9, or 10. Even and odd addends and even and odd sums are also considered in this lesson.

Lesson 5C: Match-Ups with 8

This lesson provides practice with the thinking strategies for facts with an addend of 8.

Lesson 5D: Number Design with 3, 8, and 9

In this lesson, students incorporate the facts with an addend of 8 with those having an addend of either 3 or 9. Students identify and apply appropriate thinking strategies for these facts.

Lesson 5E: Jellybean Jumble with 0, 1, 2, 3, 8, 9, 10, the Doubles, and the Near-Doubles

This lesson incorporates facts having an addend of 8 with facts introduced in Levels 1-4. Students identify and apply appropriate thinking strategies for these facts.

Lesson 5F: Secret Message with 0, 1, 2, 3, 8, 9, 10, the Doubles, and the Near-Doubles

In this lesson, students continue to complete facts introduced so far in the program.

Lesson 5G: The Level 5 Number Challenge

This challenge assesses the students' ability to identify and apply appropriate thinking strategies to the facts introduced in Levels 1-5. Students also review models and vocabulary introduced so far in the program.

ADDITION GRID

The addition facts considered in this level are the following:

+	0	1	2	3	4	5	6	7	8	9	10
0	0	1	2	3	4	5	6	7	8	9	10
1	1	2	3	4	5	6	7	8	9	10	11
2	2	3	4	5	6	7	8	9	10	11	12
3	3	4	5	6	7	8	9	10	11	12	13
4	4	5	6	7	8	9			12	13	14
5	5	6	7	8	9	10	11		13	14	15
6	6	7	8	9		11	12	13	14	15	16
7	7	8	9	10			13	14	15	16	17
8	8	9	10	11	12	13	14	15	16	17	18
9	9	10	11	12	13	14	15	16	17	18	19
10	10	11	12	13	14	15	16	17	18	19	20

LESSON 5A: TEN-FRAME RALLY WITH 8

TEACHER LESSON

In this lesson, students are introduced to the build-10 thinking strategy for facts with an addend of 8.

Checking the Addition Grid

Have the students check their addition grid and find the facts with an addend of 8 they have already completed.

0 + 8 and 8 + 0
1 + 8 and 8 + 1
2 + 8 and 8 + 2
7 + 8 and 8 + 7
8 + 8
9 + 8 and 8 + 9
10 + 8 and 8 + 10

Ask the students to complete these facts and explain their thinking strategies. In this lesson and in lesson 5B, students will develop thinking strategies for the remaining facts with an addend of 8.

Interpreting the Operation of Addition

Present the following story problem to the students:

■ There are 8 passengers in 1 ten-frame train and 4 passengers in another ten-frame train. How many passengers altogether are in the two trains?

Have the students draw a picture illustrating this problem. Have them represent it as a number sentence.

■ 8 + 4 = 12
There are 12 passengers altogether.

Note: This story problem illustrates the additive structure; part-part-whole. Other additive structures are possible and are discussed in the Introduction to the program.

Introducing the Thinking Strategy: Build-10

Ask the students: How can the build-10 strategy be used to complete the fact 8 + 4?

■ Move 2 passengers from the second train to fill the first train. This leaves 2 passengers in the second train. One ten-frame with 10 and another ten-frame with 2 represent 12.

Explain to the students that they can use the build-10 strategy to complete a fact with an addend of 8.

Divide the class into cooperative working groups. Distribute ten-frame mats and counters, as well as a copy of the activity sheet, Ten-Frame Rally, to each student. Explain to students they will use ten-frames to complete addition facts with an addend of 8. They will also have to explain their thinking strategy for completing facts with an addend of 8.

Applying the Thinking Strategy: Build-10

After the students have completed the activity sheet, discuss how they can apply the build-10 strategy to facts with an addend of 8. The build-10 thinking strategy for facts with an addend of 8 is to build-10 by taking 2 from the number added with 8 and adding it to 8.

Have the students complete the fact 8 + 4 using the build-10 thinking strategy.

8 + 4 (addend of 8)

■ Build-10:
Build 10 by taking 2 from 4 and giving it to 8.
8 + 2 = 10 and 4 − 2 = 2
10 + 2 = 12
SO, 8 + 4 = 12

Have the students note they can use the build-10 thinking strategy when the addend of 8 is the first addend or the second. Remind the students that the order of the addends does not affect the sum.

Ten-Frame Flash

To provide more practice with finding two less than a number, play Ten-Frame Flash with the students. Show the students a ten-frame, and ask them for the number that is two less than the number indicated on the ten-frame. Have them answer with their response cards.

Encouraging Class Discussion

Engaging students in whole-class discussions is an integral part of the program. Prompts for encouraging class discussions can be found on page 2 of the Introduction.

INTRODUCING THE STUDENT ACTIVITY SHEET

Students will have completed the activity sheet during the lesson.

Note: Some students may note the last fact on the activity sheet, 5 + 8, has an addend of 5. It can also be completed as follows:

COMPLETING THE ADDITION GRID

Have the students fill in their addition grid for the addition facts with an addend of 8 that have not been completed in previous levels.

Ten-Frame Rally

Complete the addition facts by placing 10 dots in one of the ten-frames and building 10. In some places, you will have to fill in the blanks. When you are finished, answer the question at the bottom of the page.

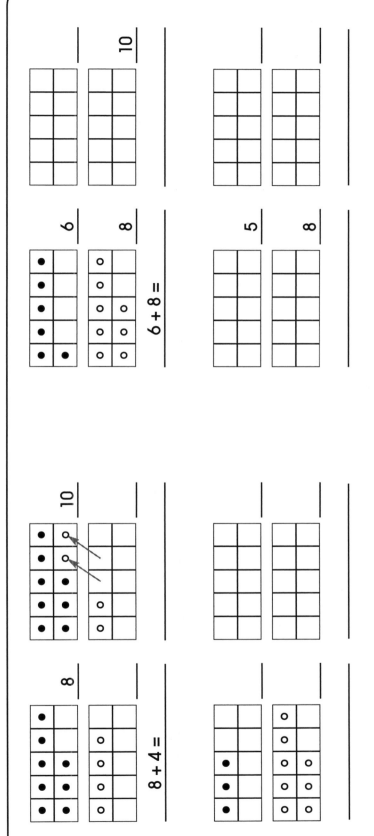

6 + 8 =

8 + 4 =

What thinking strategy do you use when you add a number with 8? Explain your answer.

LESSON 5B: WACKY WEBS WITH 8, 9, AND 10

TEACHER LESSON

In this lesson, students compare the thinking strategies of facts with addends of 8, 9, and 10. They also consider even and odd addends and sums.

Practicing the Thinking Strategy: Addend of 10

Present the addition fact 6 + 10 to the students. Have the students note that the fact has an addend of 10. Ask them to complete this fact and explain their thinking strategy.

6 + 10 (addend of 10)

- Pattern of 10:
  A set of 6 and a set of 10 is 16.
  SO, 6 + 10 = 16

Practicing the Thinking Strategies: Addend of 9

Present the addition fact 6 + 9 to the students. Have the students note that the fact has an addend of 9. Ask them to complete this fact and explain their thinking strategies.

6 + 9 (addend of 9)

- Build-10:
  Build 10 by taking 1 from 6.
  9 + 1 = 10 and 6 − 1 = 5
  10 + 5 = 15
  SO, 6 + 9 = 15

- Helping Fact:
  6 + 10 = 16
  9 = 10 − 1
  16 − 1 = 15
  SO, 6 + 9 = 15

Practicing the Thinking Strategies: Addend of 8

Present the addition fact 6 + 8 to the students. Have the students note that the fact has an addend of 8. Ask them to complete this fact and explain their thinking strategies.

6 + 8 (addend of 8)

- Build-10:
  Build 10 by taking 2 from 6.
  8 + 2 = 10 and 6 − 2 = 4
  10 + 4 = 14
  SO, 6 + 8 = 14

- Helping Fact:
  6 + 10 = 16
  8 = 10 − 2
  16 − 2 = 14
  SO, 6 + 8 = 14

Note: Some students may note that the addends of this fact differ by two. Facts with addends that differ by 2 can also be completed using the Robin Hood thinking strategy. This strategy is introduced in the next level.

Comparing Strategies for Facts with an Addend of 8 and 9

Have the students compare the build-10 strategy and the helping fact strategy for completing the facts 6 + 9 and 6 + 8.

- When the fact has an addend of 9, subtract 1 from 6 and add the 1 to 9 to build 10. You also subtract 1 from the sum of the helping fact.

- When the fact has an addend of 8, subtract 2 from 6 and add the 2 to 8 to build 10. You also subtract 2 from the sum of the helping fact.

Even and Odd Numbers

Have the students name the even numbers that are less than or equal to 20.

- The numbers 0, 2, 4, 6, 8, 10, 12, 14, 16, 18, and 20 are even numbers.

Have the students name the odd numbers that are less than or equal to 20.

- The numbers 1, 3, 5, 7, 9, 11, 13, 15, 17, and 19 are odd numbers.

Have the students examine the addition sentences 9 + 6 = 15 and 8 + 6 = 14.

Ask: Are the addends and the sums even or odd?

- The addend 9 is odd, and the addend 6 is even. The sum 15 is odd.

- The addends 8 and 6 are both even. The sum 14 is even.

Note: A detailed explanation of even and odd sums, including rules, is given in Lesson 6G.

Encouraging Class Discussion

Engaging students in whole-class discussions is an integral part of the program. Prompts for encouraging class discussions can be found on page 2 of the Introduction.

INTRODUCING THE STUDENT ACTIVITY SHEET

Distribute a copy of the sheet, Wacky Webs, to each student. Have the students read the instructions and complete the activity.

Wacky Webs

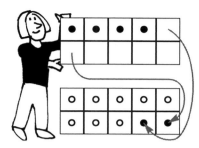

The numbers 0, 2, 4, 6, 8, 10, 12, 14, 16, 18, and 20 are **EVEN** numbers.

The numbers 1, 3, 5, 7, 9, 11, 13, 15, 17, and 19 are **ODD** numbers.

Below, fill in the outer cells of each web by adding the numbers in the inner cells with the number in the middle.

Colour all of the cells that have an **EVEN** number.

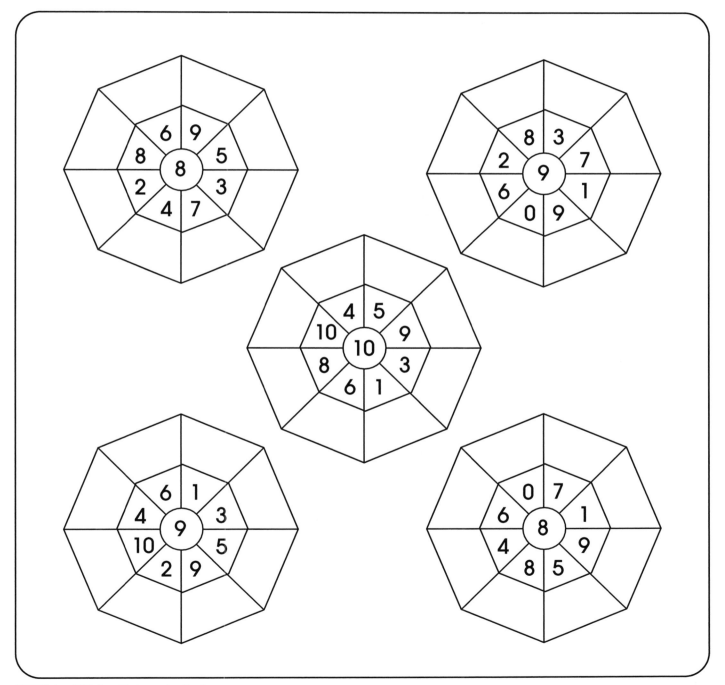

LESSON 5C: MATCH-UPS WITH 8

TEACHER LESSON

In this lesson, the students practice the thinking strategies for facts with an addend of 8.

Identifying and Applying Thinking Strategies

Present the students with the following addition facts:

5 + 8
8 + 8
2 + 8

Have the students note that all the facts have an addend of 8. Ask them to complete these facts and explain their thinking strategies. Remind them that when they know more than one strategy for completing a fact, they can choose the thinking strategy that works best for them.

(a) 5 + 8 (addend of 8)

■ Build-10:
Build 10 by taking 2 from 5.
8 + 2 = 10 and 5 − 2 = 3
10 + 3 = 13
SO, 5 + 8 = 13

■ Helping Fact:
5 + 10 = 15
8 = 10 − 2
15 − 2 = 13
SO, 5 + 8 = 13

■ Helping Fact:
5 + 5 = 10
8 = 5 + 3
10 + 3 = 13
SO, 8 + 5 = 13

Note: The ten-frame model is very effective for modelling facts with an addend of 5. Encourage students who want to complete the fact by picturing the following two ten-frames to do so:

(b) 8 + 8 (double fact/addend of 8)

■ Special Picture:
Picture a box of crayons with 2 rows of 8 crayons.
SO, 8 + 8 = 16

■ Build-10:
Build 10 by taking 2 from 8.
8 + 2 = 10 and 8 − 2 = 6
10 + 6 = 16
SO, 8 + 8 = 16

■ Helping Fact:
10 + 10 = 20
8 = 10 − 2
20 − 2 − 2 = 16
SO, 8 + 8 = 16

Note: Discuss with students which thinking strategy they prefer to use, and have them justify their choice.

(c) 2 + 8 (addend of 2/addend of 8)

■ Two-More-Than:
Two more than 8 is 10.
SO, 2 + 8 = 10

Note: Students can also complete this fact with the build-10 strategy or helping fact thinking strategy. Ask the students if they agree that the two-more-than strategy is more efficient than the other two.

Note: Some students will complete this fact by picturing the ten-frame. Encourage them to do so.

Encouraging Class Discussion

Engaging students in whole-class discussions is an integral part of the program. Prompts for encouraging class discussions can be found on page 2 of the Introduction.

INTRODUCING THE STUDENT ACTIVITY SHEET

Distribute a copy of the sheet, Match-Ups, to each student. Have the students read the instructions and complete the activity.

POWER FACTS

Have students practice the fifth set of Power Facts (page 137) at least once a day. They can also continue to practice the first four sets of Power Facts. Students can practice in class and at home.

PARTNER BINGO

Partner Bingo, Level 5A, provides more practice for the addition facts with an addend of 8 (pages 163-164). Have the students complete the facts in order and cross out only one square on their card for each fact. Partner Bingo can be played in class or at home.

CARD GAMES

Card Games, Level 5, provide more practice for the facts with an addend of 8 (pages 212-213). Students can play in class or at home.

STUDENT JOURNAL

Have students choose a fact with an addend of 8 and explain their thinking strategies for completing it.

THINKING STRATEGIES: ADDITION

Match-Ups

Complete each addition fact by connecting the dot beside the fact to the dot beside its sum.

When you have completed the "match-ups," answer the question at the bottom of the page.

5 + 8 •	• 14
8 + 8 •	• 16
8 + 6 •	• 13
2 + 8 •	• 10
8 + 4 •	• 11
7 + 8 •	• 15
8 + 3 •	• 12
8 + 9 •	• 17
0 + 8 •	• 9
10 + 8 •	• 18
8 + 1 •	• 8

4 + 8 •	• 12
9 + 8 •	• 14
8 + 3 •	• 16
6 + 8 •	• 17
8 + 8 •	• 11
8 + 5 •	• 13
8 + 7 •	• 15
1 + 8 •	• 10
8 + 10 •	• 8
2 + 8 •	• 9
8 + 0 •	• 18

What thinking strategy did you use for completing the fact 5 + 8? Explain your answer.

LESSON 5D: NUMBER DESIGN WITH 3, 8, AND 9

TEACHER LESSON

In this lesson, students incorporate the facts with addends of 8 with those having an addend of either 3 or 9.

Identifying Thinking Strategies

Now that the thinking strategies for facts with an addend of 8 have been developed, have the students complete the addition facts with an addend of 8 together with facts having addends of 3 and 9.

Have them consider the following six facts. There are two facts with an addend of 8, two with an addend of 9, and two with an addend of 3. Have the students identify these facts.

$$\begin{array}{cccccc} 4 & 7 & 9 & 8 & 7 & 3 \\ +8 & +3 & +4 & +5 & +9 & +6 \end{array}$$

addend of 8

$$\begin{array}{cc} 4 & 8 \\ +8 & +5 \end{array}$$

addend of 3

$$\begin{array}{cc} 7 & 3 \\ +3 & +6 \end{array}$$

addend of 9

$$\begin{array}{cc} 9 & 7 \\ +4 & +9 \end{array}$$

Applying Thinking Strategies

Ask the students how they would apply thinking strategies for the facts they identified.

(a) 4 + 8 (addend of 8)

- Build-10:
  Build 10 by taking 2 from 4.
  $8 + 2 = 10$ and $4 - 2 = 2$
  $10 + 2 = 12$
  SO, $4 + 8 = 12$

- Helping Fact:
  $4 + 10 = 14$
  $8 = 10 - 2$
  $14 - 2 = 12$
  SO, $4 + 8 = 12$

Have students use similar thinking strategies to complete the fact 8 + 5.

(b) 7 + 3 (addend of 3)

- Count on 3:
  $7 \rightarrow 8, 9, 10$
  SO, $7 + 3 = 10$

Note: Some students will complete the fact 7 + 3 by picturing the ten-frame. Encourage them to do so.

Have students use the three-more-than strategy to complete the fact 3 + 6.

(c) 9 + 4 (addend of 9)

- Build-10:
  Build 10 by taking 1 from 4.
  $9 + 1 = 10$ and $4 - 1 = 3$
  $10 + 3 = 13$
  SO, $9 + 4 = 13$

- Helping Fact:
  $10 + 4 = 14$
  $9 = 10 - 1$
  $14 - 1 = 13$
  SO, $9 + 4 = 13$

Have the students use similar thinking strategies to complete the fact 7 + 9.

Encouraging Class Discussion

Engaging students in whole-class discussions is an integral part of the program. Prompts for encouraging class discussions can be found on page 2 of the Introduction.

INTRODUCING THE STUDENT ACTIVITY SHEET

Distribute a copy of the sheet, Number Design, to each student. Have the students read the instructions and complete the activity.

CHALLENGE FACTS

Use the Challenge Facts, Level 5B (page 190), to help the students identify facts that have addends of 0, 1, 2, 3, 8, 9, 10, are doubles, and are near-doubles. Have the students place shapes around the facts. For example, have them place circles around all the facts with an addend of 8 and then complete them. Next, have them place triangles around all the near-double facts, and so on. They can also use different coloured pencils to identify the facts.

Number Design

Complete the addition facts below. When you are finished, choose the colours for the Colour Key, and colour the design.

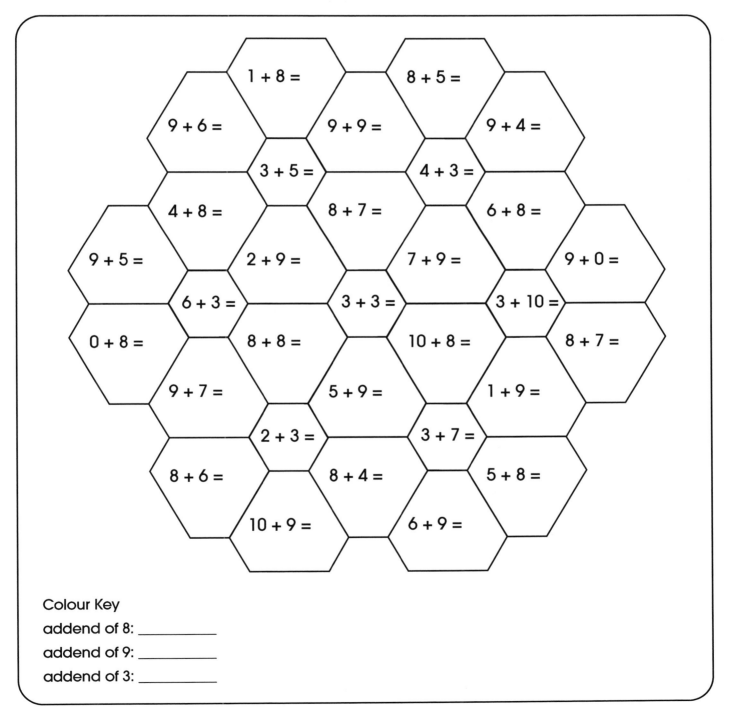

1 + 8 =

8 + 5 =

9 + 6 =

9 + 9 =

9 + 4 =

3 + 5 =

4 + 3 =

4 + 8 =

8 + 7 =

6 + 8 =

9 + 5 =

2 + 9 =

7 + 9 =

9 + 0 =

6 + 3 =

3 + 3 =

3 + 10 =

0 + 8 =

8 + 8 =

10 + 8 =

8 + 7 =

9 + 7 =

5 + 9 =

1 + 9 =

2 + 3 =

3 + 7 =

8 + 6 =

8 + 4 =

5 + 8 =

10 + 9 =

6 + 9 =

Colour Key

addend of 8: _____

addend of 9: _____

addend of 3: _____

LESSON 5E: JELLYBEAN JUMBLE WITH 0, 1, 2, 3, 8, 9, 10, THE DOUBLES, AND THE NEAR-DOUBLES

TEACHER LESSON

In this lesson, students complete facts introduced so far in the program by identifying and applying thinking strategies.

Identifying and Applying Thinking Strategies

Present the students with the following addition facts:

0 + 8
4 + 9
7 + 8
6 + 6
2 + 4
1 + 10

Have the students complete the facts. The students must be able to recognize and apply an appropriate thinking strategy for each fact, then explain their thinking strategies. Have the students first note whether the facts have an addend of 0, 1, 2, 3, 8, 9, 10, or are doubles or near-doubles.

(a) 0 + 8 (addend of 0)

■   Pattern of 0:
The sum of 0 and a number is the number.
SO, 0 + 8 = 8

(b) 4 + 9 (addend of 9)

■   Build-10:
Build 10 by taking 1 from 4.
9 + 1 = 10 and 4 − 1 = 3
10 + 3 = 13
SO, 4 + 9 = 13

■   Helping Fact:
10 + 4 = 14
9 = 10 − 1
14 − 1 = 13
SO, 4 + 9 = 13

(c) 7 + 8 (near-double/addend of 8)

■   Three-Step Strategy:
Step 1: The smaller addend is 7.
Step 2: 7 + 7 = 14
Step 3: 14 + 1 = 15
   SO, 7 + 8 = 15

Note: Students can complete the double fact 7 + 7 using the special picture of a calendar or the helping fact 5 + 5.

■   Build-10:
Build 10 by taking 2 from 7.
8 + 2 = 10 and 7 − 2 = 5
10 + 5 = 15
SO, 7 + 8 = 15

■   Helping Fact:
7 + 10 = 17
8 = 10 − 2
17 − 2 = 15
SO, 7 + 8 = 15

Note: Discuss with students which thinking strategy they prefer, and have them justify their choice.

(d) 6 + 6 (double fact)

■   Special Picture:
Picture an egg carton with 2 rows of 6 eggs.
SO, 6 + 6 = 12

■   Helping Fact :
5 + 5 = 10
6 = 5 + 1
10 + 1 + 1 = 12
SO, 6 + 6 = 12

(e) 2 + 4 (addend of 2)

■   Two-More-Than:
Two more than 4 is 6.
SO, 2 + 4 = 6

(f) 1 + 10 (addend of 1/addend of 10)

■   One-More-Than:
One more than 10 is 11.
SO, 1 + 10 = 11

■   Pattern of 10:
A set of 1 and a set of 10 is 11.
SO, 1 + 10 = 11

Note: Discuss with students which thinking strategy they prefer, and have them justify their choice.

Encouraging Class Discussion

Engaging students in whole-class discussions is an integral part of the program. Prompts for encouraging class discussions can be found on page 2 of the Introduction.

INTRODUCING THE STUDENT ACTIVITY SHEET

Distribute a copy of the sheet, Jellybean Jumble, to each student. Have the students read the instructions and complete the activity.

Jellybean Jumble

Complete the addition facts below. You will find that the sum of one of the three facts in each group is different from the sums of the other two facts. Colour the jellybean in each group that has the different sum.

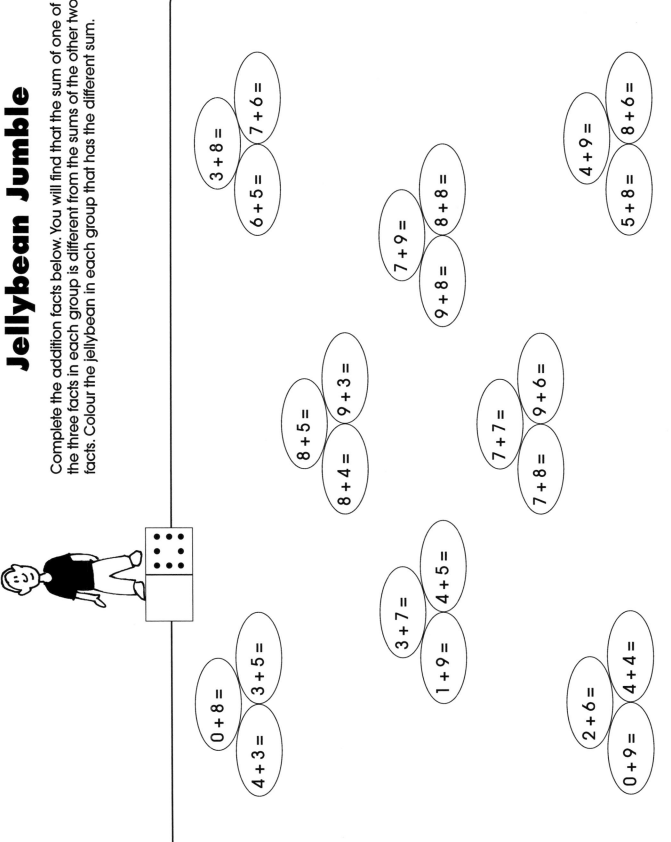

3 + 8 =
7 + 6 =
6 + 5 =

7 + 9 =
8 + 8 =
9 + 8 =

4 + 9 =
8 + 6 =
5 + 8 =

8 + 5 =
9 + 3 =
8 + 4 =

7 + 7 =
9 + 6 =
7 + 8 =

0 + 8 =
3 + 5 =
4 + 3 =

3 + 7 =
4 + 5 =
1 + 9 =

2 + 6 =
4 + 4 =
0 + 9 =

LESSON 5F: SECRET MESSAGE WITH 0, 1, 2, 3, 8, 9, 10, THE DOUBLES, AND THE NEAR-DOUBLES

TEACHER LESSON

In this lesson, students complete facts introduced so far in the program by identifying and applying the appropriate thinking strategies.

Preparing for the Level 5 Number Challenge

Encourage students to practice the fifth set of Power Facts (page 137). Students can also play Partner Bingo, Level 5 (pages 163-166), either in class or at home, to prepare for the Level 5 Challenge.

Identifying and Applying Thinking Strategies

Present the students with the following addition facts:

3 + 8
9 + 8
5 + 6

Have the students complete the facts and explain their thinking strategies.

(a) 3 + 8 (addend of 3/addend of 8)

- Count on 3:
  8 → 9, 10, 11
  SO, 3 + 8 = 11

- Build-10:
  Build 10 by taking 2 from 3.
  8 + 2 = 10 and 3 − 2 = 1
  10 + 1 = 11
  SO, 3 + 8 = 11

- Helping Fact:
  3 + 10 = 13
  8 = 10 − 2
  13 − 2 = 11
  SO, 3 + 8 = 11

Note: Discuss with students which thinking strategy they prefer, and have them justify their choice.

(b) 9 + 8 (addend of 9/addend of 8/near-double fact)

- Build-10:
  Build 10 by taking 1 from 8.
  9 + 1 = 10 and 8 − 1 = 7
  10 + 7 = 17
  SO, 9 + 8 = 17

- Helping Fact:
  10 + 8 = 18
  9 = 10 − 1
  18 − 1 = 17
  SO, 9 + 8 = 17

- Three-Step Strategy:
  Step 1: The smaller addend is 8.
  Step 2: 8 + 8 = 16
  Step 3: 16 + 1 = 17
  SO, 9 + 8 = 17

Note: The thinking strategies for an addend of 8 are not included for this fact. Have the students discuss why it is more efficient to consider strategies for an addend of 9 than for an addend of 8.

Note: Discuss with students which thinking strategy they prefer, and have them justify their choice.

(c) 5 + 6 (double fact/addend of 5)

- Three-Step Strategy:
  Step 1: The smaller addend is 5.
  Step 2: 5 + 5 = 10
  Step 3: 10 + 1 = 11
  SO, 5 + 6 = 11

Note: Students can complete the double fact 5 + 5 with the special picture of two hands.

Note: Some students will note this fact has an addend of 5 and complete this fact by picturing a ten-frame with ten counters and one more counter. Encourage them to do so.

Encouraging Class Discussion

Engaging students in whole-class discussions is an integral part of the program. Prompts for encouraging class discussions can be found on page 2 of the Introduction.

INTRODUCING THE STUDENT ACTIVITY SHEET

Distribute a copy of the sheet, Secret Message, to each student. Have the students read the instructions and complete the activity.

PARTNER BINGO

Students can practice all facts introduced in the program so far by playing Partner Bingo, Level 5B (pages 165-166). Have the students complete the facts in order and cross out only one square on their card for each fact. Partner Bingo can be played in class or at home.

Secret Message

Complete the addition facts. In the Code Key, find the number that matches the sum of the first fact. Write the letter that is above that number in the first blank. Now, find the number in the Code Key that matches the sum of the second fact. Write the letter that is above it in the second blank. Continue with each addition fact until you have filled in all of the remaining blanks with a letter from the Code Key. When you are finished, you will find the secret message.

Why does the cloud feel shy?

‾1‾ ‾2‾ ‾3‾   ‾4‾ ‾5‾ ‾6‾ ‾7‾ ‾8‾   ‾9‾ ‾10‾   ‾11‾ ‾12‾ ‾13‾ ‾14‾

‾15‾ ‾16‾ ‾17‾ ‾18‾   ‾19‾ ‾20‾ ‾21‾   ‾22‾ ‾23‾ ‾24‾ ‾25‾ ‾26‾   ‾27‾ ‾28‾ ‾29‾ ‾30‾ ‾31‾ ‾32‾

Code Key	S	G	U	H	R	L	I	T	A	N	E	D	W	O	C	Y
	0	4	6	7	8	9	10	11	12	13	14	15	16	17	18	19

① 3 + 8
② 3 + 4
③ 6 + 8
④ 9 + 9
⑤ 4 + 5
⑥ 8 + 9
⑦ 1 + 5
⑧ 9 + 6

⑨ 5 + 5
⑩ 0 + 0
⑪ 7 + 10
⑫ 5 + 8
⑬ 3 + 6
⑭ 10 + 9
⑮ 8 + 8
⑯ 7 + 7

⑰ 6 + 6
⑱ 1 + 7
⑲ 7 + 3
⑳ 6 + 7
㉑ 2 + 2
㉒ 5 + 6
㉓ 0 + 7
㉔ 3 + 3

㉕ 9 + 4
㉖ 8 + 7
㉗ 5 + 9
㉘ 4 + 4
㉙ 10 + 6
㉚ 8 + 6
㉛ 4 + 8
㉜ 6 + 2

LESSON 5G: THE LEVEL 5 NUMBER CHALLENGE

The Level 5 Number Challenge includes the addition facts introduced in Level 5, as well as those introduced in the first four levels.

Before students take the Level 5 Number Challenge, have them complete addition facts with an addend of 0, 1, 2, 3, 8, 9, 10, or that are doubles or near-doubles. Choose facts that the students find most challenging. The following are often difficult for students to complete:

$$6 + 8$$
$$4 + 9$$
$$7 + 7$$
$$6 + 10$$
$$1 + 9$$
$$8 + 5$$
$$7 + 6$$

Have the student discuss the different thinking strategies they can use with these addition facts.

INSTRUCTIONS FOR THE LEVEL 5 CHALLENGE

Distribute a copy of the challenge sheet to each student. Explain the challenge: There are nine facts at the top of the page. Below, there are nine boxes with a clue in each box. Complete the facts, then match each completed fact with one of the clues, and place it in that box. Cross out each fact after it has been placed in its box. For students who would like an extra challenge, have them add the sums of the three facts in each row, then add the sums of the three facts in each column. (See answer key for the mystery number.)

SUGGESTIONS FOR MORE PRACTICE

Students will have more opportunities to practice the addition facts of this level as they work through the last level of the program. However, if the students need more practice, consider the following suggestions:

- Check that students understand and can apply the build-10 strategy and the helping fact strategy for facts with an addend of 8.

- Write seven addition facts in a row, each with a missing addend. Have the students place a 0, 1, 2, 3, 8, 9, 10, the same addend, or an addend that differs by 1 for each missing addend. Have the students complete the facts. For example, consider the following:

	4	9		6		
+ 8	+	+	+ 0	+	+ 10	+ 5

8	4	9	8	6	8	8
+ 8	+ 8	+ 8	+ 0	+ 8	+ 10	+ 5

- Identify the facts that students find difficult. Help them develop thinking strategies for these facts. Have the students list the facts they find difficult, and encourage them to practice these facts both with a classmate in school and a parent at home.

- Have students continue to practice the first five levels of Power Facts.

- Have students play Partner Bingo in class or at home. There are 4 Partner Bingos for this level of the program (pages 163-166).

- Have students choose facts and make up posters for the facts.

Level 5 Number Challenge

Complete the addition facts below. Then, read the clue in each box, and find the fact that matches it. Place each completed fact into the box with its matching clue.

6 + 8	4 + 5	8 + 9	7 + 3	8 + 8	6 + 9	5 + 3	8 + 4	7 + 6

This fact is shown with the following picture: 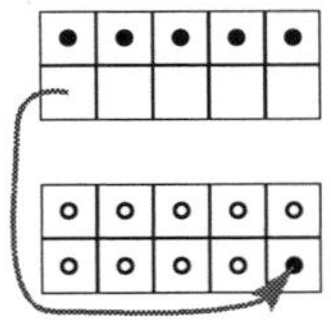	This fact is shown with the following picture: 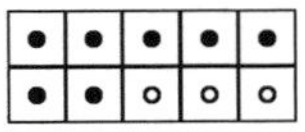	The sum of this fact is one more than the sum of 6 + 6.
This is the near-double fact with addends of 4 and 5.	This fact is shown with the following picture: 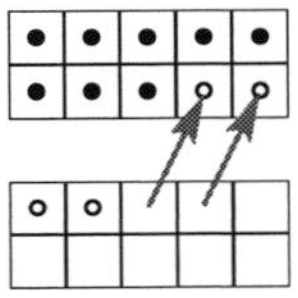	This is the fact with the greatest sum.
This is the fact that joins 6 and 8.	This fact has the greatest even sum.	This fact is shown with the following picture: 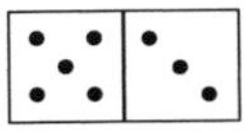

LEVEL 6: REMAINING FACTS

LEVEL 6 OVERVIEW

There are only three basic addition facts, and their turnarounds, that have not yet been introduced. These facts have addends of 4, 5, 6, and 7.

        4 + 6 and 6 + 4
        4 + 7 and 7 + 4
        5 + 7 and 7 + 5

The fact 4 + 6 and its turnaround have a sum of 10. Extra activities and games are provided for facts with a sum of 10.

The fact 5 + 7 and its turnaround have an addend of 5. Ten-frame models can help with completing this fact.

The facts 4 + 6 and 5 + 7 and their turnarounds have addends that differ by 2. Facts with addends that differ by 2 are called *Robin Hood facts* and can be completed with the Robin Hood thinking strategy.

As well, various helping fact strategies can be used to complete these facts.

Ten-Frame Flash

Students can use ten-frames to picture both facts with a sum of 10 and with an addend of 5. Refer to the pages of ten-frames dots (pages 220-222).

Play Ten-Frame Flash for facts with an addend of 5.

(a) Show the students one of the ten-frames for a few seconds. Then cover the ten-frame, and ask the students how many dots are required to complete the ten-frame. Have the students answer using their response boards.

Play Ten-Frame Flash for facts with a sum of 10.

(b) Show the students two ten-frames for a few seconds. Make sure one of the ten-frames has five dots. The ten-frame with five dots can be either the first or second ten-frame. Ask the students how many dots they see. Have the students answer using their response boards.

The Robin Hood Thinking Strategy

Facts with addends that differ by 2 can be called *Robin Hood facts*. For example, consider the fact 4 + 6. The addends 4 and 6 differ by 2. The addend 4 is one less than 5 and the addend 6 is one more than 5. Take 1 from the "rich" (the addend 6), and give it to the "poor" (the addend 4). The fact 4 + 6 has the same sum as the double fact 5 + 5.

Introducing the Remaining Facts

Students can use the following thinking strategies to complete these facts.

(a) 4 + 6 (6 + 4)

■ Robin Hood Strategy:
    Take 1 from 6 and give it to 4.
    6 − 1 = 5 and 4 + 1 = 5
    5 + 5 = 10
    SO, 4 + 6 = 10

■ Helping Fact:
    3 + 6 = 9
    4 = 3 + 1
    9 + 1 = 10
    SO, 4 + 6 = 10

■ Helping Fact:
    4 + 4 = 8
    6 = 4 + 2
    8 + 2 = 10
    SO, 4 + 6 = 10

Note: Students may prefer to use other facts as helping facts.

Note: Some students will complete this fact by picturing the ten-frame (4 counters and 6 counters complete the ten-frame). Encourage them to do so.

(b) 4 + 7 (7 + 4)

■ Helping Fact:
    3 + 7 = 10
    4 = 3 + 1
    10 + 1 = 11
    SO, 4 + 7 = 11

Note: Students may prefer to use other facts as helping facts.

Note: Students can also complete this fact using the build-10 thinking strategy by taking 3 from 4 to build 10.

(c) 5 + 7 (7 + 5/addend of 5)

■ Robin Hood Strategy:
    Take 1 from 7 and give it to 5.
    7 − 1 = 6 and 5 + 1 = 6
    6 + 6 = 12
    SO, 5 + 7 = 12

■ Helping Fact:
    3 + 7 = 105 = 3 + 2
    10 + 2 = 12
    SO, 5 + 7 = 12

■ Helping Fact:
    5 + 5 = 10
    7 = 5 + 2
    10 + 2 = 12
    SO, 5 + 7 = 12

Note: Students can picture this helping strategy with the following two ten-frames. Encourage them to do so.

Note: Students may prefer to use other facts as helping facts.

CARD GAMES: SUMS OF 10

Card Games, Level 6, provide more practice for the facts with a sum of 10 (pages 214-215). In addition to these games, there are a number of excellent card games that can help the students complete addition facts with a sum of 10. The following are examples of two such games.

The Game of 10

This is a card game for two or more players. Use the Level 6 playing cards (pages 214-215) or a regular deck of playing cards without the face cards: Place the cards facedown. The first player turns over the first card from the deck and places it faceup on the table. (If the card is a 10, the player keeps it.) The next player turns up the next card. If the player turns up a 10 or can make a 10 with that card and the card faceup on the table, he/she does so and takes the card(s). If the player cannot do so, he/she leaves the card faceup on the table together with the first card, and the turn goes to the next player. The game continues in this manner, each player turning over a card and trying to make a 10 with the cards faceup on the table. The game is played until all the cards are turned over. The player with the most cards wins.

Variation: Players can make 10 with just 2 cards or with combinations of more than 2 cards.

Pyramid

This can be played as a one-player game or cooperatively played with more than one player. Use the Level 6 playing cards (pages 214-215) or a regular deck of playing cards without the face cards. Set up a pyramid with the cards with one card on top, two cards overlapping the bottom edge of the card on top, then three cards overlapping the bottom edge of the two cards, and so on. The cards are placed faceup. Continue until there are six cards at the bottom of the pyramid. Note that the six cards at the bottom of the pyramid are the only cards that are completely uncovered. The remaining cards are placed facedown in a pile on the table. The player picks up any two uncovered cards with a sum of 10. As cards on the bottom of the pyramid are picked, more cards are uncovered. The player then turns over the first card from the ones remaining in the pile. If that card and an uncovered card have a sum of 10, the player picks up both cards. The player continues to turn over cards from the pile, one at a time, trying to make 10 with the uncovered cards on the table. If all of the cards from the pyramid have been picked up from the table and the cards from the pile have been turned over, the player wins the game.

Variation: Once students are comfortable with pairs of numbers that add to 10, this game can be extended to include combinations of numbers that add to 10.

Level 6 consists of the following lessons:

Lesson 6A: Ten-Frame Rally with the Remaining Facts

This lesson models the remaining facts with ten-frames.

Lesson 6B: Ten-Frame Rally with Sums of 10

In this lesson, students use ten-frames to model facts with a sum of 10.

Lesson 6C: Cool Loops with Sums of 10

This lesson introduces the Robin Hood thinking strategy as well as games for facts with a sum of 10.

Lesson 6D: Match-Ups with the Remaining Facts

This lesson provides practice with the thinking strategies for the remaining facts.

Lesson 6E: Number Design with the Doubles, the Near-Doubles, and the Robin Hood Facts

In this lesson, students incorporate Robin Hood facts with double and near-double facts. Students identify and apply appropriate thinking strategies for these facts.

Lesson 6F: Jellybean Jumble with Facts 0-10

In this lesson, students incorporate the remaining facts with those introduced in previous levels.

Lesson 6G: Wacky Webs with Facts 0-10

In this lesson, students complete the basic addition facts by identifying and applying thinking strategies. They examine even and odd addends and even and odd sums.

Lesson 6H: Secret Message with Facts 0-10

In this lesson, students continue to complete the basic addition facts.

Lesson 6I: The Level 6 Number Challenge

This challenge assesses the students' ability to identify and apply appropriate thinking strategies to the facts introduced in Levels 1-6. Students also review models and vocabulary introduced in the program.

ADDITION GRID

The addition facts considered in this level are the following:

+	0	1	2	3	4	5	6	7	8	9	10
0	0	1	2	3	4	5	6	7	8	9	10
1	1	2	3	4	5	6	7	8	9	10	11
2	2	3	4	5	6	7	8	9	10	11	12
3	3	4	5	6	7	8	9	10	11	12	13
4	4	5	6	7	8	9	10	11	12	13	14
5	5	6	7	8	9	10	11	12	13	14	15
6	6	7	8	9	10	11	12	13	14	15	16
7	7	8	9	10	11	12	13	14	15	16	17
8	8	9	10	11	12	13	14	15	16	17	18
9	9	10	11	12	13	14	15	16	17	18	19
10	10	11	12	13	14	15	16	17	18	19	20

LESSON 6A: TEN-FRAME RALLY WITH THE REMAINING FACTS

TEACHER LESSON

In this lesson, students use ten-frames to model the remaining facts.

The Remaining Basic Addition Facts

Have the students check their addition grid. Ask them to name the facts that are not yet completed. The facts are the following:

4 + 6 and 6 + 4
4 + 7 and 7 + 4
5 + 7 and 7 + 5

Interpreting the Operation of Addition

Present the following story problem to the students:

■ Amanda had some erasers. She gave 4 erasers to her sister Amy. Now Amanda has 6 erasers left. How many erasers did Amanda have to begin with?

Have the students draw a picture illustrating this problem. Have them represent it as a number sentence.

■ 6 + 4 = 10
Amanda had 10 erasers altogether.

Note: This story problem is an example of the structure of separation, where the initial quantity is unknown. This is an example of a structure involving addition that often receives less attention than other structures.

Modelling with Ten-Frames

Divide the class into cooperative working groups. Distribute a copy of the activity sheet to each student, as well as counters and two ten-frame mats. Have the students use the ten-frames to model the remaining facts, then complete their activity sheet.

After the students have completed the activity sheet, discuss the facts they modelled on their ten-frames.

■ 4 + 6 = 10

Have the students note that 4 counters and 6 counters fill a 10-frame: 4 counters leave one square not filled in the first row, while 6 counters fill that square in the first row and all the squares in the second row.

Have the students note that 4 is one less than 5, while 6 is one more than 5. Have the students note that these addends differ by 2. Facts with addends that differ by 2 can be called *Robin Hood facts*. The Robin Hood thinking strategy is explained in more detail in Lesson 6C.

■ 7 + 4 = 11

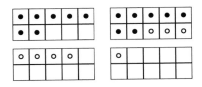

The addend 7 is modelled with 7 counters. The 7 counters complete the first row of the ten-frame and 2 squares of the second row. The addend 4 is modelled with 4 more counters. Since there is room for only 3 more counters in the ten-frame, students must place the last counter in the first square of a second ten-frame. The number 11 is represented by one ten-frame with 10 counters and 1 more counter.

■ 5 + 7 = 12

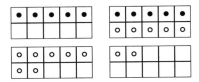

Have the students note that the fact has an addend of 5. The first ten-frame has 5 counters in the first row, while the second ten-frame has 5 counters in the first row and 2 counters in the second row. The two rows of 5 counters make 10 counters, and 2 more counters represent the number 12. Have the students note that 5 + 7 = 5 + 5 + 2.

Note: Thinking strategies for these facts are also considered in Lesson 6D.

Ten-Frame Flash

Play Ten-Frame Flash for addition facts with an addend of 5. Show the students two ten-frames for a few seconds, with one of the ten-frames having five dots. The ten-frame with five dots can be either the first or second ten-frame. Ask the students how many dots they see, and have them answer using their response boards.

Encouraging Class Discussion

Engaging students in whole-class discussions is an integral part of the program. Prompts for encouraging class discussions can be found on page 2 of the Introduction.

INTRODUCING THE STUDENT ACTIVITY SHEET

Students will have completed the activity sheet during the lesson.

COMPLETING THE ADDITION GRID

Have the students fill in their addition grid for the remaining addition facts.

Ten-Frame Rally

Complete the addition facts with ten-frames. Explain your thinking strategies at the bottom of the page.

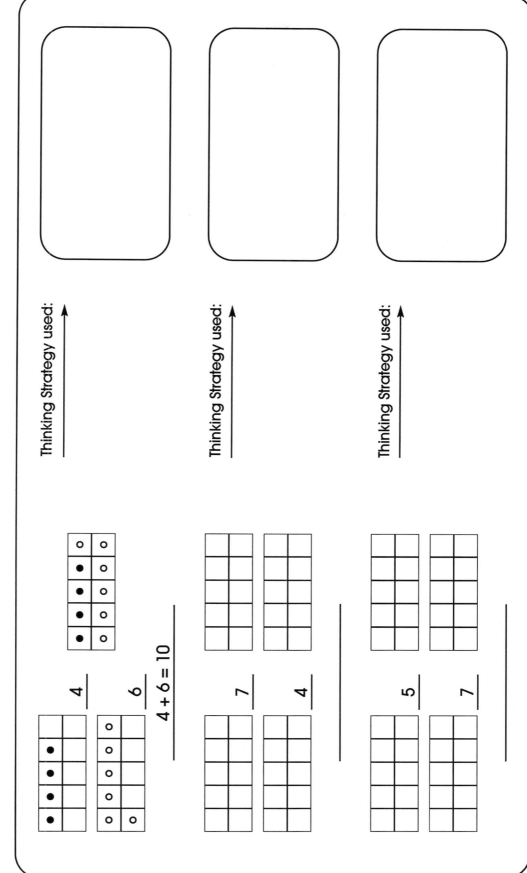

Thinking Strategy used: →

Thinking Strategy used: →

Thinking Strategy used: →

4

6

4 + 6 = 10

7

4

5

7

LESSON 6B: TEN-FRAME RALLY WITH SUMS OF 10

TEACHER LESSON

In this lesson, students use ten-frames to model facts with sums of 10.

Introducing Facts with Sums of 10

Most of the addition facts with a sum of 10 have already been introduced in previous levels of the program. The only basic fact with a sum of 10 that has not yet been introduced is 6 + 4 and its turnaround 4 + 6.

Modelling with Ten-Frames

Present the addition fact 5 + 5 to the students. Have each student model the fact with a ten-frame mat and counters of two colours. Have the students place 5 counters of one colour in the first row and 5 counters of the second colour in the second row.

5 + 5 = 10

Next, have them replace the first counter of the second row with a counter of the first colour. Ask: What addition sentence do these counters represent?

4 + 6 = 10

Now, have the students replace a counter of the first row with a counter of the colour of the second row. Ask: What addition sentence do these counters represent?

3 + 7 = 10

Continue to replace counters of the first row with counters of the colour of the second row. Each time, have the students name the addition sentence the counters represent. When all of the counters that have the same colour as the second row replace the counters of the first row, the ten-frame looks like the following and shows the addition fact 0 + 10 = 10:

Ten-Frame Train

Remind the students about the ten-frame train. Show ten-frame train cars with different numbers of passengers in them. Each time, ask the students how many more passengers are required to fill the train cars.

Ten-Frame Flash

Refer to the pages of ten-frames dots (pages 220-222). Show the students one of the ten-frames for a few seconds. Then cover the ten-frame, and ask the students how many dots are required to complete the ten-frame. Have the students answer with their response boards.

The Sum-of-10 Rainbow

Have the students write the numbers from 0 to 10 sequentially in a row, but have them write the 5 twice. Have them join each pair of numbers with a sum of 10 with curved lines, starting with the two 5s. The curved lines form the sum-of-10 rainbow.

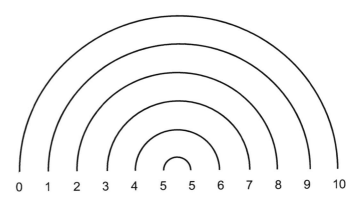

Have the students note that 5 + 5 = 10. Next, have them note that 4 + 6 = 10. Remind them that 4 is one less than 5, and 6 is one more than 5. Now, point out that in each subsequent pair, one number is the same less than 5 as the other is greater than 5.

Encouraging Class Discussion

Engaging students in whole-class discussions is an integral part of the program. Prompts for encouraging class discussions can be found on page 2 of the Introduction.

INTRODUCING THE STUDENT ACTIVITY SHEET

Distribute a copy of the sheet, Ten-Frame Rally, to each student. Have the students read the instructions and complete the activity.

Note: The students can complete this activity in cooperative working pairs.

Ten-Frame Rally

The addition buddy is showing 5 + 5 with a ten-frame. Use the ten-frames below to show the other addition facts that have a sum of 10. Name the addition facts that you show. Make sure each ten-frame shows a different addition sum.

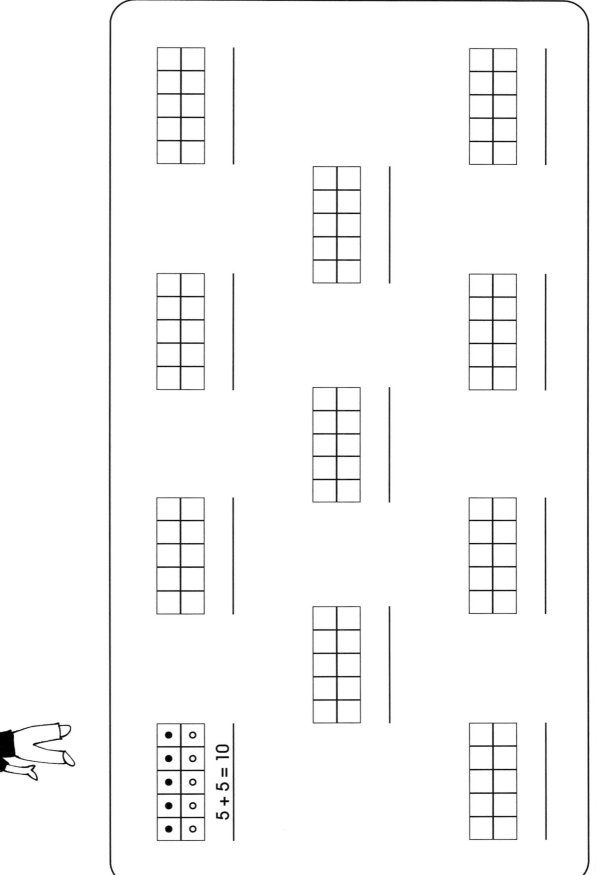

5 + 5 = 10

LESSON 6C: COOL LOOPS WITH SUMS OF 10

TEACHER LESSON

In this lesson, students are introduced to the Robin Hood thinking strategy, as well as to games for completing facts with sums of 10.

Introducing the Thinking Strategy: Robin Hood

Divide the class into pairs of students. Give each pair of students 10 cubes. Have one student from the pair take 4 cubes and the other student take 6 cubes. Ask the pairs: What can you do so that each of you has the same number of cubes?

- The student with 6 cubes can give 1 cube to his/her partner. Each student then has 5 cubes.

Tell the students that "taking one from the rich and giving it to the poor" is called the *Robin Hood thinking strategy*. If the students are not familiar with the story of Robin Hood, tell them the story.

Have the students model the fact 4 + 6 with a ten-frame. Ask the students to note the following:

- The addends differ by 2.
- 4 is one less than 5, and 6 is one more than 5.

Note: Make sure students understand that if they subtract 1 from 6 and add it to 4, they now are considering the fact 5 + 5.

Have the students use the Robin Hood strategy to complete the fact 4 + 6.

4 + 6   (Robin Hood fact)

- Robin Hood Strategy:
  Take 1 from 6 and give it to 4.
  6 − 1 = 5 and 4 + 1 = 5
  5 + 5 = 10
  SO, 4 + 6 = 10

Note: This Robin Hood strategy can be used for any fact in which the addends differ by 2.

Ten-Frame Team Games

There are a number of team games the students can play to practice the facts with sums of 10. Consider the following:

Match to 10: Divide the class into two or three teams. Make sure there are an even number of students on each team. Give each student a ten-frame containing 0 to 10 dots. Have the students find a partner on their team by matching up their ten-frames so the combined dots add to 10. The team that "matches up" first wins. Remind students that as partners their dots must add to 10. (This game can also be played with cards numbered 1 to 10 rather than with ten-frames.)

Making 10: Divide the class into two or three teams. Give each student a ten-frame containing 1 to 10 dots, then present a ten-frame with dots from 1 to 10 on the chalkboard or overhead. Explain that the object of the game is to make 10. Have the students check whether their ten-frame and your ten-frame have 10 dots in total. Students who have a "winning" ten-frame can show the ten-frame. The first student to show a winning ten-frame is awarded a point for his/her team. For the game to be fair, make sure each team has been given the same ten-frames. Have the students name the addition sentence each time.

Pairs of Numbers that Add to 10

Have the students name pairs of numbers with a sum of 10. Remind students that the order of the numbers does not matter; for example, the pair of numbers 9 and 1 are considered to be the same as the pair of numbers 1 and 9. There are six pairs:

0 and 10	1 and 9	2 and 8
3 and 7	4 and 6	5 and 5

Encouraging Class Discussion

Engaging students in whole-class discussions is an integral part of the program. Prompts for encouraging class discussions can be found on page 2 of the Introduction.

INTRODUCING THE STUDENT ACTIVITY SHEET

Distribute a copy of the sheet, Cool Loops, to each student. Have the students read the instructions and complete the activity.

Note: The loops form a pattern that students can use to check their work.

STUDENT JOURNAL

Have students explain their thinking strategies for completing the fact 4 + 6.

Cool Loops

Below, circle each pair of numbers that has a sum of 10. The numbers must be beside each other horizontally, vertically, or diagonally. When you are finished, solve the problem at the bottom of the page.

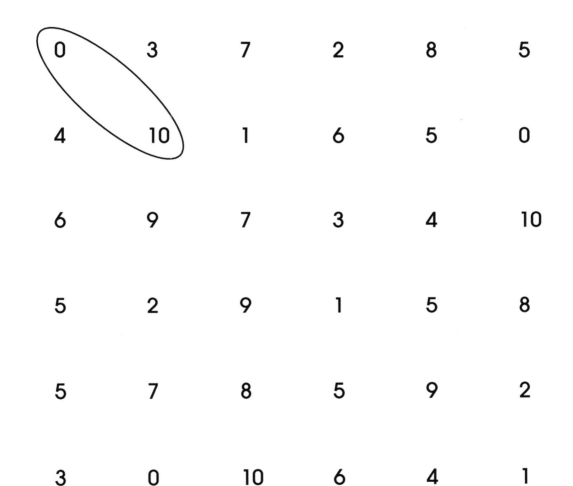

0	3	7	2	8	5
4	10	1	6	5	0
6	9	7	3	4	10
5	2	9	1	5	8
5	7	8	5	9	2
3	0	10	6	4	1

Name each pair of numbers with a sum of 10.

LESSON 6D: MATCH-UPS WITH THE REMAINING FACTS

TEACHER LESSON

In this lesson, students are introduced to thinking strategies for the remaining facts.

Introducing the Thinking Strategies: Remaining Facts

Present the students with the following addition facts:

$$7 + 5$$
$$4 + 6$$
$$7 + 4$$

Ask students what thinking strategies can be used to complete these facts. List their responses on the chalkboard. Add the following if students do not suggest them:

(a) 7 + 5 (Robin Hood fact/addend of 5)

- Robin Hood Strategy:
  Take 1 from 7 and give it to 5.
  $7 - 1 = 6$ and $5 + 1 = 6$
  $6 + 6 = 12$
  SO, $7 + 5 = 12$

- Helping Fact:
  $7 + 3 = 10$
  $5 = 3 + 2$
  $10 + 2 = 12$
  SO, $7 + 5 = 12$

- Helping Fact:
  $5 + 5 = 10$
  $7 = 5 + 2$
  $10 + 2 = 12$
  SO, $7 + 5 = 12$

Note: This fact has an addend of 5. The second helping fact strategy can be pictured with one ten-frame having 10 counters and 2 more counters. Encourage students to picture the ten-frame for facts with an addend of 5.

(b) 4 + 6 (6 + 4)

- Robin Hood Strategy:
  Take 1 from 6 and give it to 4.
  $6 - 1 = 5$ and $4 + 1 = 5$
  $5 + 5 = 10$
  SO, $4 + 6 = 10$

- Helping Fact:
  $3 + 6 = 9$
  $4 = 3 + 1$
  $9 + 1 = 10$
  SO, $4 + 6 = 10$

- Helping Fact:
  $4 + 4 = 8$
  $6 = 4 + 2$
  $8 + 2 = 10$
  SO, $4 + 6 = 10$

Note: Students can also complete the fact $4 + 6$ by picturing the ten-frame (4 counters and 6 counters fill the ten-frame). Encourage them to do so.

(c) 7 + 4 (7 + 4)

- Helping Fact:
  $7 + 3 = 10$
  $4 = 3 + 1$
  $10 + 1 = 11$
  SO, $7 + 4 = 11$

Note: Students can also complete this fact by picturing the ten-frame (7 counters and 3 counters make 10 counters, and there is one more counter, representing the number 11.) Encourage them to do so.

Note: Students can also complete this fact by using the build-10 thinking strategy (by taking 3 from 4 to build 10).

Note: Students may prefer to use other facts as helping facts.

Encouraging Class Discussion

Engaging students in whole-class discussions is an integral part of the program. Prompts for encouraging class discussions can be found on page 2 of the Introduction.

INTRODUCING THE STUDENT ACTIVITY SHEET

Distribute a copy of the sheet, Match-Ups, to each student. Have the students read the instructions and complete the activity.

POWER FACTS

Have students practice the sixth set of Power Facts (page 138) at least once a day. They can also continue to practice the first five sets of Power Facts. Students can practice in class and at home.

PARTNER BINGO

Partner Bingo, Level 6A, provides more practice for the remaining addition facts (pages 167-171). There is one Partner Bingo for facts with addends of 4, 6, and 7. There are 2 Partner Bingos for facts with an addend of 5. Encourage the students to complete facts with an addend of 5 by picturing the ten-frame. Have the students complete the facts in order and cross out only one square on their card for each fact. Partner Bingo can be played in class or at home.

CARD GAMES

Card Games, Level 6, provide more practice for the doubles (pages 214-215). Students can play in class or at home.

STUDENT JOURNAL

Have students choose two of the remaining facts and explain their thinking strategies for completing them.

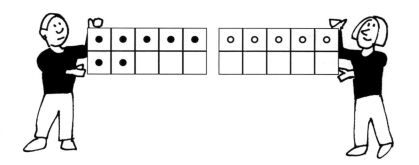

Match-Ups

Complete each addition fact by connecting the dot beside the fact to the dot beside its sum.

7 + 5 •	• 13	6 + 4 •	• 12
5 + 5 •	• 14	4 + 8 •	• 10
4 + 7 •	• 11	5 + 6 •	• 11
7 + 7 •	• 10	8 + 5 •	• 14
8 + 5 •	• 12	6 + 8 •	• 13

5 + 4 •	• 13	7 + 6 •	• 14
3 + 7 •	• 9	6 + 8 •	• 12
7 + 4 •	• 10	5 + 7 •	• 10
5 + 7 •	• 11	6 + 4 •	• 11
4 + 9 •	• 12	4 + 7 •	• 13

5 + 8 •	• 12	7 + 4 •	• 13
6 + 4 •	• 10	8 + 5 •	• 11
3 + 9 •	• 13	5 + 7 •	• 14
8 + 6 •	• 11	4 + 6 •	• 10
4 + 7 •	• 14	10 + 4 •	• 12

LESSON 6E: NUMBER DESIGN WITH THE DOUBLES, THE NEAR-DOUBLES, AND THE ROBIN HOOD FACTS

TEACHER LESSON

In this lesson, students incorporate the Robin Hood facts with double facts and near-double facts.

Identifying Thinking Strategies

Now that the thinking strategies for the remaining facts have been developed, have the students complete these addition facts together with double facts and near-double facts.

Have students consider the following six facts. Two are Robin Hood facts, two are near-double facts, and two are double facts. Have the students identify these facts.

$$
\begin{array}{cccccc}
6 & 5 & 4 & 5 & 6 & 7 \\
+\,4 & +\,4 & +\,4 & +\,7 & +\,7 & +\,7
\end{array}
$$

Robin Hood

$$
\begin{array}{cc}
6 & 5 \\
+\,4 & +\,7
\end{array}
$$

near-double

$$
\begin{array}{cc}
5 & 6 \\
+\,4 & +\,7
\end{array}
$$

double fact

$$
\begin{array}{cc}
4 & 7 \\
+\,4 & +\,7
\end{array}
$$

Applying Thinking Strategies

Ask the students how they would apply thinking strategies for the facts they identified.

(a) 6 + 4 (Robin Hood fact)

■ Robin Hood Strategy:
Take 1 from 6 and give it to 4.
6 − 1 = 5 and 4 + 1 = 5
5 + 5 = 10
SO, 6 + 4 = 10

Have the students use a similar thinking strategy to complete the fact 5 + 7.

Note: Students can also complete these facts using other thinking strategies.

(b) 5 + 4 (near-double fact)

■ Three-Step Strategy:
Step 1: The smaller addend is 4.
Step 2: 4 + 4 = 8
Step 3: 8 + 1 = 9
        SO, 5 + 4 = 9

Note: Students can use the special picture of a spider to complete the double fact 4 + 4.

Note: This fact has an addend of 5, and students can complete this fact by picturing the ten-frame (1 more counter is required to fill the ten-frame). Encourage them to do so.

Have students use a similar thinking strategy to complete the fact 6 + 7.

(c) 4 + 4 (double fact)

■ Special Picture:
Picture a spider with 4 legs on each side.
SO, 4 + 4 = 8

Have students use a similar thinking strategy to complete the fact 7 + 7.

Encouraging Class Discussion

Engaging students in whole-class discussions is an integral part of the program. Prompts for encouraging class discussions can be found on page 2 of the Introduction.

INTRODUCING THE STUDENT ACTIVITY SHEET

Distribute a copy of the sheet, Number Design, to each student. Have the students read the instructions and complete the activity.

Note: The activity sheet also contains facts with an addend of 10.

CHALLENGE FACTS

Use the Challenge Facts, Level 6B (pages 196-199), to help the students identify facts. Have them place shapes around the facts. For example, have them place circles around all the facts that are Robin Hood facts and then complete them. Next, have them place rectangles around all the near-double facts, and so on. They can also use different coloured pencils to identify the facts.

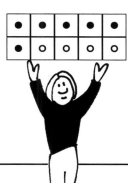

Number Design

Complete the addition facts below. When you are finished, choose the colours for the Colour Key, and colour the design.

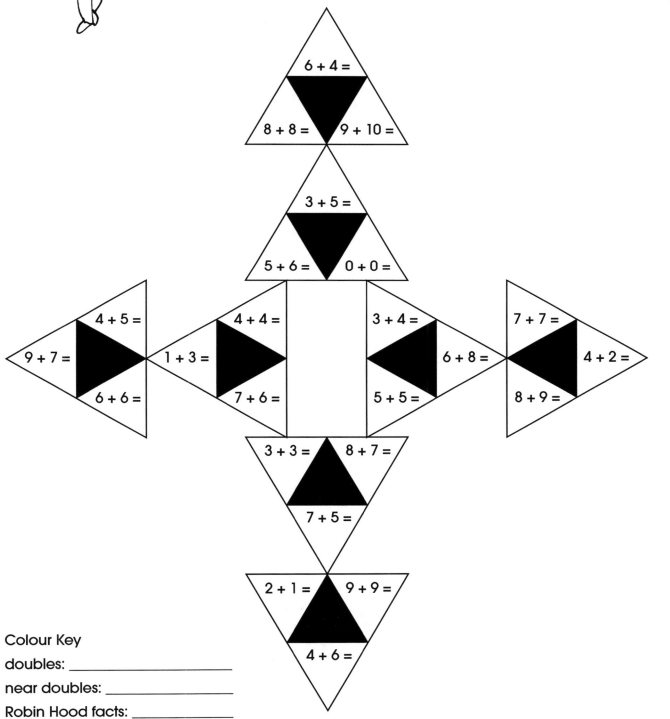

6 + 4 =

8 + 8 =   9 + 10 =

3 + 5 =

5 + 6 =   0 + 0 =

4 + 5 =   4 + 4 =   3 + 4 =   7 + 7 =

9 + 7 =   1 + 3 =   6 + 8 =   4 + 2 =

6 + 6 =   7 + 6 =   5 + 5 =   8 + 9 =

3 + 3 =   8 + 7 =

7 + 5 =

2 + 1 =   9 + 9 =

4 + 6 =

Colour Key

doubles: _____

near doubles: _____

Robin Hood facts: _____

LESSON 6F: JELLYBEAN JUMBLE WITH FACTS 0-10

TEACHER LESSON

In this lesson, students complete the basic addition facts by identifying and applying thinking strategies.

Identifying and Applying Thinking Strategies

Present the students with the following addition facts:

5 + 7
9 + 7
6 + 6
5 + 8

Have the students complete the facts and then explain their thinking strategies. Discuss with students which thinking strategy they prefer, and have them justify their choice.

(a) 5 + 7 (Robin Hood fact/addend of 5)

■ Robin Hood Strategy:

Take 1 from 7 and give it to 5.
7 − 1 = 6 and 5 + 1 = 6
6 + 6 = 12
SO, 5 + 7 = 12

■ Helping Fact:

3 + 7 = 10
5 = 3 + 2
10 + 2 = 12
SO, 5 + 7 = 12

■ Helping Fact:

5 + 5 = 10
7 = 5 + 2
10 + 2 = 12
SO, 5 + 7 = 12

Note: Some students will note that this fact has an addend of 5 and complete this fact by picturing a ten-frame with 10 counters and 2 more counters. Encourage them to do so.

Note: Students can use other facts as helping facts.

(b) 9 + 7 (addend of 9/Robin Hood fact)

■ Build-10:

Build 10 by taking 1 from 7.
9 + 1 = 10 and 7 − 1 = 6
10 + 6 = 16
SO, 9 + 7 = 16

■ Helping Fact:

10 + 7 = 17
9 = 10 − 1
17 − 1 = 16
SO, 9 + 7 = 16

■ Robin Hood Strategy:

Take 1 from 9 and give it to 7.
9 − 1 = 8 and 7 + 1 = 8
8 + 8 = 16
SO, 9 + 7 = 16

Note: Students can complete the double fact 8 + 8 with the special picture of crayons or the helping fact 10 + 10.

(c) 6 + 6 (double fact)

■ Special Picture:

Picture an egg carton with 2 rows of 6 eggs.
SO, 6 + 6 = 12

■ Helping Fact:

5 + 5 = 10
6 = 5 + 1
10 + 1 + 1 = 12
SO, 6 + 6 = 12

(d) 5 + 8 (addend of 8/addend of 5)

■ Build-10:

Build 10 by taking 2 from 5.
8 + 2 = 10 and 5 − 2 = 3
10 + 3 = 13
SO, 5 + 8 = 13

■ Helping Fact:

5 + 10 = 15
8 = 10 − 2
15 − 2 = 13
SO, 5 + 8 = 13

■ Helping Fact:

5 + 5 = 10
8 = 5 + 3
10 + 3 = 13
SO, 5 + 8 = 13

Note: Some students will note this fact has an addend of 5 and complete this fact by picturing a ten-frame with 10 counters and 3 more counters. Encourage them to do so.

Encouraging Class Discussion

Engaging students in whole-class discussions is an integral part of the program. Prompts for encouraging class discussions can be found on page 2 of the Introduction.

INTRODUCING THE STUDENT ACTIVITY SHEET

Distribute a copy of the sheet, Jellybean Jumble, to each student. Have the students read the instructions and complete the activity.

Jellybean Jumble

Complete the addition facts below. You will find that the sum of one of the four facts in each group is different from the sums of the other three facts. Colour the jellybean in each group that has the different sum.

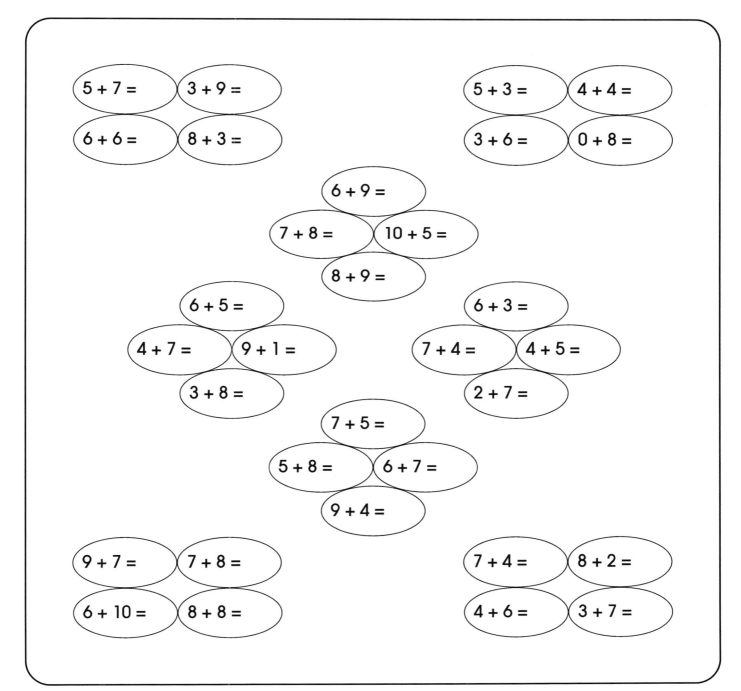

5 + 7 =   3 + 9 =

6 + 6 =   8 + 3 =

5 + 3 =   4 + 4 =

3 + 6 =   0 + 8 =

6 + 9 =

7 + 8 =   10 + 5 =

8 + 9 =

6 + 5 =

4 + 7 =   9 + 1 =

3 + 8 =

6 + 3 =

7 + 4 =   4 + 5 =

2 + 7 =

7 + 5 =

5 + 8 =   6 + 7 =

9 + 4 =

9 + 7 =   7 + 8 =

6 + 10 =   8 + 8 =

7 + 4 =   8 + 2 =

4 + 6 =   3 + 7 =

LESSON 6G: WACKY WEBS WITH FACTS 0-10

TEACHER LESSON

In this lesson, students complete the basic addition facts and examine even and odd addends and sums.

Identifying and Applying Thinking Strategies

Present the students with the following addition facts:

7 + 4
5 + 9

Have the students complete the facts and explain the thinking strategies they used.

(a) 7 + 4 (remaining fact)

■ Helping Fact:
7 + 3 = 10
4 = 3 + 1
10 + 1 = 11
SO, 7 + 4 = 11

Note: Students may prefer to use other facts as helping facts.

Note: Students can also complete this fact by using the build-10 thinking strategy (by taking 3 from 4 to build 10).

(b) 5 + 9 (addend of 9)

■ Build-10:
Build 10 by taking 1 from 5.
9 + 1 = 10 and 5 − 1 = 4
10 + 4 = 14
SO, 5 + 9 = 14

■ Helping Fact:
5 + 10 = 15
9 = 10 − 1
15 − 1 = 14
SO, 5 + 9 = 14

Note: Some students will note this fact has an addend of 5 and complete this fact by picturing a ten-frame with 10 counters and 4 more counters. Encourage them to do so.

Even and Odd Numbers

Ask the students: Can you name the even numbers that are less than or equal to 20? (0, 2, 4, 6, 8, 10, 12, 14, 16, 18, 20)

Ask the students: Can you name the ending numerals of the even numbers? (0, 2, 4, 6, 8)

Ask the students: Can you name the odd numbers that are less than or equal to 20? (1, 3, 5, 7, 9, 11, 13, 15, 17, 19)

Ask the students: Can you name the ending numerals of the odd numbers? (1, 3, 5, 7, 9)

Even and Odd Addends and Sums

Have the students model the following addition sentences with cube trains:

7 + 4 = 11
5 + 9 = 14
4 + 8 = 12

Ask them whether the addends and sums are even or odd.

■ 7 + 4 = 11 (The addend 7 is odd and the addend 4 is even. The sum 11 is odd.)

■ 5 + 9 = 14 (The addends 5 and 9 are odd. The sum 14 is even.)

■ 4 + 8 = 12 (The addends 4 and 8 are both even. The sum 12 is even.)

Ask: What patterns do you notice for the sums of even and odd numbers? Justify these patterns.

■ The sum of an odd number and an even number is odd: When an odd number of cubes is divided into two equal groups, there is one left. When an odd and even number are added together, there is always one left.

■ The sum of two odd numbers is even: When an odd number of cubes is divided into two groups, there is one left. When two odd numbers are added together, two cubes are left (one from each group). One can be placed in the first group; the other can be placed in the second group. The two groups will be equal, and the sum is even.

■ The sum of two even numbers is even: Each cube train can be divided into two equal groups; therefore, their sum can be divided into two equal groups.

Note: The sum of an even number and an odd number is also odd.

Encouraging Class Discussion

Engaging students in whole-class discussions is an integral part of the program. Prompts for encouraging class discussions can be found on page 2 of the Introduction.

INTRODUCING THE STUDENT ACTIVITY SHEET

Distribute a copy of the sheet, Wacky Webs, to each student. Have the students read the instructions and complete the activity.

Wacky Webs

The numbers ending in 0, 2, 4, 6, and 8 are **EVEN** numbers.

The numbers ending in 1, 3, 5, 7, and 9 are **ODD** numbers.

Below, fill in the outer cells of each web by adding the numbers in the inner cells with the number in the middle.

Colour all of the cells that have an **EVEN** number.

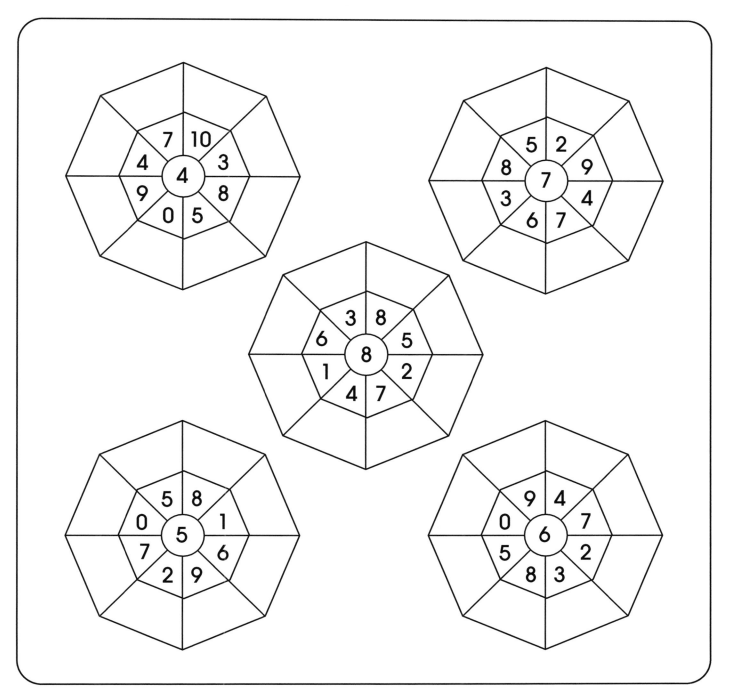

LESSON 6H: SECRET MESSAGE WITH FACTS 0-10

TEACHER LESSON

In this lesson, students complete the basic addition facts by identifying and applying thinking strategies.

Preparing for the Level 6 Number Challenge

Encourage students to practice the sixth set of Power Facts (page 138). Students can also play Partner Bingo, Level 6 (pages 167-177), either in class or at home, to prepare for the Level 6 Challenge.

Identifying and Applying Thinking Strategies

Present the students with the following addition facts:

4 + 6
8 + 6
4 + 5

Have the students complete the facts and explain their thinking strategies. Discuss with students which thinking strategy they prefer, and have them justify their choice.

(a) 4 + 6 (Robin Hood fact)

■ Robin Hood Strategy:

Take 1 from 6 and give it to 4.
6 − 1 = 5 and 4 + 1 = 5
5 + 5 = 10
SO, 4 + 6 = 10

■ Helping Fact:

3 + 6 = 9
4 = 3 + 1
9 + 1 = 10
SO, 4 + 6 = 10

■ Helping Fact:

4 + 4 = 8
6 = 4 + 2
8 + 2 = 10
SO, 4 + 6 = 10

Note: Students may prefer to use other facts as helping facts.

Note: Students can complete this fact by picturing the ten-frame (4 counters and 6 counters complete the ten-frame). Encourage them to do so.

(b) 8 + 6 (addend of 8/Robin Hood fact)

■ Build-10:

Build 10 by taking 2 from 6.
8 + 2 = 10 and 6 − 2 = 4
10 + 4 = 14
SO, 8 + 6 = 14

■ Helping Fact:

10 + 6 = 16
8 = 10 − 2
16 − 2 = 14
SO, 8 + 6 = 14

■ Robin Hood Strategy:

Take 1 from 8 and give it to 6.
8 − 1 = 7 and 6 + 1 = 7
7 + 7 = 14
SO, 8 + 6 = 14

Note: Students can use the special picture of 2 weeks of 7 days to complete the double fact 7 + 7, or they can use the helping fact 5 + 5.

(c) 4 + 5 (near-double)

■ Three-Step Strategy:

Step 1: The smaller addend is 4.
Step 2: 4 + 4 = 8
Step 3: 8 + 1 = 9
        SO, 4 + 5 = 9

Note: Students can use the special picture of a spider to complete the double fact 4 + 4.

Note: Students can complete this fact by picturing the ten-frame (1 more counter is required to fill the ten-frame). Encourage them to do so.

Encouraging Class Discussion

Engaging students in whole-class discussions is an integral part of the program. Prompts for encouraging class discussions can be found on page 2 of the Introduction.

INTRODUCING THE STUDENT ACTIVITY SHEET

Distribute a copy of the sheet, Secret Message, to each student. Have the students read the instructions and complete the activity.

PARTNER BINGO

Students can practice the basic facts by playing Partner Bingo, Level 6B (pages 172-177). Have the students complete the facts in order and cross out only one square on their card for each fact. Partner Bingo can be played in class or at home.

Secret Message

Complete the addition facts. In the Code Key, find the number that matches the sum of the first fact. Write the letter that is above that number in the first blank. Now, find the number in the Code Key that matches the sum of the second fact. Write the letter that is above it in the second blank. Continue with each addition fact until you have filled in the remaining blanks with a letter from the Code Key. When you are finished, you will find the secret message.

Why are the students wearing bathing suits to school?

$\overline{1}$ $\overline{2}$ $\overline{3}$ $\overline{4}$　　$\overline{5}$ $\overline{6}$ $\overline{7}$　　$\overline{8}$ $\overline{9}$ $\overline{10}$ $\overline{11}$ $\overline{12}$ $\overline{13}$ $\overline{14}$　　$\overline{15}$ $\overline{16}$

$\overline{17}$ $\overline{18}$ $\overline{19}$ $\overline{20}$ $\overline{21}$ $\overline{22}$　　$\overline{23}$ $\overline{24}$　　$\overline{25}$　　$\overline{26}$ $\overline{27}$ $\overline{28}$　　$\overline{29}$ $\overline{30}$ $\overline{31}$ $\overline{32}$

Code Key	Y	D	V	N	E	C	T	R	O	A	I	L	H	P	S	G
	4	5	6	7	8	9	10	11	12	13	14	15	16	17	18	19

①　4　+6

②　8　+8

③　5　+3

④　2　+2

⑤　4　+9

⑥　3　+8

⑦　1　+7

⑧　0　+5

⑨　2　+9

⑩　7　+7

⑪　2　+4

⑫　9　+5

⑬　1　+6

⑭　10　+9

⑮　4　+6

⑯　6　+6

⑰　9　+9

⑱　3　+6

⑲　9　+7

⑳　8　+4

㉑　7　+5

㉒　9　+6

㉓　6　+8

㉔　3　+4

㉕　6　+7

㉖　4　+5

㉗　8　+5

㉘　5　+6

㉙　8　+9

㉚　4　+8

㉛　3　+9

㉜　8　+7

LESSON 61: THE LEVEL 6 NUMBER CHALLENGE

The Level 6 Number Challenge is the last challenge in the program. It involves all the basic addition facts, and it includes addition facts introduced in Level 6 as well as those introduced throughout the program.

Before students take the Level 6 Number Challenge, have them complete the basic addition facts. Choose facts that the students find most challenging. The following are often difficult for students to complete:

    4 + 6
    8 + 4
    5 + 7
    4 + 9
    6 + 8
    7 + 4
    5 + 8

Have the student discuss the different thinking strategies they can use with these addition facts.

INSTRUCTIONS FOR THE LEVEL 6 CHALLENGE

Distribute a copy of the challenge sheet to each student. Explain the challenge: There are nine facts at the top of the page. Below, there are nine boxes with a clue in each box. Complete the facts, then match each completed fact with one of the clues, and place it in that box. Cross out each fact after it has been placed in its box. For students who would like an extra challenge, have them add the sums of the three facts in each row, then add the sums of the three facts in each column. (See answer key for the mystery number.)

SUGGESTIONS FOR MORE PRACTICE

If students have not yet mastered the addition facts, consider the following suggestions:

- Check that students can model the facts introduced in Level 6 with ten-frames.

- Write seven addition facts in a row, each with a missing addend. Have the students place the same number for each of the missing addends. Have the students complete the facts. For example, consider the following:

9		7		0		6
+	+ 5	+	+ 8	+	+ 4	+

9	5	7	5	0	5	6
+ 5	+ 5	+ 5	+ 8	+ 5	+ 4	+ 5

- Identify the facts that students find difficult. Help them develop thinking strategies for these facts. Have the students list the facts they find difficult, and encourage them to practice these facts both with a classmate in school and with a parent at home.

- Have students continue to practice all six sets of Power Facts.

- Have students play Partner Bingo in class or at home. There are 11 Partner Bingos for this level of the program (pages 167-177).

- Have students play card games. In addition to the card games introduced in the program, they can play the card game, Addition War, with a regular deck of cards. This game is played like the card game War, except that each player turns over two cards. Each player names the sum of the cards he/she has turned over. The player with the larger sum wins all four cards. The game is played without face cards.

Level 6 Number Challenge

Complete the addition facts below. Then, read the clue in each box, and find the fact that matches it. Place each completed fact into the box with its matching clue.

5	8	8	4	5	7	8	5	9
+ 7	+ 8	+ 10	+ 6	+ 8	+ 4	+ 6	+ 4	+ 8

The sum of this fact is one more than 10.	This fact is shown with the following picture: 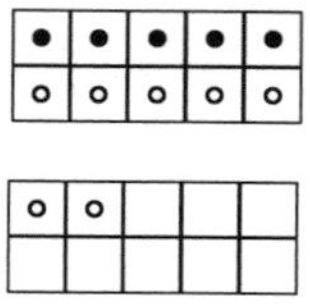	This is the near-double fact with addends of 8 and 9.
This fact is shown with the following picture: 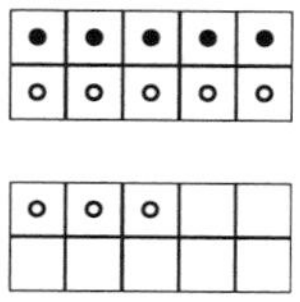	This is the fact that joins 8 and 10.	This fact is shown with the following picture: 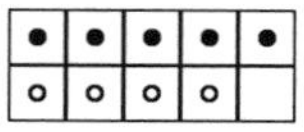
This fact is a double fact.	This fact has a sum of 10.	This fact is shown with the following picture: 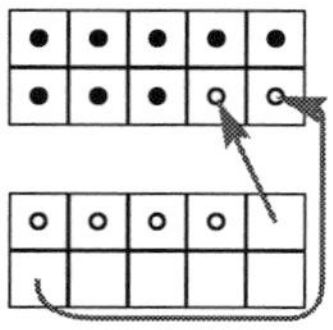

APPENDIX
A

TEACHER RESOURCES

ADDITION GRID

_____has learned the addition facts from 1-10!

+	0	1	2	3	4	5	6	7	8	9	10
0											
1											
2											
3											
4											
5											
6											
7											
8											
9											
10											

POWER FACTS: LEVEL 1

9 + 1 = 10	4 + 3 = 7	2 + 6 = 8	9 + 0 = 9
2 + 7 = 9	1 + 8 = 9	3 + 1 = 4	3 + 3 = 6
3 + 5 = 8	0 + 0 = 0	6 + 3 = 9	1 + 7 = 8
0 + 6 = 6	3 + 2 = 5	2 + 8 = 10	5 + 2 = 7
1 + 2 = 3	3 + 7 = 10	4 + 2 = 6	1 + 6 = 7

THINKING STRATEGIES

Level 1 introduces facts with an addend of 0, 1, 2, or 3.

THINKING STRATEGY: ADDEND OF 1

The thinking strategy for an addition fact with an addend of 1 is based on the one-more-than relationship.

Consider, for example, the fact 9 + 1.

9 + 1 (addend of 1)

- One-More-Than:
  One more than 9 is 10.
  SO, 9 + 1 = 10

THINKING STRATEGY: ADDEND OF 2

The thinking strategy for an addition fact with an addend of 2 is based on the two-more-than relationship.

Consider, for example, the fact 2 + 7.

2 + 7 (addend of 2)

- Two-More-Than:
  Two more than 7 is 9.
  SO, 2 + 7 = 9

If students have not yet developed the two-more-than relationship, suggest they count on 2 as follows: Have them start with the greater addend, 7. Have the students say 7, pause, and say 8, 9.

THINKING STRATEGY: ADDEND OF 3

The thinking strategy for an addition fact with an addend of 3 is the count on strategy.

Consider, for example, the fact 3 + 5.

3 + 5 (addend of 3)

- Count on 3:
  5 → 6, 7, 8
  SO, 3 + 5 = 8

Suggest the students count on 3 as follows. Have them start with the greater addend, 5. Have the students say 5, pause, and say 6, 7, 8.

THINKING STRATEGY: ADDEND OF 0

The thinking strategy for an addition fact with an addend of 0 is the pattern of 0.

Consider, for example, the fact 0 + 6.

0 + 6 (addend of 0)

- Pattern of 0:
  The sum of 0 and a number is the number.
  SO, 0 + 6 = 6

POWER FACTS: LEVEL 2

4 + 10 = 14	6 + 2 = 8	8 + 1 = 9	7 + 3 = 10
4 + 9 = 13	5 + 3 = 8	1 + 9 = 10	3 + 9 = 12
3 + 4 = 7	8 + 9 = 17	7 + 2 = 9	10 + 5 = 15
2 + 9 = 11	7 + 1 = 8	3 + 6 = 9	0 + 8 = 8
0 + 0 = 0	9 + 9 = 18	6 + 9 = 15	8 + 2 = 10

THINKING STRATEGIES

Level 2 introduces facts with an addend of 9 or 10.

THINKING STRATEGY: ADDEND OF 10

The thinking strategy for an addition fact with an addend of 10 is the pattern of 10.

Consider, for example, the fact 10 + 4

10 + 4 (addend of 10)

- Pattern of 10:
  A set of 10 and a set of 4 is 14.
  SO, 10 + 4 = 14

THINKING STRATEGIES: ADDEND OF 9

The primary thinking strategies for facts with an addend of 9 are the build-10 and helping fact strategies. These strategies are based on the place-value relationship with 10. Consider, for example, the fact 4 + 9.

4 + 9 (addend of 9)

- Build-10:
  Build 10 by taking 1 from 4.
  9 + 1 = 10 and 4 − 1 = 3
  10 + 3 = 13
  SO, 4 + 9 = 13

- Helping Fact:
  4 + 10 = 14
  9 = 10 − 1
  14 − 1 = 13
  SO, 4 + 9 = 13

Encourage the students to use these thinking strategies whether the 9 or 10 is the first addend or the second.

POWER FACTS: LEVEL 3

5 + 5 = 10	4 + 4 = 8	10 + 10 = 20	1 + 1 = 2
6 + 6 = 12	8 + 8 = 16	9 + 8 = 17	2 + 2 = 4
9 + 7 = 16	2 + 5 = 7	1 + 0 = 1	3 + 7 = 10
2 + 7 = 9	6 + 3 = 9	3 + 3 = 6	9 + 9 = 18
1 + 9 = 10	5 + 9 = 14	7 + 7 = 14	2 + 8 = 10

THINKING STRATEGIES

Level 3 introduces the double facts. The double facts are facts with equal addends. Double facts can be completed with the special picture strategy; some can also be completed with a helping fact strategy. Students can continue to complete the double facts introduced in Level 1 and Level 2 with the thinking strategies developed in those levels.

SPECIAL PICTURE STRATEGY

The double facts can be related to special pictures. The special pictures provide visual cues for the doubles.

3 + 3 = 6	a bug with 3 legs on each side
4 + 4 = 8	a spider with 4 legs on each side
5 + 5 = 10	a person with 5 fingers on each hand
6 + 6 = 12	an egg carton with 2 rows of 6 eggs
7 + 7 = 14	a calendar with 2 weeks of 7 days
8 + 8 = 16	a box of crayons with 2 rows of 8 crayons
9 + 9 = 18	an 18-wheeler double with 9 wheels on each side

RAP SONG

The following song might help the students remember the special pictures.

3 + 3 – Don't YOU bug me!

4 + 4 – There's a spider on my door!

5 + 5 – Ten fingers are ALIVE!

6 + 6 – Twelve eggs – let's mix!

7 + 7 – Fourteen days in heaven!

8 + 8 – Sixteen crayons are great!

9 + 9 – 18-wheelers drive fine!

10 + 10 – Twenty and we can start again!

THINKING STRATEGIES: DOUBLE FACTS

The helping fact strategy can also be used to complete some double facts. Consider, for example, the fact 6 + 6.

6 + 6 (double fact)

■ Special Picture:
  Picture an egg carton with 2 rows of 6 eggs.
  SO, 6 + 6 = 12

■ Helping Fact:
  5 + 5 = 10
  6 = 5 + 1
  10 + 1 + 1 = 12
  SO, 6 + 6 = 12

POWER FACTS: LEVEL 4

6 + 6 = 12	1 + 0 = 1	3 + 4 = 7	8 + 9 = 17
6 + 7 = 13	2 + 8 = 10	9 + 9 = 18	7 + 7 = 14
9 + 4 = 13	4 + 5 = 9	2 + 7 = 9	3 + 7 = 10
2 + 10 = 2	7 + 8 = 15	6 + 9 = 15	2 + 1 = 3
9 + 1 = 10	3 + 6 = 9	8 + 8 = 16	6 + 5 = 11

THINKING STRATEGY

THINKING STRATEGY: NEAR-DOUBLES

Level 4 introduces the near-double facts. In near-double facts, addends differ by one. Many near-double facts have been introduced in the first three levels of the program. Students can continue to complete these facts with the strategies developed in those levels, or they can use the near-double strategy introduced in this level. The near-double strategy involves three steps.

Consider, for example, the fact 7 + 6.

7 + 6 (near double)

■ Three-Step Strategy:

Step 1: Identify the smaller addend.
  The smaller addend is 6.

Step 2: Double the smaller addend.
  6 + 6 (double fact)

Step 3: Add 1 to the sum of the double.
  SO, 12 + 1 = 13

Remind students they can complete the double fact 6 + 6 with the special picture of an egg carton or with the helping fact 5 + 5.

POWER FACTS: LEVEL 5

10 + 5 = 15	8 + 6 = 14	4 + 9 = 13	3 + 8 = 11
9 + 5 = 14	2 + 0 = 2	7 + 8 = 15	5 + 6 = 11
8 + 5 = 13	9 + 10 = 19	1 + 8 = 9	9 + 8 = 17
7 + 3 = 10	4 + 8 = 12	9 + 6 = 15	2 + 7 = 9
5 + 4 = 9	9 + 7 = 16	8 + 8 = 16	7 + 6 = 1

THINKING STRATEGIES

Level 5 introduces facts with an addend of 8. Many of these facts have been introduced in previous levels of the program. There are only four facts with an addend of 8 (and their |turnarounds) that are yet to be introduced. They are the following:

3 + 8	8 + 3
4 + 8	8 + 4
5 + 8	8 + 5
6 + 8	8 + 6

THINKING STRATEGIES: ADDEND OF 8

Students can use either the build-10 strategy or a helping fact strategy for these facts.

Consider, for example, the fact 8 + 5.

8 + 5 (addend of 8)

- Build-10:
  Build 10 by taking 2 from 5.
  8 + 2 = 10 and 5 − 2 = 3
  10 + 3 = 13
  SO, 8 + 5 = 13

- Helping Fact:
  10 + 5 = 15
  8 = 10 − 2
  15 − 2 = 13
  SO, 8 + 5 = 13

Several strategies can be used to complete many of the facts with an addend of 8. Encourage students to choose the strategy they prefer to complete these facts.

POWER FACTS: LEVEL 6

$4 + 7 = 11$ $5 + 9 = 14$ $8 + 4 = 12$ $3 + 6 = 9$

$8 + 7 = 15$ $3 + 8 = 11$ $10 + 0 = 10$ $7 + 5 = 12$

$9 + 3 = 12$ $3 + 5 = 8$ $4 + 6 = 10$ $8 + 9 = 17$

$7 + 7 = 14$ $6 + 7 = 13$ $5 + 8 = 13$ $4 + 5 = 9$

$6 + 8 = 14$ $2 + 8 = 10$ $6 + 9 = 15$ $3 + 7 = 10$

THINKING STRATEGIES

THINKING STRATEGIES: REMAINING FACTS

Three facts and their turnarounds have not yet been introduced in the program. They are:

$4 + 6$ and $6 + 4$
$4 + 7$ and $7 + 4$
$5 + 7$ and $7 + 5$

The following thinking strategies can be used to complete these facts.

(a) 4 + 6 (Robin Hood fact)

■ Robin Hood Strategy:

Take 1 from 6 and give it to 4.
$6 - 1 = 5$ and $4 + 1 = 5$
$5 + 5 = 10$
SO, $4 + 6 = 10$

■ Helping Fact:

$3 + 6 = 9$
$4 = 3 + 1$
$9 + 1 = 10$
SO, $4 + 6 = 10$

■ Helping Fact:

$4 + 4 = 8$
$6 = 4 + 2$
$8 + 2 = 10$
SO, $4 + 6 = 10$

(b) 4 + 7

■ Helping Fact:

$3 + 7 = 10$
$4 = 3 + 1$
$10 + 1 = 11$
SO, $4 + 7 = 11$

(c) 5 + 7 (Robin Hood fact)

■ Robin Hood Strategy:

Take 1 from 7 and give it to 5.
$7 - 1 = 6$ and $5 + 1 = 6$
$6 + 6 = 12$
SO, $5 + 7 = 12$

■ Helping Fact:

$3 + 7 = 10$
$5 = 3 + 2$
$10 + 2 = 12$
SO, $5 + 7 = 12$

■ Helping Fact:

$5 + 5 = 10$
$7 = 5 + 2$
$10 + 2 = 12$
SO, $5 + 7 = 12$

STUDENT						
LEVEL 1	□ 1+1 □ 1+4 □ 8+1 □ 1+9 □ 3+2 □ 2+5 □ 2+7 □ 8+2 □ 1+3 □ 3+3 □ 3+4 □ 5+3 □ 6+3 □ 3+7 □ 0+0 □ 0+3	(same)	(same)	(same)	(same)	(same)
LEVEL 2	□ 10+2 □ 5+10 □ 2+9 □ 9+3 □ 9+4 □ 5+9 □ 6+9 □ 9+7 □ 9+8 □ 9+9	(same)	(same)	(same)	(same)	(same)
LEVEL 3	□ 0+0 □ 2+2 □ 4+4 □ 5+5 □ 6+6 □ 7+7 □ 8+8 □ 10+10	(same)	(same)	(same)	(same)	(same)
LEVEL 4	□ 4+5 □ 5+4 □ 5+6 □ 6+5 □ 6+7 □ 7+6 □ 7+8 □ 8+7	(same)	(same)	(same)	(same)	(same)
LEVEL 5	□ 8+3 □ 3+8 □ 8+4 □ 4+8 □ 8+5 □ 5+8 □ 8+6 □ 6+8	(same)	(same)	(same)	(same)	(same)
LEVEL 6	□ 4+6 □ 6+4 □ 4+7 □ 7+4 □ 5+7 □ 7+5	(same)	(same)	(same)	(same)	(same)

SELF-ASSESSMENT PROGRESS REPORT FOR STUDENTS • FACTS WITH 0, 1, 2, AND 3

Complete each fact, and explain your thinking strategy. Place a check mark beside each fact you have mastered.

☐ 2 + 5 =

☐ 0 + 6 =

☐ 3 + 7 =

☐ 8 + 1 =

☐ 6 + 3 =

☐ 2 + 2 =

☐ 0 + 0 =

☐ 3 + 3 =

☐ 1 + 9 =

☐ 7 + 2 =

SELF-ASSESSMENT PROGRESS REPORT FOR STUDENTS • FACTS WITH 9 AND 10

Complete each fact, and explain your thinking strategy. Place a check mark beside each fact you have mastered.

☐ 9 + 6 =

☐ 10 + 4 =

☐ 8 + 9 =

☐ 4 + 9 =

☐ 0 + 9 =

☐ 9 + 5 =

☐ 9 + 9 =

☐ 3 + 9 =

☐ 10 + 9 =

SELF-ASSESSMENT PROGRESS REPORT FOR STUDENTS • DOUBLE FACTS

Complete each fact, and explain your thinking strategy. Place a check mark beside each fact you have mastered.

☐ 6 + 6 =

☐ 8 + 8 =

☐ 4 + 4 =

☐ 9 + 9 =

☐ 5 + 5 =

☐ 7 + 7 =

☐ 10 + 10 =

SELF-ASSESSMENT PROGRESS REPORT FOR STUDENTS • NEAR-DOUBLE FACTS

Complete each fact, and explain your thinking strategy. Place a check mark beside each fact you have mastered.

☐ 9 + 8 =

☐ 7 + 6 =

☐ 6 + 5 =

☐ 0 + 1 =

☐ 4 + 5 =

☐ 3 + 4 =

☐ 7 + 8 =

SELF-ASSESSMENT PROGRESS REPORT FOR STUDENTS • FACTS WITH 8

Complete each fact, and explain your thinking strategy. Place a check mark beside each fact you have mastered.

☐ 5 + 8 =

☐ 8 + 7 =

☐ 3 + 8 =

☐ 8 + 6 =

☐ 8 + 10 =

☐ 8 + 4 =

☐ 9 + 8 =

SELF-ASSESSMENT PROGRESS REPORT FOR STUDENTS • REMAINING FACTS

Complete each fact, and explain your thinking strategy. Place a check mark beside each fact you have mastered.

☐ 4 + 7 =

☐ 6 + 4 =

☐ 5 + 7 =

LETTER TO PARENTS/GUARDIANS

Dear Parents/Guardians:

We have started a program called *Thinking Strategies: Addition*. This program is based on the latest research and uses thinking strategies to help children learn the addition facts. An important component of the program is parent-involvement opportunities.

What Is the Latest Research on Mastering the Facts?

The latest research gives the following three steps in mastering the facts:

1. developing a strong understanding of the operations and number relationships
2. developing efficient thinking strategies for fact retrieval
3. practicing the use and selection of those strategies

What Is a Thinking Strategy?

A thinking strategy is a way of thinking that helps complete a fact quickly. For a strategy to be a thinking strategy, it must be done mentally, and it must be efficient.

By involving more senses when introducing the facts, the greater the likelihood your child will remember how to complete the facts. Different strategies work for different students. The program *Thinking Strategies: Addition* provides a variety of strategies; your child can choose what works best for him/her. Some strategies are visual; for example, special pictures are used to complete the double facts. Some strategies are auditory and involve rhymes. Many strategies involve patterns and facts students have yet to master that connect with facts they already know how to complete.

The ten-frame model is a powerful model in building mastery of the addition facts and is introduced at the beginning of the program. The ten-frame is an array of 2 rows and 5 columns in which counters or dots are placed to illustrate numbers. The number 7, for example, is displayed on a ten-frame by placing a counter in each frame on the top row, beginning on the left. Once the first row is full, the 2 remaining counters are placed in the second row frames, again beginning on the left. In this way, the number 7 is displayed as 5 (in the first row) and 2 (in the second row).

How Does the Program Work?

Using six levels, the program teaches students many strategies for completing the facts. The levels are based on the ease of learning the facts rather than on a numerical order. For example, facts with an addend (number being added) of 9 are introduced early in the program.

From the beginning, the students learn that the order of the addends in a fact does not affect the answer. For example, 5 + 2 and 2 + 5 both equal 7. In the program, students learn both these facts together. In this way, the number of facts students have to learn is cut almost in half.

The Power Facts

For each level of the program, your child will bring home a set of Power Facts. Power Facts include the facts introduced in that level as well as some of the more difficult facts introduced in earlier levels. The Power Facts are given in rows and columns. It is important to change the order in which you ask the facts. One day, ask the facts vertically from top to bottom, another day from bottom to top. A third day ask the facts horizontally left to right, and then from right to left. Please practice a set of Power Facts with your child at least once a day. Thinking strategies for the facts introduced in that level are also included.

Practicing the Facts

When you practice the facts with your child, have him/her say the entire fact, not just the answer, when responding; for example, "2 + 5 = 7" rather than just "7." Stating the entire fact helps students learn the facts. Also, encourage your child to note patterns and connections, and to use thinking strategies to master the addition facts.

The Level Challenges

A Level Challenge is at the end of each level. Help your child prepare for each challenge by making sure he or she knows the Power Facts for that level. You can also use Partner Bingos and card games to practice each set of facts. These will be sent home with your child. Feel free to ask for extra copies if your child would like more practice.

Better Learning and More Fun

By working together with your child on the addition facts, you will be reinforcing important learning tools while helping your child. You will also share in the fun and enjoyment of the program.

Please call me if you want more information about the program. Thank you for your help.

APPENDIX
B

PARTNER BINGO

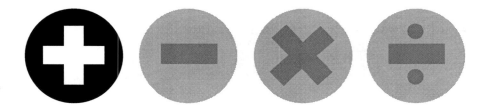

PARTNER BINGO 1

Level 1

Find a partner.

Answer question 1, and cross out one of the answers on your card (Partner #1).

Have your partner answer question 1, and cross out one of the answers on his/her card (Partner #2).

Take turns answering questions and crossing out one answer each time.

The winner is the first one who has a row, column, or diagonal crossed out.

Partner #1

① 3 + 2 = _____
② 1 + 9 = _____
③ 2 + 8 = _____
④ 1 + 2 = _____
⑤ 6 + 3 = _____
⑥ 5 + 2 = _____
⑦ 4 + 0 = _____
⑧ 2 + 7 = _____
⑨ 4 + 3 = _____
⑩ 3 + 5 = _____
⑪ 1 + 6 = _____
⑫ 7 + 3 = _____
⑬ 8 + 1 = _____
⑭ 4 + 2 = _____
⑮ 2 + 6 = _____
⑯ 0 + 1 = _____

Partner #1

7	8	0	3	9
10	2	9	7	0
6	7	+	10	1
0	2	10	8	4
5	9	4	2	5

Partner #2

① 1 + 4 = _____
② 6 + 2 = _____
③ 3 + 3 = _____
④ 0 + 0 = _____
⑤ 3 + 7 = _____
⑥ 2 + 5 = _____
⑦ 7 + 1 = _____
⑧ 3 + 6 = _____
⑨ 0 + 5 = _____
⑩ 7 + 2 = _____
⑪ 3 + 4 = _____
⑫ 1 + 5 = _____
⑬ 2 + 3 = _____
⑭ 9 + 1 = _____
⑮ 5 + 3 = _____
⑯ 1 + 1 = _____

Partner #2

9	1	10	8	7
2	4	3	5	9
5	8	+	7	3
10	6	0	1	5
3	9	8	4	6

PARTNER BINGO 2

Find a partner.

Answer question 1, and cross out one of the answers on your card (Partner #1).

Have your partner answer question 1, and cross out one of the answers on his/her card (Partner #2).

Take turns answering questions and crossing out one answer each time.

The winner is the first one who has a row, column, or diagonal crossed out.

Partner #1

① 2 + 5 = _____   ⑨ 0 + 7 = _____
② 1 + 3 = _____   ⑩ 2 + 4 = _____
③ 3 + 7 = _____   ⑪ 3 + 6 = _____
④ 8 + 1 = _____   ⑫ 1 + 1 = _____
⑤ 0 + 2 = _____   ⑬ 5 + 1 = _____
⑥ 3 + 3 = _____   ⑭ 4 + 3 = _____
⑦ 2 + 8 = _____   ⑮ 2 + 6 = _____
⑧ 5 + 3 = _____   ⑯ 2 + 3 = _____

Partner #1

1	0	7	6	2
7	2	3	10	7
8	1	+	9	0
10	5	4	0	6
3	6	8	4	9

Partner #2

① 6 + 3 = _____   ⑨ 2 + 6 = _____
② 5 + 0 = _____   ⑩ 0 + 10 = _____
③ 8 + 2 = _____   ⑪ 8 + 1 = _____
④ 3 + 4 = _____   ⑫ 3 + 5 = _____
⑤ 2 + 7 = _____   ⑬ 2 + 3 = _____
⑥ 2 + 1 = _____   ⑭ 1 + 7 = _____
⑦ 7 + 3 = _____   ⑮ 5 + 2 = _____
⑧ 1 + 4 = _____   ⑯ 2 + 2 = _____

Partner #2

1	7	6	5	4
10	3	9	10	6
8	2	+	7	3
5	9	8	6	10
9	10	1	5	8

PARTNER BINGO 3

Find a partner.

Answer question 1, and cross out one of the answers on your card (Partner #1).

Have your partner answer question 1, and cross out one of the answers on his/her card (Partner #2).

Take turns answering questions and crossing out one answer each time.

The winner is the first one who has a row, column, or diagonal crossed out.

Partner #1

1. 7 + 2 = _____
2. 2 + 1 = _____
3. 3 + 3 = _____
4. 1 + 9 = _____
5. 6 + 3 = _____
6. 2 + 5 = _____
7. 3 + 0 = _____
8. 7 + 1 = _____
9. 4 + 3 = _____
10. 2 + 6 = _____
11. 3 + 7 = _____
12. 1 + 8 = _____
13. 4 + 1 = _____
14. 3 + 5 = _____
15. 8 + 2 = _____
16. 0 + 4 = _____

Partner #1

8	1	4	7	10
3	8	5	1	9
9	0	+	10	7
2	6	10	9	6
6	8	3	0	2

Partner #2

1. 3 + 4 = _____
2. 0 + 5 = _____
3. 6 + 1 = _____
4. 1 + 1 = _____
5. 7 + 3 = _____
6. 2 + 2 = _____
7. 1 + 4 = _____
8. 5 + 3 = _____
9. 2 + 7 = _____
10. 3 + 1 = _____
11. 5 + 2 = _____
12. 3 + 6 = _____
13. 0 + 0 = _____
14. 2 + 4 = _____
15. 6 + 2 = _____
16. 2 + 3 = _____

Partner #2

4	3	0	7	9
10	8	4	5	1
6	5	+	6	2
9	4	5	1	7
1	7	3	8	5

PARTNER BINGO 4

Level 2A

Find a partner.

Answer question 1, and cross out one of the answers on your card (Partner #1).

Have your partner answer question 1, and cross out one of the answers on his/her card (Partner #2).

Take turns answering questions and crossing out one answer each time.

The winner is the first one who has a row, column, or diagonal crossed out.

Partner #1

① 9 + 3 = _____   ⑨ 2 + 9 = _____

② 5 + 9 = _____   ⑩ 9 + 4 = _____

③ 9 + 9 = _____   ⑪ 9 + 9 = _____

④ 9 + 6 = _____   ⑫ 7 + 9 = _____

⑤ 4 + 9 = _____   ⑬ 9 + 5 = _____

⑥ 9 + 7 = _____   ⑭ 8 + 9 = _____

⑦ 3 + 9 = _____   ⑮ 6 + 9 = _____

⑧ 9 + 8 = _____   ⑯ 9 + 10 = _____

Partner #1

17	16	18	11	9
11	10	15	17	14
9	12	+	19	12
13	18	16	10	15
14	13	9	17	18

Partner #2

① 7 + 9 = _____   ⑨ 9 + 3 = _____

② 9 + 4 = _____   ⑩ 8 + 9 = _____

③ 10 + 9 = _____   ⑪ 9 + 6 = _____

④ 9 + 3 = _____   ⑫ 4 + 9 = _____

⑤ 9 + 8 = _____   ⑬ 9 + 0 = _____

⑥ 6 + 9 = _____   ⑭ 5 + 9 = _____

⑦ 9 + 9 = _____   ⑮ 9 + 7 = _____

⑧ 5 + 9 = _____   ⑯ 1 + 9 = _____

Partner #2

9	13	15	16	11
14	11	17	19	14
16	18	+	11	13
9	12	10	14	15
17	11	12	13	18

PARTNER BINGO 5

Level 2A

Find a partner.

Answer question 1, and cross out one of the answers on your card (Partner #1).

Have your partner answer question 1, and cross out one of the answers on his/her card (Partner #2).

Take turns answering questions and crossing out one answer each time.

The winner is the first one who has a row, column, or diagonal crossed out.

Partner #1

① 6 + 9 = _____
② 9 + 4 = _____
③ 9 + 8 = _____
④ 5 + 9 = _____
⑤ 9 + 9 = _____
⑥ 7 + 9 = _____
⑦ 9 + 3 = _____
⑧ 9 + 6 = _____
⑨ 9 + 8 = _____
⑩ 10 + 9 = _____
⑪ 9 + 7 = _____
⑫ 3 + 9 = _____
⑬ 9 + 6 = _____
⑭ 5 + 9 = _____
⑮ 4 + 9 = _____
⑯ 9 + 1 = _____

Partner #1

13	14	16	9	11
10	15	9	12	15
17	16	+	14	9
12	19	13	11	16
18	11	15	14	17

Partner #2

① 9 + 9 = _____
② 7 + 9 = _____
③ 3 + 9 = _____
④ 9 + 6 = _____
⑤ 9 + 4 = _____
⑥ 8 + 9 = _____
⑦ 2 + 9 = _____
⑧ 5 + 9 = _____
⑨ 9 + 3 = _____
⑩ 9 + 9 = _____
⑪ 4 + 9 = _____
⑫ 7 + 9 = _____
⑬ 9 + 5 = _____
⑭ 3 + 9 = _____
⑮ 6 + 9 = _____
⑯ 9 + 0 = _____

Partner #2

13	9	10	12	15
15	16	13	19	14
14	10	+	16	11
19	12	15	17	18
18	14	12	13	10

PARTNER BINGO 6

Find a partner.

Answer question 1, and cross out one of the answers on your card (Partner #1).

Have your partner answer question 1, and cross out one of the answers on his/her card (Partner #2).

Take turns answering questions and crossing out one answer each time.

The winner is the first one who has a row, column, or diagonal crossed out.

Partner #1

1. 6 + 10 = _____
2. 7 + 3 = _____
3. 9 + 8 = _____
4. 2 + 5 = _____
5. 3 + 9 = _____
6. 0 + 5 = _____
7. 7 + 9 = _____
8. 5 + 3 = _____
9. 9 + 9 = _____
10. 7 + 2 = _____
11. 9 + 5 = _____
12. 1 + 8 = _____
13. 2 + 4 = _____
14. 10 + 10 = _____
15. 3 + 3 = _____
16. 0 + 0 = _____

Partner #1

6	12	15	18	10
14	11	7	17	6
16	20	+	9	13
17	15	0	19	8
13	9	16	11	5

Partner #2

1. 9 + 9 = _____
2. 2 + 6 = _____
3. 0 + 1 = _____
4. 5 + 9 = _____
5. 2 + 3 = _____
6. 1 + 1 = _____
7. 8 + 2 = _____
8. 10 + 7 = _____
9. 9 + 2 = _____
10. 3 + 5 = _____
11. 1 + 10 = _____
12. 4 + 3 = _____
13. 4 + 9 = _____
14. 3 + 7 = _____
15. 9 + 6 = _____
16. 5 + 1 = _____

Partner #2

3	14	4	15	11
15	8	5	18	20
13	16	+	3	10
10	7	1	6	17
20	8	2	11	5

PARTNER BINGO 7

Level 2B

Find a partner.

Answer question 1, and cross out one of the answers on your card (Partner #1).

Have your partner answer question 1, and cross out one of the answers on his/her card (Partner #2).

Take turns answering questions and crossing out one answer each time.

The winner is the first one who has a row, column, or diagonal crossed out.

Partner #1

① 9 + 5 = _____
② 3 + 7 = _____
③ 1 + 9 = _____
④ 3 + 3 = _____
⑤ 5 + 2 = _____
⑥ 9 + 9 = _____
⑦ 10 + 4 = _____
⑧ 6 + 3 = _____

⑨ 2 + 8 = _____
⑩ 7 + 9 = _____
⑪ 1 + 5 = _____
⑫ 10 + 9 = _____
⑬ 3 + 2 = _____
⑭ 4 + 0 = _____
⑮ 9 + 3 = _____
⑯ 1 + 7 = _____

Partner #1

7	16	17	10	12
4	9	14	8	6
18	15	+	19	10
6	5	3	20	18
17	12	10	14	15

Partner #2

① 5 + 3 = _____
② 8 + 9 = _____
③ 2 + 7 = _____
④ 1 + 6 = _____
⑤ 10 + 8 = _____
⑥ 3 + 4 = _____
⑦ 2 + 2 = _____
⑧ 9 + 4 = _____

⑨ 5 + 10 = _____
⑩ 7 + 3 = _____
⑪ 1 + 0 = _____
⑫ 2 + 9 = _____
⑬ 8 + 1 = _____
⑭ 9 + 6 = _____
⑮ 6 + 2 = _____
⑯ 10 + 10 = _____

Partner #2

16	7	8	20	3
1	19	4	15	9
18	4	+	14	7
10	6	19	13	9
8	17	15	16	11

PARTNER BINGO 8

Level 3A

Find a partner.

Answer question 1, and cross out one of the answers on your card (Partner #1).

Have your partner answer question 1, and cross out one of the answers on his/her card (Partner #2).

Take turns answering questions and crossing out one answer each time.

The winner is the first one who has a row, column, or diagonal crossed out.

Partner #1

①　6 + 6 = _____　⑨　9 + 9 = _____

②　7 + 7 = _____　⑩　5 + 5 = _____

③　8 + 8 = _____　⑪　6 + 6 = _____

④　9 + 9 = _____　⑫　8 + 8 = _____

⑤　3 + 3 = _____　⑬　3 + 3 = _____

⑥　1 + 1 = _____　⑭　7 + 7 = _____

⑦　8 + 8 = _____　⑮　10 + 10 = _____

⑧　7 + 7 = _____　⑯　4 + 4 = _____

Partner #1

14	16	0	4	12
20	2	12	14	2
6	10	+	16	10
16	4	14	6	18
8	18	4	12	2

Partner #2

①　2 + 2 = _____　⑨　4 + 4 = _____

②　4 + 4 = _____　⑩　7 + 7 = _____

③　6 + 6 = _____　⑪　3 + 3 = _____

④　7 + 7 = _____　⑫　2 + 2 = _____

⑤　8 + 8 = _____　⑬　9 + 9 = _____

⑥　0 + 0 = _____　⑭　8 + 8 = _____

⑦　3 + 3 = _____　⑮　6 + 6 = _____

⑧　9 + 9 = _____　⑯　5 + 5 = _____

Partner #2

2	18	14	4	16
4	12	6	10	20
14	16	+	2	8
10	2	8	16	12
6	18	20	0	4

PARTNER BINGO 9

Level 3A

Find a partner.

Answer question 1, and cross out one of the answers on your card (Partner #1).

Have your partner answer question 1, and cross out one of the answers on his/her card (Partner #2).

Take turns answering questions and crossing out one answer each time.

The winner is the first one who has a row, column, or diagonal crossed out.

Partner #1

① 3 + 3 = _____   ⑨ 7 + 7 = _____

② 6 + 6 = _____   ⑩ 4 + 4 = _____

③ 8 + 8 = _____   ⑪ 3 + 3 = _____

④ 4 + 4 = _____   ⑫ 6 + 6 = _____

⑤ 9 + 9 = _____   ⑬ 9 + 9 = _____

⑥ 7 + 7 = _____   ⑭ 2 + 2 = _____

⑦ 0 + 0 = _____   ⑮ 8 + 8 = _____

⑧ 8 + 8 = _____   ⑯ 10 + 10 = _____

Partner #1

16	6	4	20	10
8	10	12	6	8
18	14	+	2	12
2	12	18	0	16
16	4	10	6	14

Partner #2

① 7 + 7 = _____   ⑨ 8 + 8 = _____

② 0 + 0 = _____   ⑩ 6 + 6 = _____

③ 2 + 2 = _____   ⑪ 7 + 7 = _____

④ 6 + 6 = _____   ⑫ 4 + 4 = _____

⑤ 8 + 8 = _____   ⑬ 8 + 8 = _____

⑥ 1 + 1 = _____   ⑭ 10 + 10 = _____

⑦ 4 + 4 = _____   ⑮ 9 + 9 = _____

⑧ 9 + 9 = _____   ⑯ 5 + 5 = _____

Partner #2

0	20	12	8	6
12	14	6	16	18
4	8	+	18	4
18	10	2	6	16
6	16	18	12	14

PARTNER BINGO 10

Level 3B

Find a partner.

Answer question 1, and cross out one of the answers on your card (Partner #1).

Have your partner answer question 1, and cross out one of the answers on his/her card (Partner #2).

Take turns answering questions and crossing out one answer each time.

The winner is the first one who has a row, column, or diagonal crossed out.

Partner #1

① 6 + 6 = _____
② 2 + 1 = _____
③ 7 + 9 = _____
④ 5 + 5 = _____
⑤ 4 + 3 = _____
⑥ 1 + 8 = _____
⑦ 7 + 3 = _____
⑧ 9 + 9 = _____
⑨ 0 + 1 = _____
⑩ 9 + 4 = _____
⑪ 3 + 3 = _____
⑫ 2 + 8 = _____
⑬ 7 + 7 = _____
⑭ 6 + 2 = _____
⑮ 8 + 8 = _____
⑯ 1 + 1 = _____

Partner #1

20	10	17	16	1
13	16	9	11	2
18	4	+	15	10
12	10	5	7	8
3	19	14	9	6

Partner #2

① 7 + 7 = _____
② 10 + 9 = _____
③ 3 + 5 = _____
④ 1 + 3 = _____
⑤ 2 + 7 = _____
⑥ 9 + 8 = _____
⑦ 6 + 6 = _____
⑧ 6 + 3 = _____
⑨ 2 + 2 = _____
⑩ 1 + 9 = _____
⑪ 8 + 8 = _____
⑫ 9 + 6 = _____
⑬ 0 + 0 = _____
⑭ 5 + 9 = _____
⑮ 3 + 7 = _____
⑯ 4 + 4 = _____

Partner #2

12	6	9	14	4
4	13	7	15	17
0	14	+	10	2
10	17	16	5	8
18	8	19	15	9

PARTNER BINGO 11

Level 3B

Find a partner.

Answer question 1, and cross out one of the answers on your card (Partner #1).

Have your partner answer question 1, and cross out one of the answers on his/her card (Partner #2).

Take turns answering questions and crossing out one answer each time.

The winner is the first one who has a row, column, or diagonal crossed out.

Partner #1

1. $5 + 5 =$ ____
2. $4 + 9 =$ ____
3. $1 + 2 =$ ____
4. $0 + 9 =$ ____
5. $5 + 3 =$ ____
6. $8 + 8 =$ ____
7. $2 + 6 =$ ____
8. $3 + 3 =$ ____
9. $0 + 0 =$ ____
10. $6 + 3 =$ ____
11. $7 + 7 =$ ____
12. $2 + 5 =$ ____
13. $10 + 10 =$ ____
14. $6 + 6 =$ ____
15. $9 + 1 =$ ____
16. $6 + 9 =$ ____

Partner #1

6	10	9	14	6
19	8	12	5	7
18	9	+	8	1
15	4	20	2	13
16	0	17	10	3

Partner #2

1. $6 + 6 =$ ____
2. $0 + 1 =$ ____
3. $8 + 8 =$ ____
4. $9 + 2 =$ ____
5. $4 + 1 =$ ____
6. $8 + 9 =$ ____
7. $5 + 5 =$ ____
8. $3 + 5 =$ ____
9. $7 + 7 =$ ____
10. $2 + 8 =$ ____
11. $6 + 9 =$ ____
12. $4 + 4 =$ ____
13. $2 + 2 =$ ____
14. $3 + 4 =$ ____
15. $7 + 3 =$ ____
16. $9 + 9 =$ ____

Partner #2

11	16	6	18	10
2	12	9	4	19
9	8	+	17	6
10	3	5	15	1
8	10	14	7	13

PARTNER BINGO 12

Find a partner.

Answer question 1, and cross out one of the answers on your card (Partner #1).

Have your partner answer question 1, and cross out one of the answers on his/her card (Partner #2).

Take turns answering questions and crossing out one answer each time.

The winner is the first one who has a row, column, or diagonal crossed out.

Partner #1

① 6 + 5 = _____   ⑨ 9 + 8 = _____

② 4 + 5 = _____   ⑩ 5 + 6 = _____

③ 2 + 3 = _____   ⑪ 8 + 7 = _____

④ 7 + 6 = _____   ⑫ 6 + 7 = _____

⑤ 8 + 9 = _____   ⑬ 4 + 5 = _____

⑥ 7 + 8 = _____   ⑭ 8 + 9 = _____

⑦ 5 + 4 = _____   ⑮ 7 + 8 = _____

⑧ 6 + 7 = _____   ⑯ 9 + 10 = _____

Partner #1

15	7	9	17	13
17	9	5	3	11
3	13	+	15	9
11	1	7	5	19
1	17	13	15	3

Partner #2

① 2 + 1 = _____   ⑨ 8 + 7 = _____

② 9 + 8 = _____   ⑩ 5 + 4 = _____

③ 5 + 4 = _____   ⑪ 1 + 2 = _____

④ 7 + 8 = _____   ⑫ 8 + 9 = _____

⑤ 6 + 5 = _____   ⑬ 10 + 9 = _____

⑥ 4 + 5 = _____   ⑭ 6 + 7 = _____

⑦ 7 + 6 = _____   ⑮ 4 + 3 = _____

⑧ 3 + 4 = _____   ⑯ 5 + 6 = _____

Partner #2

17	7	5	15	13
1	11	9	19	3
9	5	+	15	7
13	15	17	3	5
19	9	13	1	11

PARTNER BINGO 13

Level 4A

Find a partner.

Answer question 1, and cross out one of the answers on your card (Partner #1).

Have your partner answer question 1, and cross out one of the answers on his/her card (Partner #2).

Take turns answering questions and crossing out one answer each time.

The winner is the first one who has a row, column, or diagonal crossed out.

Partner #1

① 4 + 5 = ____   ⑨ 7 + 6 = ____
② 8 + 7 = ____   ⑩ 3 + 4 = ____
③ 5 + 6 = ____   ⑪ 8 + 7 = ____
④ 4 + 3 = ____   ⑫ 9 + 8 = ____
⑤ 6 + 7 = ____   ⑬ 5 + 4 = ____
⑥ 10 + 9 = ____   ⑭ 4 + 3 = ____
⑦ 7 + 8 = ____   ⑮ 6 + 5 = ____
⑧ 8 + 9 = ____   ⑯ 9 + 10 = ____

Partner #1

15	7	5	11	19
17	3	9	13	17
11	19	+	3	15
9	13	7	11	5
5	19	15	7	17

Partner #2

① 4 + 3 = ____   ⑨ 8 + 7 = ____
② 6 + 7 = ____   ⑩ 8 + 9 = ____
③ 8 + 9 = ____   ⑪ 3 + 4 = ____
④ 7 + 8 = ____   ⑫ 6 + 5 = ____
⑤ 3 + 2 = ____   ⑬ 2 + 3 = ____
⑥ 9 + 8 = ____   ⑭ 7 + 6 = ____
⑦ 7 + 6 = ____   ⑮ 8 + 7 = ____
⑧ 5 + 6 = ____   ⑯ 1 + 2 = ____

Partner #2

9	13	11	17	5
7	17	15	19	7
13	9	+	15	1
15	17	3	11	5
7	13	19	7	9

Find a partner.

Answer question 1, and cross out one of the answers on your card (Partner #1).

Have your partner answer question 1, and cross out one of the answers on his/her card (Partner #2).

Take turns answering questions and crossing out one answer each time.

The winner is the first one who has a row, column, or diagonal crossed out.

Partner #1

① 5 + 4 = _____   ⑨ 2 + 3 = _____
② 3 + 7 = _____   ⑩ 5 + 10 = _____
③ 7 + 9 = _____   ⑪ 8 + 9 = _____
④ 1 + 2 = _____   ⑫ 7 + 7 = _____
⑤ 5 + 0 = _____   ⑬ 0 + 0 = _____
⑥ 10 + 8 = _____   ⑭ 5 + 6 = _____
⑦ 9 + 4 = _____   ⑮ 1 + 9 = _____
⑧ 8 + 7 = _____   ⑯ 10 + 10 = _____

Partner #1

15	7	17	9	12
16	10	19	15	5
8	13	+	0	16
5	12	15	2	10
14	18	3	20	11

Partner #2

① 3 + 9 = _____   ⑨ 7 + 7 = _____
② 1 + 6 = _____   ⑩ 0 + 1 = _____
③ 5 + 3 = _____   ⑪ 4 + 3 = _____
④ 9 + 9 = _____   ⑫ 1 + 1 = _____
⑤ 7 + 8 = _____   ⑬ 6 + 9 = _____
⑥ 7 + 2 = _____   ⑭ 2 + 8 = _____
⑦ 9 + 0 = _____   ⑮ 8 + 8 = _____
⑧ 6 + 7 = _____   ⑯ 9 + 10 = _____

Partner #2

1	17	12	9	4
11	10	15	12	18
14	9	+	7	20
2	5	19	11	16
15	13	6	8	7

PARTNER BINGO 15

Level 4B

Find a partner.

Answer question 1, and cross out one of the answers on your card (Partner #1).

Have your partner answer question 1, and cross out one of the answers on his/her card (Partner #2).

Take turns answering questions and crossing out one answer each time.

The winner is the first one who has a row, column, or diagonal crossed out.

Partner #1

① 10 + 9 = _____
② 3 + 4 = _____
③ 9 + 7 = _____
④ 6 + 6 = _____
⑤ 3 + 10 = _____
⑥ 6 + 3 = _____
⑦ 7 + 8 = _____
⑧ 4 + 2 = _____
⑨ 5 + 9 = _____
⑩ 1 + 6 = _____
⑪ 2 + 8 = _____
⑫ 7 + 10 = _____
⑬ 6 + 7 = _____
⑭ 9 + 9 = _____
⑮ 5 + 4 = _____
⑯ 9 + 8 = _____

Partner #1

17	3	12	15	13
11	6	5	10	7
17	13	+	18	8
9	3	16	11	9
19	12	8	14	7

Partner #2

① 8 + 7 = _____
② 9 + 4 = _____
③ 7 + 3 = _____
④ 6 + 5 = _____
⑤ 1 + 9 = _____
⑥ 3 + 8 = _____
⑦ 8 + 9 = _____
⑧ 4 + 4 = _____
⑨ 6 + 3 = _____
⑩ 10 + 10 = _____
⑪ 7 + 6 = _____
⑫ 2 + 9 = _____
⑬ 1 + 5 = _____
⑭ 8 + 8 = _____
⑮ 6 + 9 = _____
⑯ 2 + 2 = _____

Partner #2

19	8	15	11	14
15	18	13	7	20
10	4	+	11	16
14	13	17	3	9
11	15	7	6	10

PARTNER BINGO 16

Level 5A

Find a partner.

Answer question 1, and cross out one of the answers on your card (Partner #1).

Have your partner answer question 1, and cross out one of the answers on his/her card (Partner #2).

Take turns answering questions and crossing out one answer each time.

The winner is the first one who has a row, column, or diagonal crossed out.

Partner #1

① 8 + 9 = _____
② 7 + 8 = _____
③ 4 + 8 = _____
④ 8 + 6 = _____
⑤ 0 + 8 = _____
⑥ 3 + 8 = _____
⑦ 8 + 10 = _____
⑧ 8 + 5 = _____
⑨ 6 + 8 = _____
⑩ 8 + 8 = _____
⑪ 8 + 3 = _____
⑫ 9 + 8 = _____
⑬ 5 + 8 = _____
⑭ 8 + 7 = _____
⑮ 8 + 4 = _____
⑯ 8 + 8 = _____

Partner #1

14	15	17	16	9
10	18	11	13	12
16	9	+	14	13
11	15	12	10	11
17	14	9	8	15

Partner #2

① 8 + 6 = _____
② 3 + 8 = _____
③ 9 + 8 = _____
④ 7 + 8 = _____
⑤ 8 + 4 = _____
⑥ 8 + 8 = _____
⑦ 5 + 8 = _____
⑧ 8 + 7 = _____
⑨ 8 + 4 = _____
⑩ 8 + 9 = _____
⑪ 6 + 8 = _____
⑫ 4 + 8 = _____
⑬ 0 + 8 = _____
⑭ 8 + 5 = _____
⑮ 7 + 8 = _____
⑯ 2 + 8 = _____

Partner #2

17	9	12	15	18
12	16	18	14	11
13	15	+	10	13
18	14	8	17	15
16	9	12	13	16

Level 5A

Find a partner.

Answer question 1, and cross out one of the answers on your card (Partner #1).

Have your partner answer question 1, and cross out one of the answers on his/her card (Partner #2).

Take turns answering questions and crossing out one answer each time.

The winner is the first one who has a row, column, or diagonal crossed out.

Partner #1

① 8 + 4 = _____ ⑨ 8 + 8 = _____
② 9 + 8 = _____ ⑩ 8 + 5 = _____
③ 8 + 5 = _____ ⑪ 4 + 8 = _____
④ 2 + 8 = _____ ⑫ 8 + 6 = _____
⑤ 6 + 8 = _____ ⑬ 3 + 8 = _____
⑥ 8 + 3 = _____ ⑭ 7 + 8 = _____
⑦ 8 + 7 = _____ ⑮ 5 + 8 = _____
⑧ 4 + 8 = _____ ⑯ 8 + 10 = _____

Partner #1

13	8	9	12	17
11	10	16	8	14
9	17	+	15	13
16	12	14	18	8
13	11	9	12	15

Partner #2

① 8 + 6 = _____ ⑨ 8 + 7 = _____
② 3 + 8 = _____ ⑩ 6 + 8 = _____
③ 7 + 8 = _____ ⑪ 8 + 9 = _____
④ 8 + 4 = _____ ⑫ 8 + 5 = _____
⑤ 8 + 8 = _____ ⑬ 0 + 8 = _____
⑥ 9 + 8 = _____ ⑭ 8 + 3 = _____
⑦ 5 + 8 = _____ ⑮ 4 + 8 = _____
⑧ 3 + 8 = _____ ⑯ 8 + 1 = _____

Partner #2

12	13	18	17	11
15	10	8	11	15
17	9	+	14	18
14	12	17	10	13
18	11	16	8	15

PARTNER BINGO 18

Level 5B

Find a partner.

Answer question 1, and cross out one of the answers on your card (Partner #1).

Have your partner answer question 1, and cross out one of the answers on his/her card (Partner #2).

Take turns answering questions and crossing out one answer each time.

The winner is the first one who has a row, column, or diagonal crossed out.

Partner #1

① 5 + 8 = _____   ⑨ 9 + 9 = _____
② 10 + 6 = _____   ⑩ 3 + 6 = _____
③ 7 + 7 = _____   ⑪ 1 + 1 = _____
④ 2 + 9 = _____   ⑫ 2 + 7 = _____
⑤ 7 + 8 = _____   ⑬ 0 + 8 = _____
⑥ 1 + 0 = _____   ⑭ 7 + 6 = _____
⑦ 4 + 9 = _____   ⑮ 8 + 3 = _____
⑧ 5 + 5 = _____   ⑯ 3 + 2 = _____

Partner #1

3	13	7	9	4
1	8	9	6	17
14	5	+	11	18
18	15	12	16	13
12	13	10	2	11

Partner #2

① 7 + 3 = _____   ⑨ 6 + 6 = _____
② 0 + 0 = _____   ⑩ 2 + 7 = _____
③ 5 + 4 = _____   ⑪ 4 + 8 = _____
④ 6 + 9 = _____   ⑫ 9 + 7 = _____
⑤ 10 + 10 = _____   ⑬ 8 + 2 = _____
⑥ 8 + 6 = _____   ⑭ 8 + 8 = _____
⑦ 3 + 3 = _____   ⑮ 6 + 5 = _____
⑧ 1 + 2 = _____   ⑯ 9 + 10 = _____

Partner #2

16	9	6	20	8
9	12	2	7	15
8	10	+	16	10
6	17	9	3	19
0	14	11	12	18

PARTNER BINGO 19

Level 5B

Find a partner.

Answer question 1, and cross out one of the answers on your card (Partner #1).

Have your partner answer question 1, and cross out one of the answers on his/her card (Partner #2).

Take turns answering questions and crossing out one answer each time.

The winner is the first one who has a row, column, or diagonal crossed out.

Partner #1

① 3 + 8 = _____   ⑨ 8 + 8 = _____
② 1 + 9 = _____   ⑩ 1 + 7 = _____
③ 6 + 6 = _____   ⑪ 3 + 4 = _____
④ 1 + 0 = _____   ⑫ 5 + 3 = _____
⑤ 2 + 7 = _____   ⑬ 6 + 9 = _____
⑥ 8 + 9 = _____   ⑭ 0 + 0 = _____
⑦ 9 + 10 = _____   ⑮ 8 + 7 = _____
⑧ 5 + 8 = _____   ⑯ 10 + 6 = _____

Partner #1

12	14	1	16	15
8	5	7	6	10
11	15	+	18	17
14	12	8	9	4
0	13	6	16	19

Partner #2

① 6 + 8 = _____   ⑨ 7 + 7 = _____
② 9 + 3 = _____   ⑩ 5 + 8 = _____
③ 2 + 5 = _____   ⑪ 8 + 9 = _____
④ 8 + 4 = _____   ⑫ 0 + 3 = _____
⑤ 4 + 4 = _____   ⑬ 9 + 5 = _____
⑥ 5 + 6 = _____   ⑭ 8 + 10 = _____
⑦ 3 + 7 = _____   ⑮ 6 + 7 = _____
⑧ 8 + 2 = _____   ⑯ 5 + 1 = _____

Partner #2

8	6	16	13	3
9	17	12	5	14
13	14	+	7	15
15	18	13	9	10
10	14	19	12	11

PARTNER BINGO 20

Find a partner.

Answer question 1, and cross out one of the answers on your card (Partner #1).

Have your partner answer question 1, and cross out one of the answers on his/her card (Partner #2).

Take turns answering questions and crossing out one answer each time.

The winner is the first one who has a row, column, or diagonal crossed out.

Partner #1

① 4 + 6 = _____   ⑨ 4 + 7 = _____

② 8 + 4 = _____   ⑩ 3 + 4 = _____

③ 4 + 3 = _____   ⑪ 4 + 8 = _____

④ 9 + 4 = _____   ⑫ 4 + 0 = _____

⑤ 7 + 4 = _____   ⑬ 4 + 9 = _____

⑥ 4 + 5 = _____   ⑭ 7 + 4 = _____

⑦ 2 + 4 = _____   ⑮ 4 + 6 = _____

⑧ 6 + 4 = _____   ⑯ 4 + 1 = _____

Partner #1

11	10	7	5	10
6	9	11	6	12
7	14	+	8	4
4	12	8	13	11
6	9	13	10	14

Partner #2

① 4 + 7 = _____   ⑨ 10 + 4 = _____

② 4 + 4 = _____   ⑩ 4 + 6 = _____

③ 4 + 10 = _____   ⑪ 4 + 9 = _____

④ 6 + 4 = _____   ⑫ 7 + 4 = _____

⑤ 9 + 4 = _____   ⑬ 3 + 4 = _____

⑥ 4 + 8 = _____   ⑭ 4 + 4 = _____

⑦ 4 + 3 = _____   ⑮ 8 + 4 = _____

⑧ 7 + 4 = _____   ⑯ 5 + 4 = _____

Partner #2

6	7	13	11	14
10	8	10	5	12
7	11	+	8	6
14	12	5	7	13
9	6	11	8	12

PARTNER BINGO 21

Level 6A

Find a partner.

Answer question 1, and cross out one of the answers on your card (Partner #1).

Have your partner answer question 1, and cross out one of the answers on his/her card (Partner #2).

Take turns answering questions and crossing out one answer each time.

The winner is the first one who has a row, column, or diagonal crossed out.

Partner #1

1. $8 + 5 =$ _____
2. $5 + 4 =$ _____
3. $6 + 5 =$ _____
4. $9 + 5 =$ _____
5. $5 + 7 =$ _____
6. $3 + 5 =$ _____
7. $5 + 5 =$ _____
8. $5 + 9 =$ _____
9. $7 + 5 =$ _____
10. $5 + 5 =$ _____
11. $0 + 5 =$ _____
12. $5 + 9 =$ _____
13. $6 + 5 =$ _____
14. $5 + 8 =$ _____
15. $7 + 5 =$ _____
16. $1 + 5 =$ _____

Partner #1

9	12	8	15	11
15	10	11	13	14
11	14	+	7	6
12	7	14	12	10
13	11	15	5	7

Partner #2

1. $3 + 5 =$ _____
2. $5 + 5 =$ _____
3. $5 + 10 =$ _____
4. $5 + 4 =$ _____
5. $6 + 5 =$ _____
6. $9 + 5 =$ _____
7. $5 + 7 =$ _____
8. $5 + 5 =$ _____
9. $5 + 8 =$ _____
10. $10 + 5 =$ _____
11. $5 + 6 =$ _____
12. $4 + 5 =$ _____
13. $5 + 7 =$ _____
14. $5 + 9 =$ _____
15. $6 + 5 =$ _____
16. $5 + 2 =$ _____

Partner #2

14	7	15	12	11
6	9	10	5	13
13	5	+	11	15
9	12	6	14	10
11	8	13	9	5

PARTNER BINGO 22

Level 6A

Find a partner.

Answer question 1, and cross out one of the answers on your card (Partner #1).

Have your partner answer question 1, and cross out one of the answers on his/her card (Partner #2).

Take turns answering questions and crossing out one answer each time.

The winner is the first one who has a row, column, or diagonal crossed out.

Partner #1

1. 7 + 5 = ____
2. 3 + 5 = ____
3. 5 + 8 = ____
4. 1 + 5 = ____
5. 5 + 7 = ____
6. 5 + 3 = ____
7. 6 + 5 = ____
8. 5 + 9 = ____
9. 3 + 5 = ____
10. 5 + 10 = ____
11. 7 + 5 = ____
12. 4 + 5 = ____
13. 9 + 5 = ____
14. 5 + 6 = ____
15. 8 + 5 = ____
16. 2 + 5 = ____

Partner #1

10	11	14	8	9
11	15	12	13	5
9	8	+	9	13
6	5	14	12	6
8	12	7	10	8

Partner #2

1. 8 + 5 = ____
2. 5 + 4 = ____
3. 7 + 5 = ____
4. 5 + 3 = ____
5. 5 + 9 = ____
6. 0 + 5 = ____
7. 5 + 7 = ____
8. 3 + 5 = ____
9. 9 + 5 = ____
10. 5 + 5 = ____
11. 2 + 5 = ____
12. 5 + 3 = ____
13. 5 + 7 = ____
14. 4 + 5 = ____
15. 5 + 8 = ____
16. 6 + 5 = ____

Partner #2

11	6	12	13	8
14	13	15	9	10
9	8	+	7	15
12	7	13	6	14
15	9	5	8	12

Level 6A

PARTNER BINGO 23

Find a partner.

Answer question 1, and cross out one of the answers on your card (Partner #1).

Have your partner answer question 1, and cross out one of the answers on his/her card (Partner #2).

Take turns answering questions and crossing out one answer each time.

The winner is the first one who has a row, column, or diagonal crossed out.

Partner #1

① $3 + 6 =$ _____   ⑨ $9 + 6 =$ _____

② $6 + 8 =$ _____   ⑩ $4 + 6 =$ _____

③ $6 + 4 =$ _____   ⑪ $6 + 6 =$ _____

④ $7 + 6 =$ _____   ⑫ $0 + 6 =$ _____

⑤ $6 + 9 =$ _____   ⑬ $3 + 6 =$ _____

⑥ $5 + 6 =$ _____   ⑭ $6 + 7 =$ _____

⑦ $6 + 3 =$ _____   ⑮ $4 + 6 =$ _____

⑧ $8 + 6 =$ _____   ⑯ $6 + 2 =$ _____

Partner #1

8	10	14	7	12
11	16	13	9	10
9	14	+	15	16
15	10	7	13	6
16	13	12	14	9

Partner #2

① $4 + 6 =$ _____   ⑨ $3 + 6 =$ _____

② $9 + 6 =$ _____   ⑩ $6 + 8 =$ _____

③ $5 + 6 =$ _____   ⑪ $4 + 6 =$ _____

④ $6 + 7 =$ _____   ⑫ $6 + 10 =$ _____

⑤ $6 + 3 =$ _____   ⑬ $7 + 6 =$ _____

⑥ $8 + 6 =$ _____   ⑭ $8 + 6 =$ _____

⑦ $6 + 6 =$ _____   ⑮ $6 + 3 =$ _____

⑧ $6 + 4 =$ _____   ⑯ $6 + 1 =$ _____

Partner #2

8	14	15	10	16
10	13	7	9	13
12	15	+	8	14
9	8	10	12	11
14	16	12	9	16

PARTNER BINGO 24

Find a partner.

Answer question 1, and cross out one of the answers on your card (Partner #1).

Have your partner answer question 1, and cross out one of the answers on his/her card (Partner #2).

Take turns answering questions and crossing out one answer each time.

The winner is the first one who has a row, column, or diagonal crossed out.

Partner #1

① 6 + 7 = _____
② 7 + 4 = _____
③ 5 + 7 = _____
④ 8 + 7 = _____
⑤ 3 + 7 = _____
⑥ 7 + 9 = _____
⑦ 0 + 7 = _____
⑧ 7 + 5 = _____
⑨ 4 + 7 = _____
⑩ 7 + 8 = _____
⑪ 7 + 3 = _____
⑫ 5 + 7 = _____
⑬ 7 + 7 = _____
⑭ 4 + 7 = _____
⑮ 7 + 6 = _____
⑯ 7 + 2 = _____

Partner #1

11	17	15	10	11
13	16	12	17	7
10	8	+	14	12
17	15	9	11	10
12	11	13	16	8

Partner #2

① 4 + 7 = _____
② 7 + 8 = _____
③ 7 + 5 = _____
④ 1 + 7 = _____
⑤ 7 + 7 = _____
⑥ 4 + 7 = _____
⑦ 7 + 3 = _____
⑧ 6 + 7 = _____
⑨ 8 + 7 = _____
⑩ 5 + 7 = _____
⑪ 7 + 9 = _____
⑫ 4 + 7 = _____
⑬ 7 + 6 = _____
⑭ 7 + 3 = _____
⑮ 5 + 7 = _____
⑯ 7 + 10 = _____

Partner #2

11	10	9	13	12
15	12	14	7	9
7	13	+	15	17
16	9	8	12	11
12	15	11	10	7

PARTNER BINGO 25

Find a partner.

Answer question 1, and cross out one of the answers on your card (Partner #1).

Have your partner answer question 1, and cross out one of the answers on his/her card (Partner #2).

Take turns answering questions and crossing out one answer each time.

The winner is the first one who has a row, column, or diagonal crossed out.

Partner #1

① 4 + 7 = _____   ⑨ 4 + 8 = _____
② 2 + 3 = _____   ⑩ 5 + 5 = _____
③ 6 + 0 = _____   ⑪ 7 + 5 = _____
④ 10 + 2 = _____   ⑫ 3 + 4 = _____
⑤ 5 + 9 = _____   ⑬ 8 + 6 = _____
⑥ 8 + 8 = _____   ⑭ 3 + 7 = _____
⑦ 6 + 4 = _____   ⑮ 7 + 6 = _____
⑧ 5 + 3 = _____   ⑯ 9 + 8 = _____

Partner #1

13	5	9	14	12
18	10	6	8	9
12	14	+	15	10
10	12	7	11	17
15	5	16	14	18

Partner #2

① 7 + 8 = _____   ⑨ 7 + 4 = _____
② 9 + 9 = _____   ⑩ 9 + 7 = _____
③ 5 + 7 = _____   ⑪ 6 + 1 = _____
④ 3 + 8 = _____   ⑫ 3 + 8 = _____
⑤ 4 + 5 = _____   ⑬ 2 + 7 = _____
⑥ 6 + 10 = _____   ⑭ 4 + 6 = _____
⑦ 8 + 5 = _____   ⑮ 6 + 9 = _____
⑧ 7 + 7 = _____   ⑯ 10 + 10 = _____

Partner #2

12	9	16	6	11
11	8	4	18	19
10	6	+	7	16
16	15	8	14	20
4	9	11	13	15

PARTNER BINGO 26

Level 6B

Find a partner.

Answer question 1, and cross out one of the answers on your card (Partner #1).

Have your partner answer question 1, and cross out one of the answers on his/her card (Partner #2).

Take turns answering questions and crossing out one answer each time.

The winner is the first one who has a row, column, or diagonal crossed out.

Partner #1

① 2 + 8 = _____
② 7 + 7 = _____
③ 3 + 10 = _____
④ 8 + 9 = _____
⑤ 2 + 0 = _____
⑥ 3 + 8 = _____
⑦ 7 + 5 = _____
⑧ 6 + 4 = _____
⑨ 5 + 3 = _____
⑩ 4 + 7 = _____
⑪ 8 + 5 = _____
⑫ 6 + 6 = _____
⑬ 2 + 9 = _____
⑭ 6 + 7 = _____
⑮ 4 + 8 = _____
⑯ 5 + 9 = _____

Partner #1

10	13	16	11	10
11	7	13	12	9
13	8	+	15	14
12	18	11	2	16
15	9	12	14	17

Partner #2

① 7 + 5 = _____
② 8 + 4 = _____
③ 6 + 9 = _____
④ 5 + 0 = _____
⑤ 2 + 1 = _____
⑥ 3 + 7 = _____
⑦ 4 + 9 = _____
⑧ 5 + 6 = _____
⑨ 9 + 10 = _____
⑩ 6 + 4 = _____
⑪ 8 + 7 = _____
⑫ 3 + 9 = _____
⑬ 7 + 4 = _____
⑭ 4 + 3 = _____
⑮ 9 + 2 = _____
⑯ 6 + 3 = _____

Partner #2

7	12	4	12	15
9	14	11	17	10
13	11	+	15	8
10	8	12	6	19
3	5	17	11	4

PARTNER BINGO 27

Level 6B

Find a partner.

Answer question 1, and cross out one of the answers on your card (Partner #1).

Have your partner answer question 1, and cross out one of the answers on his/her card (Partner #2).

Take turns answering questions and crossing out one answer each time.

The winner is the first one who has a row, column, or diagonal crossed out.

Partner #1

1. 3 + 5 = ____
2. 4 + 2 = ____
3. 8 + 8 = ____
4. 6 + 4 = ____
5. 8 + 0 = ____
6. 8 + 6 = ____
7. 7 + 5 = ____
8. 2 + 9 = ____
9. 7 + 8 = ____
10. 4 + 1 = ____
11. 3 + 9 = ____
12. 7 + 4 = ____
13. 8 + 9 = ____
14. 9 + 4 = ____
15. 5 + 8 = ____
16. 3 + 6 = ____

Partner #1

5	16	10	18	17
11	3	12	2	20
2	15	+	6	9
13	11	7	12	13
8	14	10	7	8

Partner #2

1. 9 + 7 = ____
2. 0 + 0 = ____
3. 8 + 3 = ____
4. 5 + 4 = ____
5. 7 + 6 = ____
6. 9 + 2 = ____
7. 10 + 7 = ____
8. 4 + 4 = ____
9. 5 + 10 = ____
10. 6 + 6 = ____
11. 4 + 7 = ____
12. 6 + 8 = ____
13. 2 + 6 = ____
14. 5 + 7 = ____
15. 3 + 1 = ____
16. 4 + 6 = ____

Partner #2

2	14	11	6	13
14	8	3	9	0
16	12	+	10	4
8	7	13	11	15
11	17	15	12	20

APPENDIX B

PARTNER BINGO 28

Find a partner.

Answer question 1, and cross out one of the answers on your card (Partner #1).

Have your partner answer question 1, and cross out one of the answers on his/her card (Partner #2).

Take turns answering questions and crossing out one answer each time.

The winner is the first one who has a row, column, or diagonal crossed out.

Partner #1

① 9 + 7 = _____
② 8 + 6 = _____
③ 5 + 9 = _____
④ 4 + 7 = _____
⑤ 3 + 10 = _____
⑥ 7 + 3 = _____
⑦ 2 + 5 = _____
⑧ 9 + 9 = _____

⑨ 9 + 6 = _____
⑩ 6 + 3 = _____
⑪ 1 + 0 = _____
⑫ 8 + 9 = _____
⑬ 6 + 4 = _____
⑭ 3 + 5 = _____
⑮ 7 + 7 = _____
⑯ 4 + 8 = _____

Partner #1

1	11	6	7	19
15	10	12	8	14
14	16	+	5	10
4	17	9	18	13
19	16	14	1	5

Partner #2

① 0 + 4 = _____
② 6 + 5 = _____
③ 7 + 2 = _____
④ 8 + 3 = _____
⑤ 6 + 10 = _____
⑥ 9 + 5 = _____
⑦ 6 + 4 = _____
⑧ 4 + 3 = _____

⑨ 6 + 8 = _____
⑩ 7 + 4 = _____
⑪ 9 + 8 = _____
⑫ 3 + 6 = _____
⑬ 5 + 7 = _____
⑭ 2 + 2 = _____
⑮ 1 + 9 = _____
⑯ 5 + 8 = _____

Partner #2

11	8	4	17	9
16	9	15	19	4
13	6	+	14	11
11	14	10	3	8
2	5	12	7	10

PARTNER BINGO 29

Find a partner.

Answer question 1, and cross out one of the answers on your card (Partner #1).

Have your partner answer question 1, and cross out one of the answers on his/her card (Partner #2).

Take turns answering questions and crossing out one answer each time.

The winner is the first one who has a row, column, or diagonal crossed out.

Partner #1

① 6 + 9 = _____   ⑨ 6 + 8 = _____

② 7 + 10 = _____   ⑩ 2 + 4 = _____

③ 8 + 8 = _____   ⑪ 7 + 3 = _____

④ 3 + 6 = _____   ⑫ 5 + 6 = _____

⑤ 7 + 5 = _____   ⑬ 0 + 1 = _____

⑥ 9 + 3 = _____   ⑭ 4 + 6 = _____

⑦ 8 + 2 = _____   ⑮ 3 + 5 = _____

⑧ 4 + 7 = _____   ⑯ 5 + 4 = _____

Partner #1

16	11	4	10	9
18	12	10	1	14
6	8	+	15	19
15	2	11	18	12
10	9	3	17	14

Partner #2

① 8 + 4 = _____   ⑨ 5 + 7 = _____

② 6 + 7 = _____   ⑩ 9 + 7 = _____

③ 10 + 10 = _____   ⑪ 6 + 6 = _____

④ 2 + 3 = _____   ⑫ 1 + 8 = _____

⑤ 5 + 8 = _____   ⑬ 9 + 9 = _____

⑥ 0 + 7 = _____   ⑭ 4 + 3 = _____

⑦ 7 + 4 = _____   ⑮ 7 + 8 = _____

⑧ 8 + 9 = _____   ⑯ 3 + 5 = _____

Partner #2

14	15	9	12	7
10	12	17	4	13
20	6	+	12	11
15	16	13	3	8
7	4	19	5	18

PARTNER BINGO 30

Level 6B

Find a partner.

Answer question 1, and cross out one of the answers on your card (Partner #1).

Have your partner answer question 1, and cross out one of the answers on his/her card (Partner #2).

Take turns answering questions and crossing out one answer each time.

The winner is the first one who has a row, column, or diagonal crossed out.

Partner #1

1. $6 + 4 =$ _____
2. $7 + 6 =$ _____
3. $0 + 9 =$ _____
4. $5 + 3 =$ _____
5. $4 + 8 =$ _____
6. $1 + 0 =$ _____
7. $9 + 7 =$ _____
8. $4 + 4 =$ _____
9. $8 + 8 =$ _____
10. $3 + 6 =$ _____
11. $4 + 7 =$ _____
12. $9 + 8 =$ _____
13. $10 + 2 =$ _____
14. $9 + 6 =$ _____
15. $7 + 7 =$ _____
16. $5 + 8 =$ _____

Partner #1

11	18	12	6	16
8	9	5	13	8
14	7	+	10	0
5	15	9	2	1
13	12	3	16	17

Partner #2

1. $5 + 7 =$ _____
2. $9 + 10 =$ _____
3. $7 + 3 =$ _____
4. $8 + 8 =$ _____
5. $9 + 4 =$ _____
6. $7 + 2 =$ _____
7. $4 + 6 =$ _____
8. $1 + 8 =$ _____
9. $3 + 2 =$ _____
10. $8 + 5 =$ _____
11. $2 + 9 =$ _____
12. $6 + 3 =$ _____
13. $0 + 2 =$ _____
14. $4 + 7 =$ _____
15. $3 + 3 =$ _____
16. $7 + 8 =$ _____

Partner #2

7	5	17	10	9
6	12	10	13	14
9	11	+	18	16
1	17	5	13	11
19	2	9	20	15

APPENDIX
C

CHALLENGE FACTS

Challenge Facts 1

5 +2	8 +1	3 +6	1 +3	2 +4	5 +0	7 +2

5 +2	8 +1	3 +6	1 +3	2 +4	5 +0	7 +2
3 +7	2 +2	1 +4	2 +6	0 +9	3 +2	7 +1	4 +3
4 +1	5 +3	2 +8	0 +0	7 +3	1 +2	6 +2	1 +8
6 +0	2 +7	1 +1	3 +4	1 +5	6 +3	4 +2	0 +2
2 +3	1 +0	2 +5	1 +9	8 +2	0 +7	3 +5	6 +1

Challenge Facts 2

6 +1	7 +3	2 +2	4 +0	3 +3	1 +1	2 +8	1 +3
0 +8	2 +1	4 +3	1 +7	2 +6	7 +0	4 +2	3 +5
5 +2	0 +1	7 +2	6 +3	10 +0	3 +2	1 +6	8 +1
2 +7	3 +4	1 +9	2 +5	0 +0	4 +1	3 +7	2 +4
3 +6	8 +2	5 +1	2 +3	1 +8	6 +2	5 +3	0 +7

Challenge Facts 3

10 + 4	10 + 7	3 +10	5 +10	10 + 2	10 +10
6 +10	6 + 9	10 + 8	9 + 8	4 +10	4 + 9
9 + 7	9 + 9	5 + 9	3 + 9	9 + 8	9 + 6
0 + 9	4 + 9	7 + 9	10 + 9	9 + 5	9 + 3
9 + 9	9 + 2	9 + 4	6 + 9	1 + 9	9 + 8

Challenge Facts 4

4 + 9	8 + 9	9 + 5	7 + 9	9 + 3	10 + 9
9 + 9	6 + 9	0 + 9	9 + 2	9 + 7	5 + 9
3 + 9	9 + 10	9 + 4	8 + 9	9 + 6	1 + 9
9 + 8	2 + 9	9 + 3	9 + 0	4 + 9	10 + 9
9 + 5	9 + 7	6 + 9	9 + 9	9 + 1	2 + 9

Challenge Facts 5

2 +6	0 +7	4 +9	3 +7	1 +8
0 +0	9 +5	2 +2	9 +10	3 +4
7 +9	8 +2	6 +3	8 +0	9 +9
3 +3	1 +1	10 +7	6 +9	7 +3
9 +2	8 +9	0 +6	2 +3	5 +10

10 +2	3 +5	9 +6	
9 +8	7 +2	3 +1	
2 +5	10 +10	4 +2	
0 +4	1 +6	3 +9	
3 +6	9 +4	1 +7	

Challenge Facts 6

6 + 6	8 + 8	5 + 5	3 + 3	7 + 7	4 + 4
2 + 2	0 + 0	1 + 1	8 + 8	6 + 6	9 + 9
5 + 5	10 + 10	7 + 7	4 + 4	9 + 9	2 + 2
3 + 3	6 + 6	8 + 8	7 + 7	0 + 0	1 + 1
8 + 8	4 + 4	3 + 3	9 + 9	5 + 5	10 + 10

Challenge Facts 7

5 +5	9 +4	1 +6	10 +8	7 +3	6 +9	8 +8	3 +3

5	9	1	10	7	6	8	3
+5	+4	+6	+8	+3	+9	+8	+3
6	3	4	7	8	2	3	5
+0	+5	+2	+7	+1	+2	+9	+10
9	2	8	0	9	6	4	2
+6	+8	+8	+1	+5	+3	+4	+5
7	10	2	4	6	9	2	0
+7	+6	+9	+3	+6	+8	+7	+4
2	9	3	6	1	10	5	7
+3	+9	+7	+2	+3	+10	+3	+9

Challenge Facts 8

5 + 5	5 + 6	7 + 7	8 + 7	3 + 3	3 + 4
6 + 6	6 + 7	4 + 4	5 + 4	8 + 8	8 + 9
7 + 8	4 + 3	9 + 8	6 + 5	2 + 3	7 + 6
9 +10	4 + 5	1 + 0	8 + 7	5 + 6	1 + 2
8 + 9	3 + 2	6 + 7	5 + 4	7 + 8	3 + 4

Challenge Facts 9

6 + 7	9 + 9	2 + 4	1 + 8	3 + 7	2 + 1	4 + 4	10 + 9

Row 1:
6 + 7   9 + 9   2 + 4   1 + 8   3 + 7   2 + 1   4 + 4   10 + 9

Row 2:
2 + 8   3 + 4   5 + 5   0 + 0   9 + 6   8 + 8   2 + 5   6 + 3

Row 3:
5 + 9   6 + 6   3 + 1   7 + 8   4 + 10   9 + 3   1 + 1   5 + 4

Row 4:
3 + 5   2 + 7   7 + 9   3 + 3   1 + 0   6 + 2   8 + 9   1 + 7

Row 5:
7 + 7   0 + 8   2 + 3   4 + 9   2 + 2   5 + 6   10 + 7   9 + 2

Challenge Facts 10

7 + 8	8 + 4	1 + 8	5 + 8	8 + 8	8 + 6
3 + 8	8 + 9	8 + 4	2 + 8	8 + 5	8 +10
0 + 8	6 + 8	8 + 8	8 + 1	3 + 8	9 + 8
8 + 8	8 + 5	10 + 8	4 + 8	8 + 6	8 + 2
5 + 8	8 + 0	3 + 8	8 + 7	8 + 9	8 + 4

Challenge Facts 11

8 +9	10 +6	3 +8	5 +5	1 +7	6 +9	4 +3	8 +5
7 +7	2 +8	9 +7	2 +2	6 +8	0 +1	10 +10	2 +7
5 +8	4 +4	6 +1	8 +4	3 +7	5 +6	9 +5	3 +2
4 +9	8 +6	5 +4	0 +2	9 +9	3 +5	7 +8	6 +6
1 +8	3 +9	8 +8	6 +7	1 +2	4 +8	3 +6	9 +10

$$\begin{array}{r} 5 \\ + \\ \hline 10 \end{array} \qquad \begin{array}{r} 7 \\ + \\ \hline 10 \end{array} \qquad \begin{array}{r} 2 \\ + \\ \hline 10 \end{array} \qquad \begin{array}{r} 4 \\ + \\ \hline 10 \end{array} \qquad \begin{array}{r} 9 \\ + \\ \hline 10 \end{array} \qquad \begin{array}{r} 0 \\ + \\ \hline 10 \end{array}$$

$$\begin{array}{r} 3 \\ + \\ \hline 10 \end{array} \qquad \begin{array}{r} 1 \\ + \\ \hline 10 \end{array} \qquad \begin{array}{r} 6 \\ + \\ \hline 10 \end{array} \qquad \begin{array}{r} 10 \\ + \\ \hline 10 \end{array} \qquad \begin{array}{r} 5 \\ + \\ \hline 10 \end{array} \qquad \begin{array}{r} 7 \\ + \\ \hline 10 \end{array}$$

$$\begin{array}{r} 0 \\ + \\ \hline 10 \end{array} \qquad \begin{array}{r} 4 \\ + \\ \hline 10 \end{array} \qquad \begin{array}{r} 9 \\ + \\ \hline 10 \end{array} \qquad \begin{array}{r} 3 \\ + \\ \hline 10 \end{array} \qquad \begin{array}{r} 1 \\ + \\ \hline 10 \end{array} \qquad \begin{array}{r} 6 \\ + \\ \hline 10 \end{array}$$

$$\begin{array}{r} 2 \\ + \\ \hline 10 \end{array} \qquad \begin{array}{r} 10 \\ + \\ \hline 10 \end{array} \qquad \begin{array}{r} 3 \\ + \\ \hline 10 \end{array} \qquad \begin{array}{r} 8 \\ + \\ \hline 10 \end{array} \qquad \begin{array}{r} 4 \\ + \\ \hline 10 \end{array} \qquad \begin{array}{r} 1 \\ + \\ \hline 10 \end{array}$$

$$\begin{array}{r} 7 \\ + \\ \hline 10 \end{array} \qquad \begin{array}{r} 9 \\ + \\ \hline 10 \end{array} \qquad \begin{array}{r} 5 \\ + \\ \hline 10 \end{array} \qquad \begin{array}{r} 2 \\ + \\ \hline 10 \end{array} \qquad \begin{array}{r} 6 \\ + \\ \hline 10 \end{array} \qquad \begin{array}{r} 10 \\ + \\ \hline 10 \end{array}$$

Challenge Facts 13

7 + 4	4 + 3	9 + 4	4 + 6	0 + 4	8 + 4
4 + 2	5 + 4	4 + 7	10 + 4	3 + 4	4 + 1
4 + 6	4 + 9	2 + 4	4 + 4	4 + 8	5 + 4
1 + 4	4 + 7	4 +10	9 + 4	6 + 4	4 + 3
4 + 8	0 + 4	5 + 4	7 + 4	4 + 4	4 + 6

Challenge Facts 14

5 + 7	3 + 5	5 + 8	2 + 5	5 + 6	5 + 1
4 + 5	9 + 5	7 + 5	10 + 5	5 + 3	5 + 8
6 + 5	5 + 2	5 + 0	7 + 5	5 + 9	5 + 5
5 + 3	5 + 8	4 + 5	0 + 5	2 + 5	9 + 5
5 + 5	5 + 10	6 + 5	5 + 1	7 + 5	5 + 4

3 + 6	6 + 5	9 + 6	0 + 6	6 + 2	6 + 8
7 + 6	6 + 3	6 + 6	4 + 6	10 + 6	6 + 5
6 + 0	8 + 6	1 + 6	6 + 7	6 + 4	2 + 6
6 + 6	6 +10	3 + 6	6 + 5	0 + 6	6 + 9
6 + 4	2 + 6	6 + 8	6 + 1	3 + 6	7 + 6

4 + 7	7 + 8	2 + 7	7 + 7	7 + 5	9 + 7
7 + 1	6 + 7	7 +10	7 + 3	8 + 7	5 + 7
7 + 9	0 + 7	7 + 4	6 + 7	7 + 2	7 + 7
8 + 7	3 + 7	1 + 7	7 +10	4 + 7	7 + 2
7 + 3	7 + 7	9 + 7	7 + 5	0 + 7	7 + 6

Challenge Facts 17

6 + 5	9 + 3	5 + 8	4 + 4	8 + 10	3 + 6	7 + 8	9 + 9
3 + 10	5 + 7	4 + 1	2 + 3	6 + 6	8 + 9	6 + 0	5 + 4
8 + 8	1 + 9	7 + 6	9 + 5	8 + 2	4 + 7	3 + 3	2 + 6
5 + 3	4 + 2	5 + 5	3 + 8	9 + 7	10 + 10	4 + 6	7 + 3
4 + 9	8 + 6	4 + 3	7 + 2	0 + 1	7 + 7	6 + 9	4 + 8

Challenge Facts 18

7 + 5	8 + 8	6 + 5	3 + 7	1 + 1	5 + 9	7 + 0
2 + 8	6 + 7	3 + 9	5 + 5	7 + 8	2 + 3	6 + 3
8 + 9	4 + 6	7 + 7	1 + 2	5 + 4	4 + 8	10 + 10
3 + 4	0 + 0	1 + 6	8 + 6	9 + 9	6 + 2	8 + 5
6 + 6	10 + 9	5 + 3	9 + 4	2 + 7	4 + 4	7 + 9

Challenge Facts 19

9 +2	5 +5	2 +2	7 +9	1 +0	3 +8	6 +7	10 +10

9
+2

5
+5

2
+2

7
+9

1
+0

3
+8

6
+7

10
+10

6
+9

8
+4

3
+3

1
+2

5
+6

2
+10

8
+8

9
+3

5
+8

4
+3

2
+0

6
+6

7
+4

9
+5

1
+9

6
+8

7
+3

2
+8

9
+8

4
+10

3
+5

7
+7

4
+9

5
+7

4
+5

9
+9

10
+1

3
+6

8
+7

5
+2

6
+4

4
+4

Challenge Facts 20

9 + 9	7 + 8	1 + 5	4 + 7	8 + 3	9 + 6	5 + 5	6 + 4
8 + 6	5 + 3	4 + 9	6 + 6	0 + 9	3 + 4	7 +10	2 + 2
6 + 5	1 + 1	3 + 2	5 + 8	4 + 4	5 + 7	8 + 9	7 + 3
4 + 2	9 + 5	8 + 8	9 + 2	7 + 6	0 + 0	6 + 3	4 + 8
2 + 8	3 + 3	2 + 1	7 + 9	10 + 8	5 + 4	7 + 7	9 + 3

APPENDIX
D

PLAYING CARDS

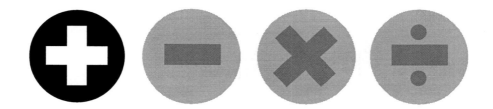

Level 1A

Level 1A

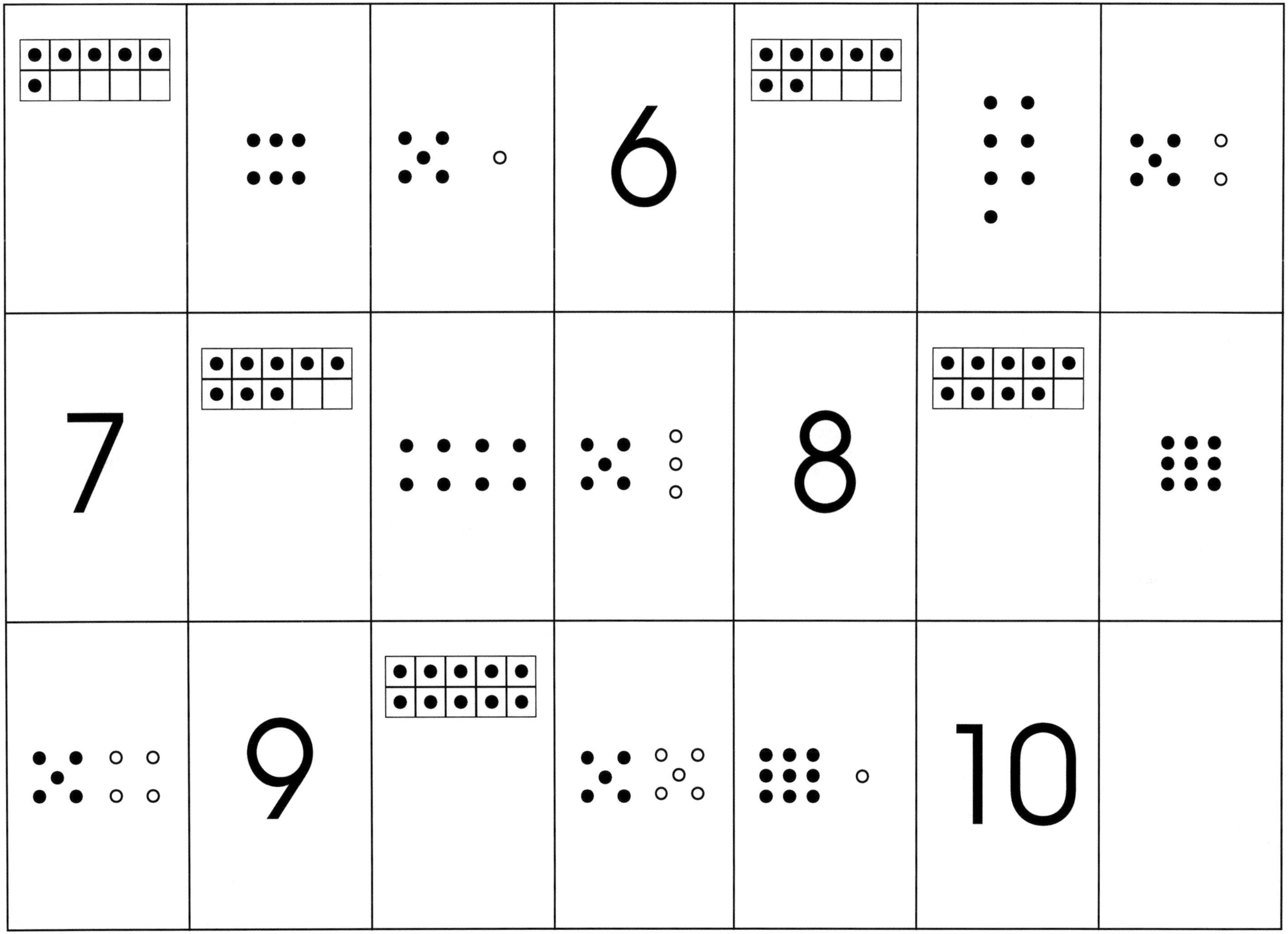

$\begin{array}{r} 1 \\ +1 \\ \hline \end{array}$		
		5
	3	$\begin{array}{r} 2 \\ +3 \\ \hline \end{array}$
	$\begin{array}{r} 1 \\ +2 \\ \hline \end{array}$	
$\begin{array}{r} 1 \\ +0 \\ \hline \end{array}$		
		4
	2	$\begin{array}{r} 1 \\ +3 \\ \hline \end{array}$

$$5 +2$$

$$10$$

$$8$$

$$7 +3$$

$$6$$

$$5 +3$$

$$6 +0$$

$$9$$

$$7$$

$$7 +2$$

Level 2

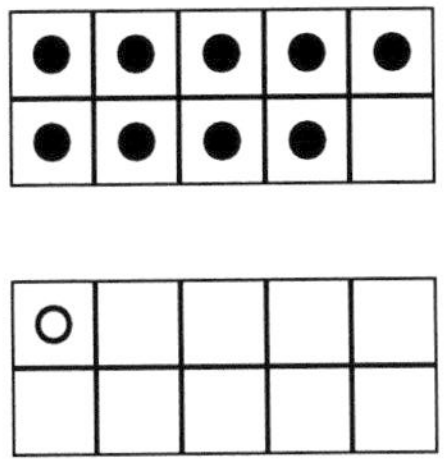	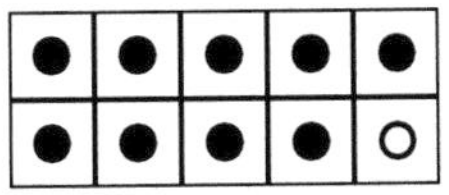	9 +1	10	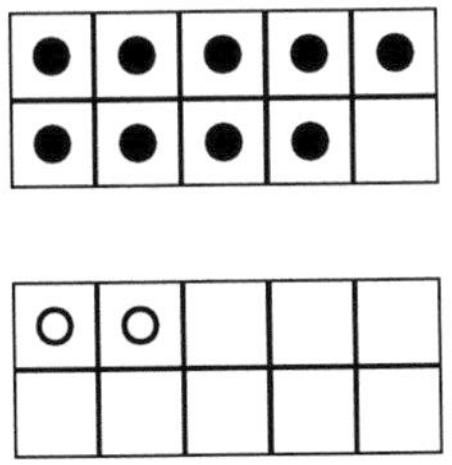	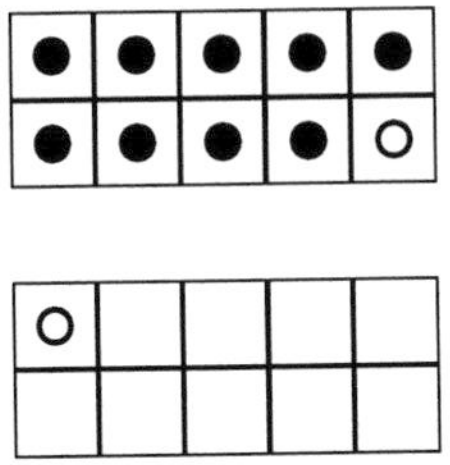	9 +2
11	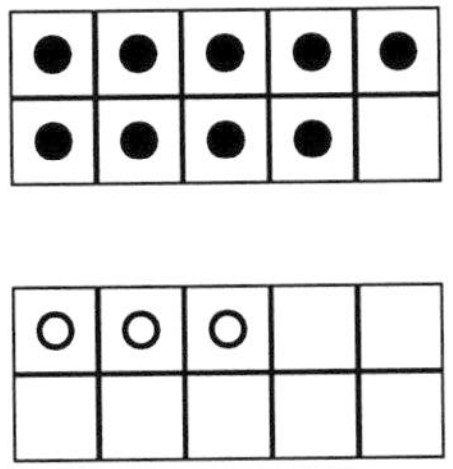	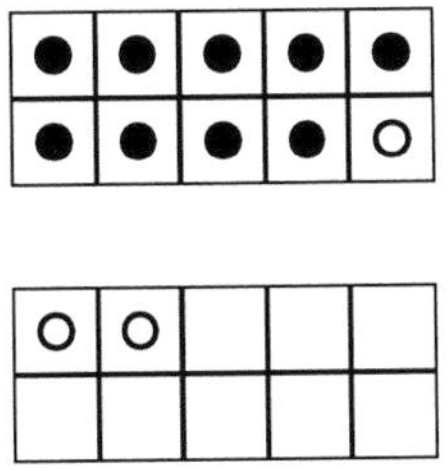	9 +3	12	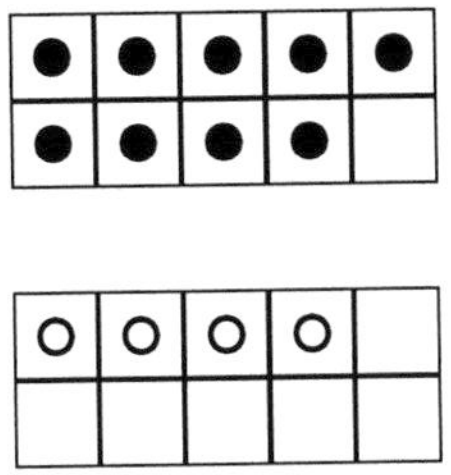	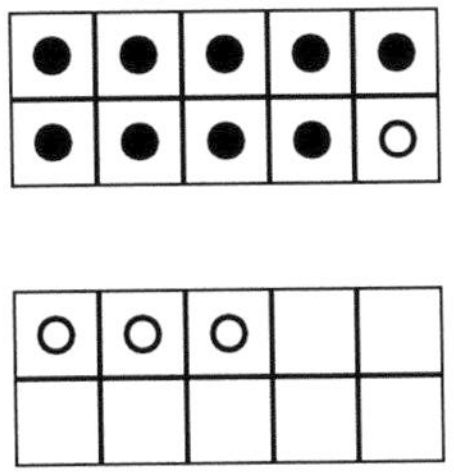
9 +4	13	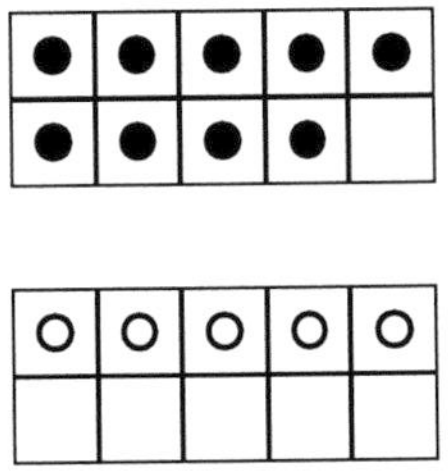	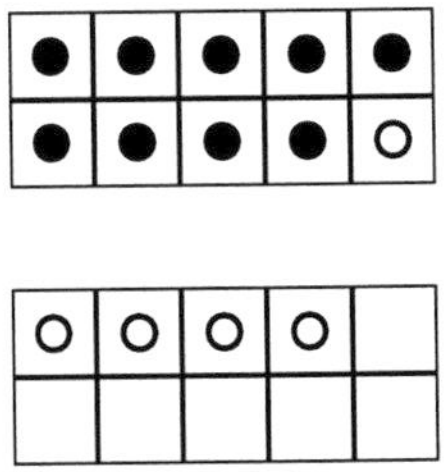	9 +5	14	

$$9 + 7$$

$$19$$

$$17$$

$$15$$

$$9 + 8$$

$$9 + 10$$

$$9 + 6$$

$$18$$

$$16$$

$$9 + 9$$

$$\begin{array}{r} 2 \\ + \\ \hline \end{array}$$

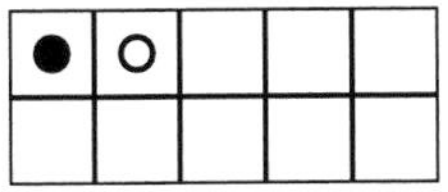

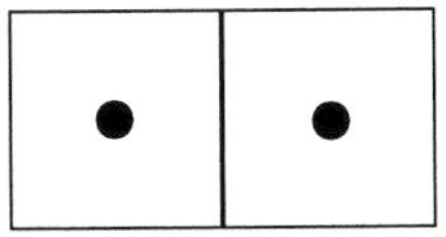

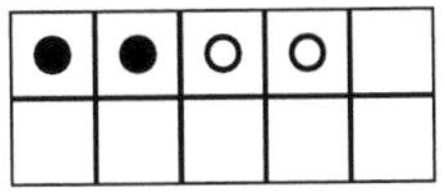

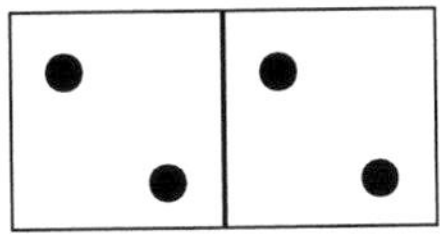

$$\begin{array}{r} 5 \\ +5 \\ \hline \end{array}$$

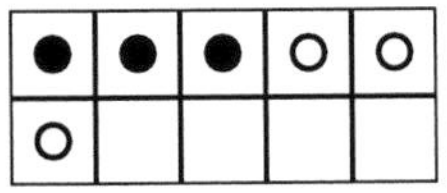

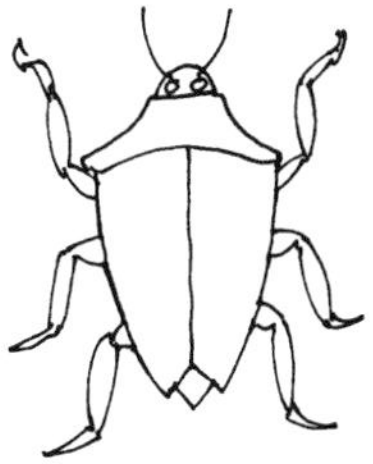

10

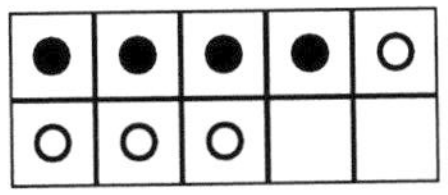

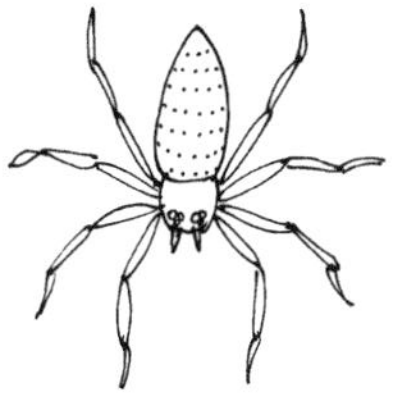

6

$$\begin{array}{r} 3 \\ +3 \\ \hline \end{array}$$

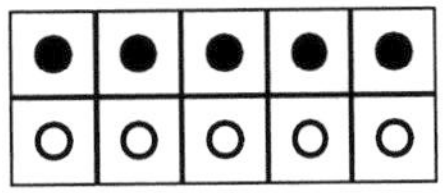

2

$$\begin{array}{r} 1 \\ +1 \\ \hline \end{array}$$

8

4

$$\begin{array}{r} 4 \\ +4 \\ \hline \end{array}$$

Level 3

$\begin{array}{r} 7 \\ +7 \\ \hline \end{array}$		
		20
	16	$\begin{array}{r} 10 \\ +10 \\ \hline \end{array}$
12	$\begin{array}{r} 8 \\ +8 \\ \hline \end{array}$	
$\begin{array}{r} 6 \\ +6 \\ \hline \end{array}$		
		18
	14	$\begin{array}{r} 9 \\ +9 \\ \hline \end{array}$

Level 4

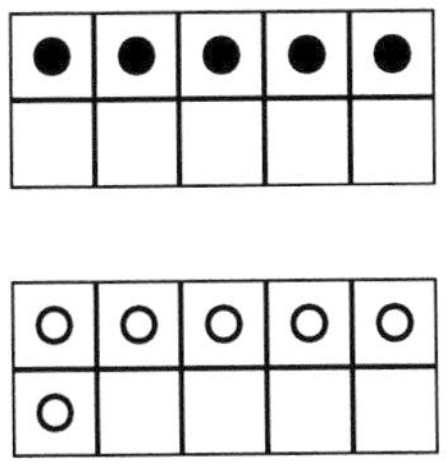	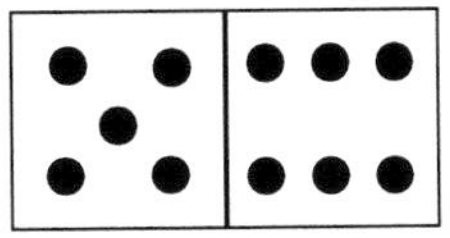	5 +6	11	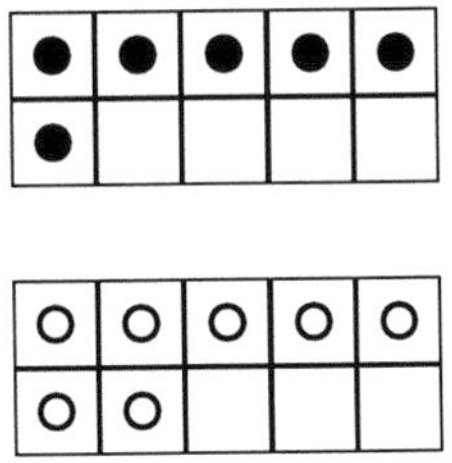	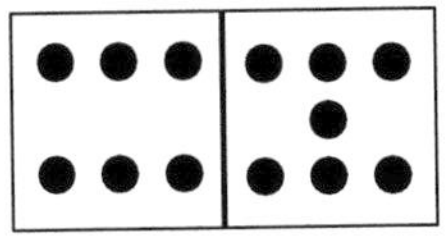	6 +7
13	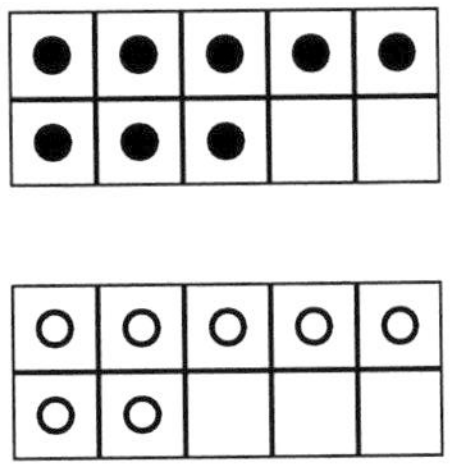	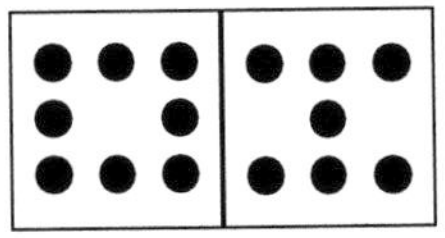	8 +7	15	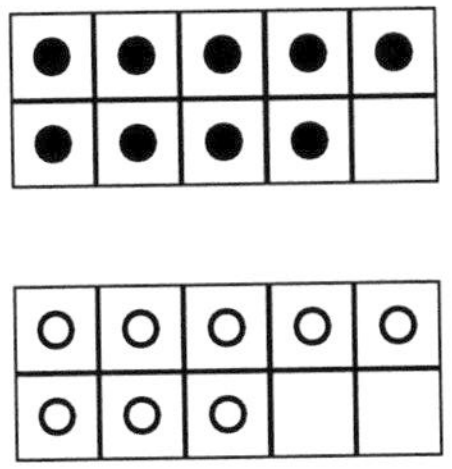	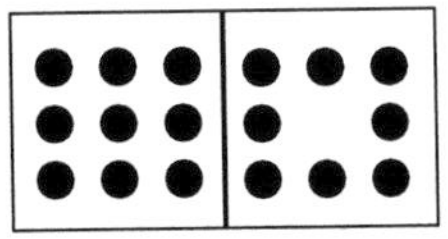
9 +8	17	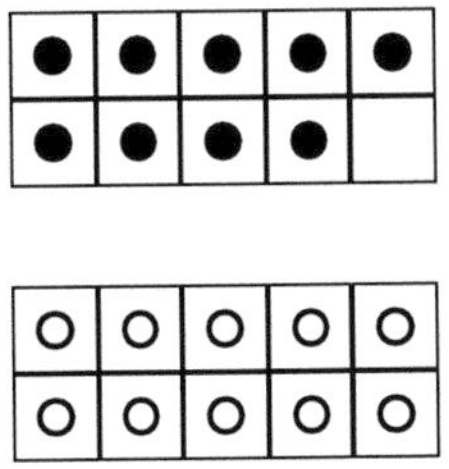	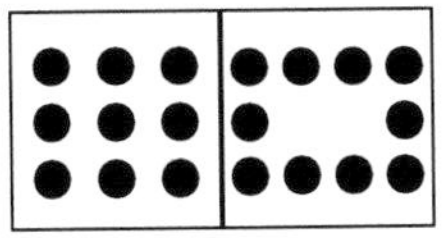	9 +10	19	

$$2 \atop +1$$

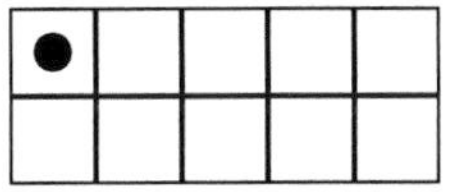

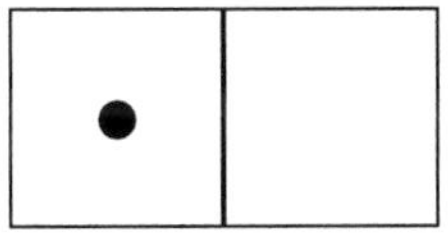

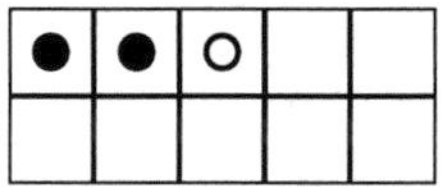

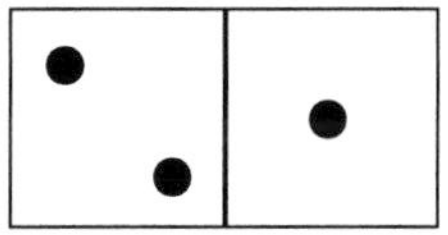

9

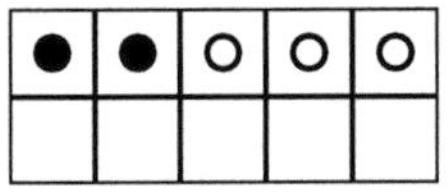

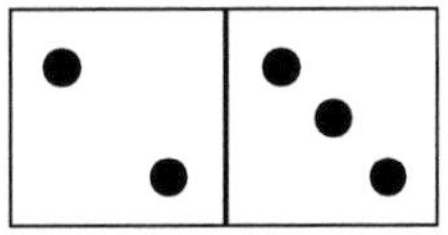

$$5 \atop +4$$

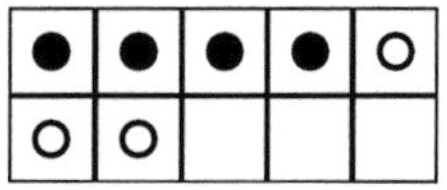

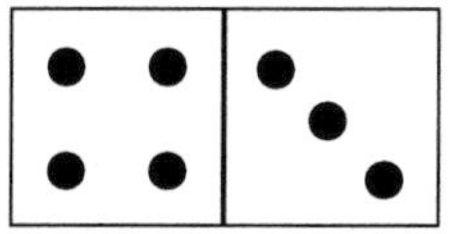

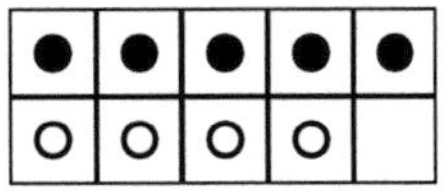

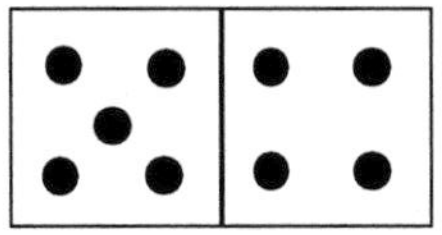

5

1

$$2 \atop +3$$

$$1 \atop +0$$

7

3

$$4 \atop +3$$

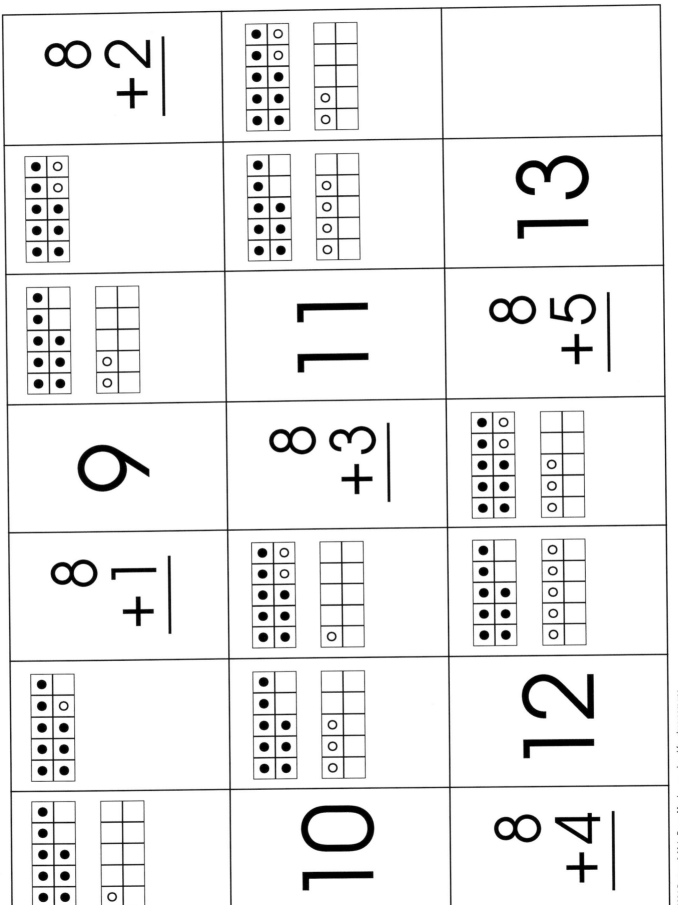

$$8 + 7$$

$$18$$

$$16$$

$$14$$

$$8 + 8$$

$$8 + 10$$

$$8 + 6$$

$$17$$

$$15$$

$$8 + 9$$

Level 6

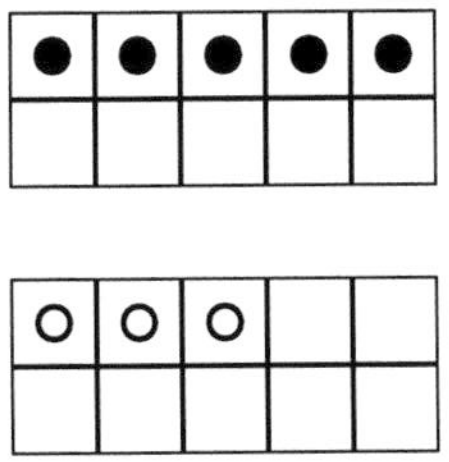	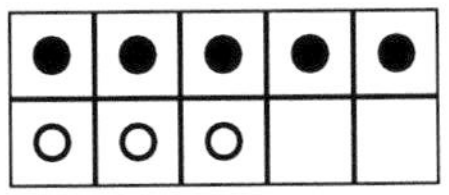	$5 + 3$	8	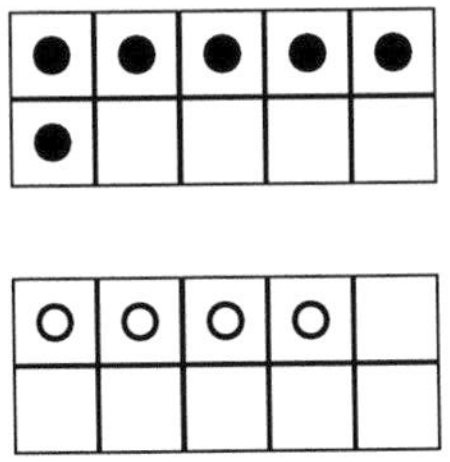	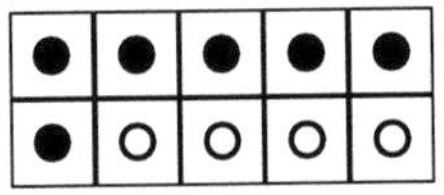	$6 + 4$
10	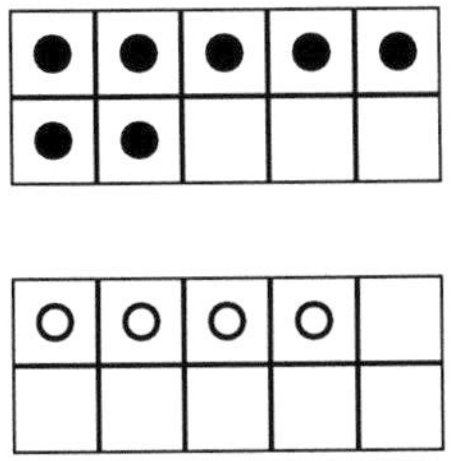	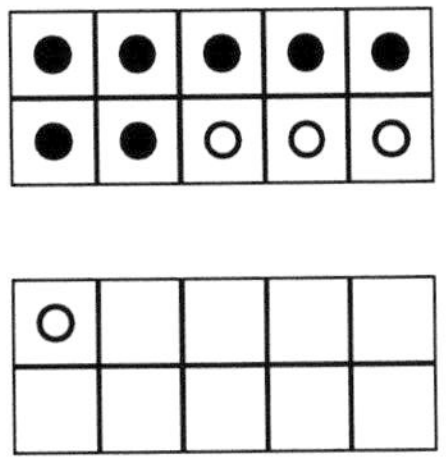	$7 + 4$	11	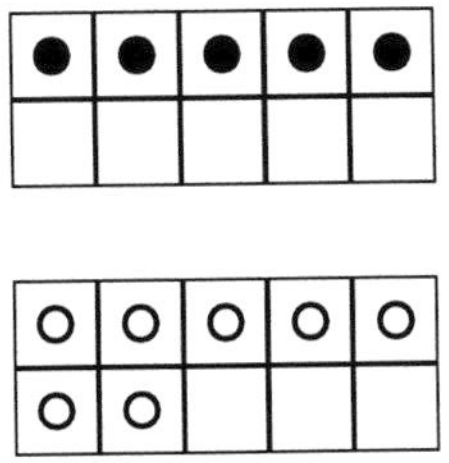	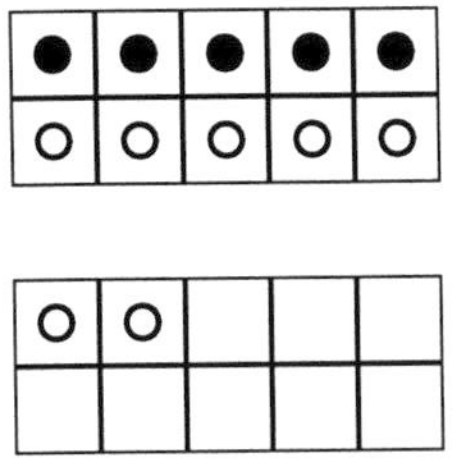
$5 + 7$	12	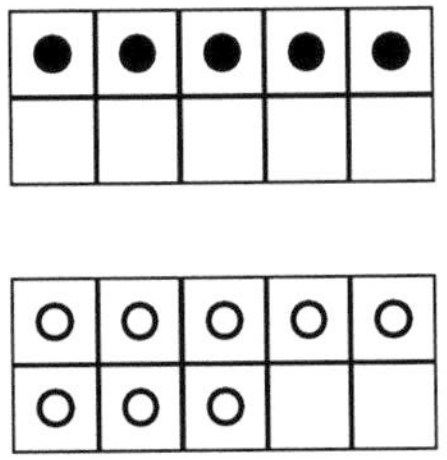	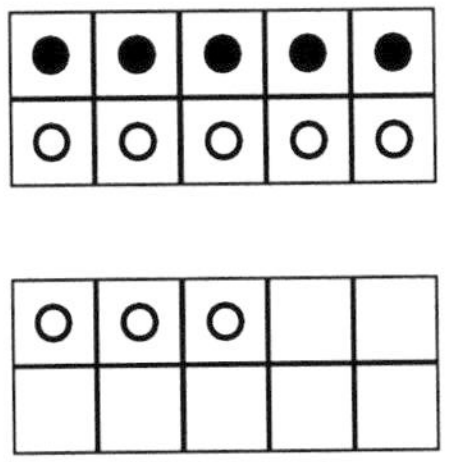	$5 + 8$	13	

$$7 + 8$$

$$9 + 9$$

$$8 + 8$$

$$6 + 8$$

$$8 + 9$$

18

16

14

17

15

APPENDIX
E

TEMPLATES

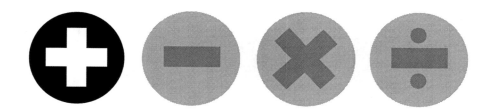

Ten-Frame Mat

Working Ten-Frames

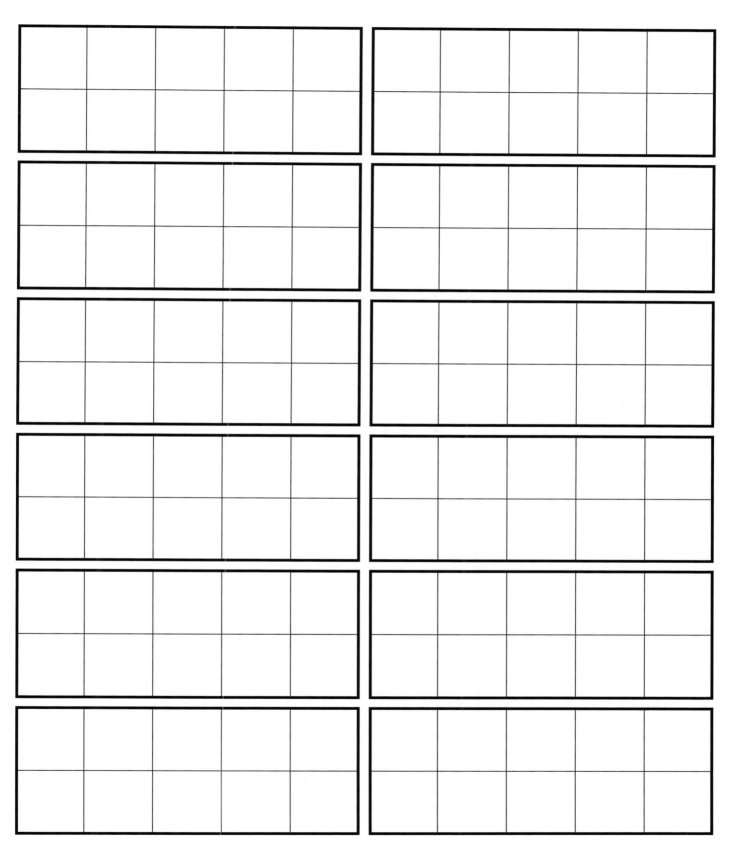

Working Ten-Frames

Working Ten-Frames

Mini Ten-Frames

Ten-Frame Train

Number Cards

0

1

2

3

Number Cards

4

5

6

7

Number Cards

8

9

10

11

Number Cards

12 | 13

14 | 15

Number Cards

16 17

18 19

Number Cards

20|30

10

Number Cards

Number Cards

APPENDIX
F

ANSWER KEYS

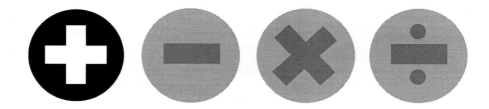

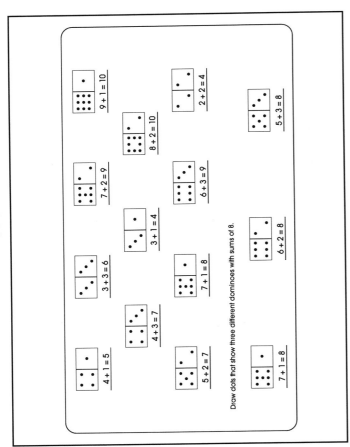

Lesson 1A, page 9

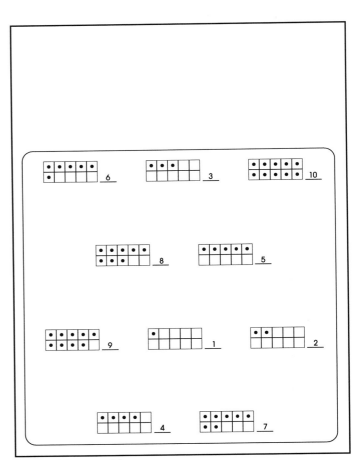

Lesson 1B, page 11

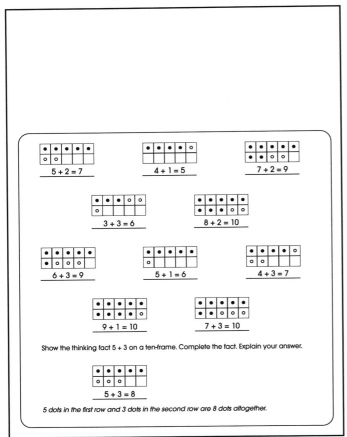

Lesson 1C, page 13

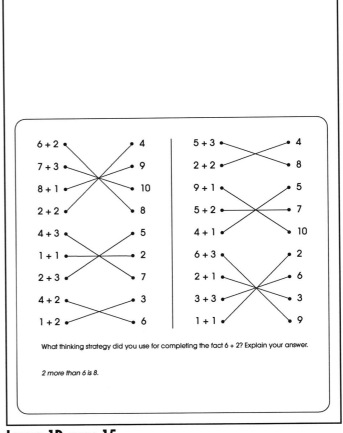

Lesson 1D, page 15

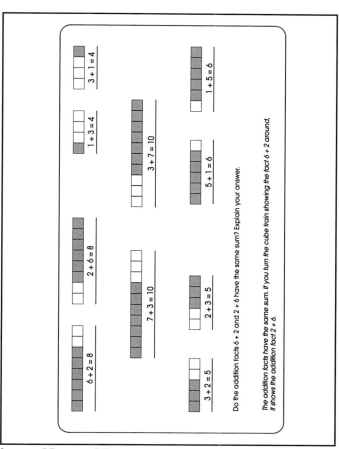

Lesson 1E, page 17

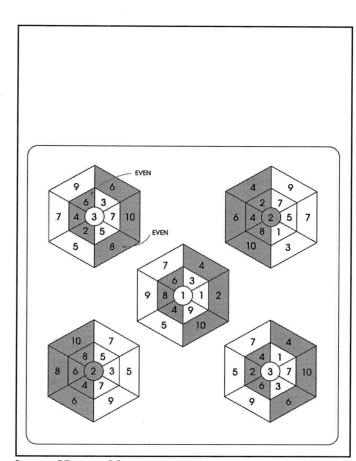

Lesson 1F, page 19

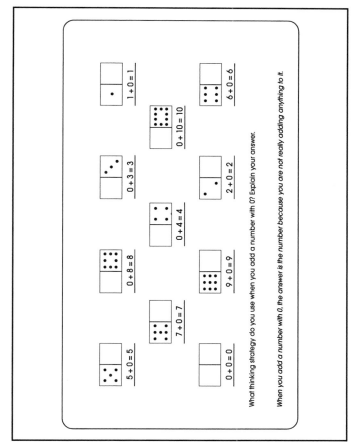

Lesson 1G, page 21

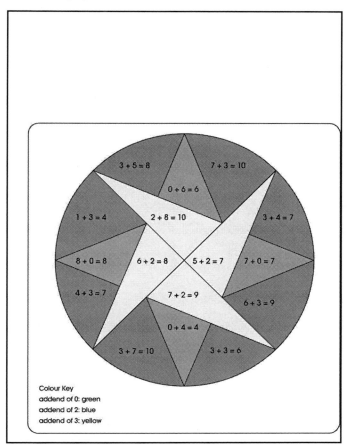

Lesson 1H, page 23

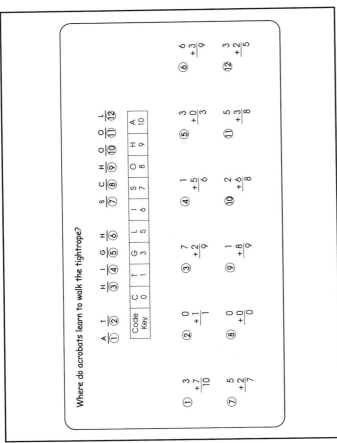

Lesson 1I, page 25

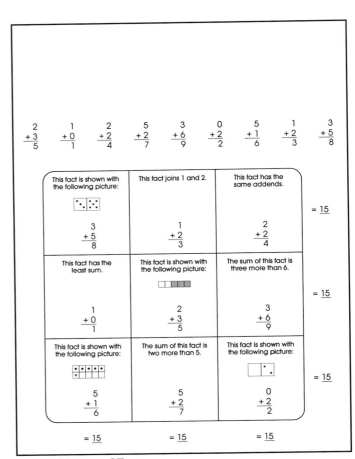

Lesson 1J, page 27

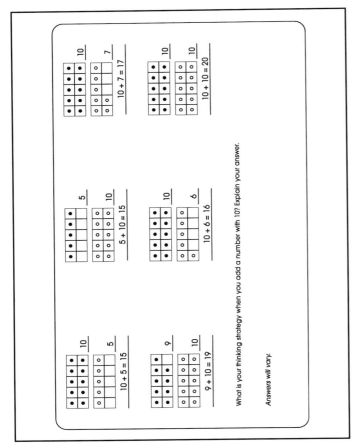

Lesson 2A, page 33

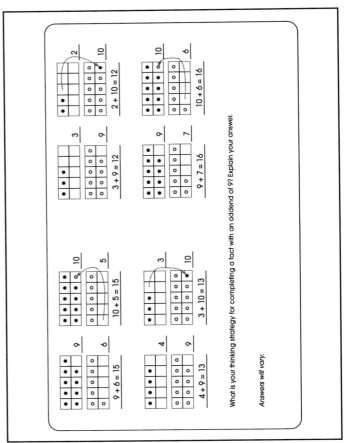

Lesson 2B, page 35

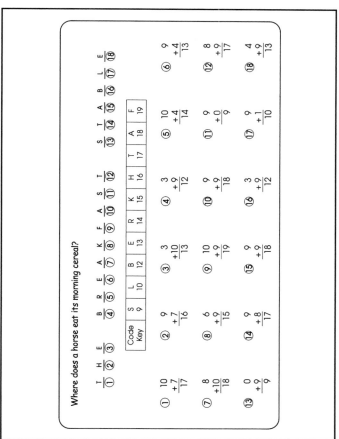

Lesson 2C, page 37

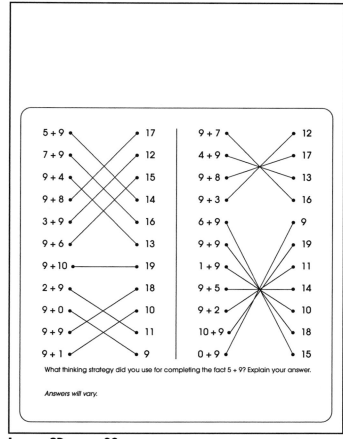

Lesson 2D, page 39

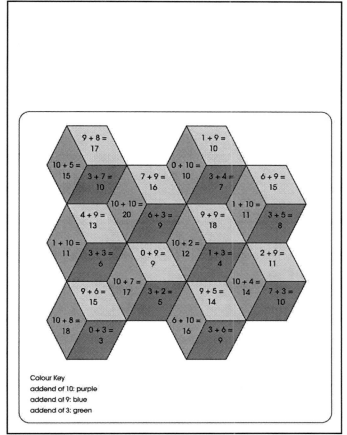

Lesson 2E, page 41

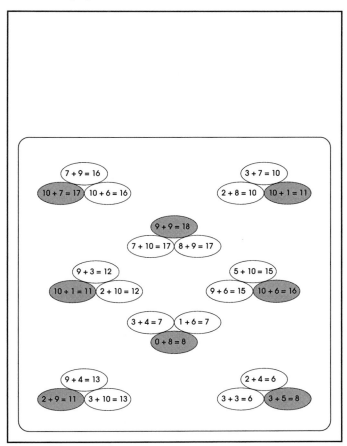

Lesson 2F, page 43

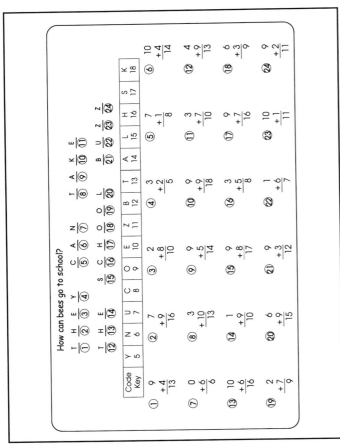

Lesson 2G, page 45

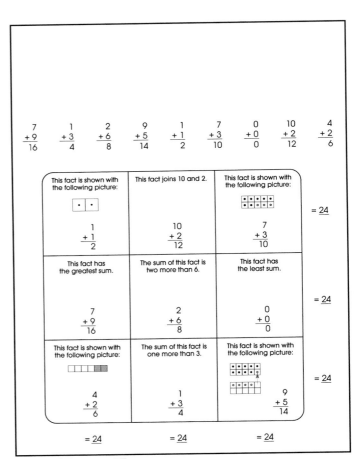

Lesson 2H, page 47

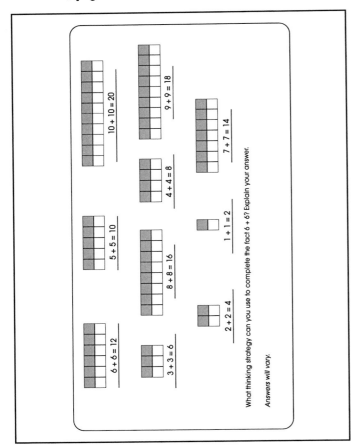

Lesson 3A, page 53

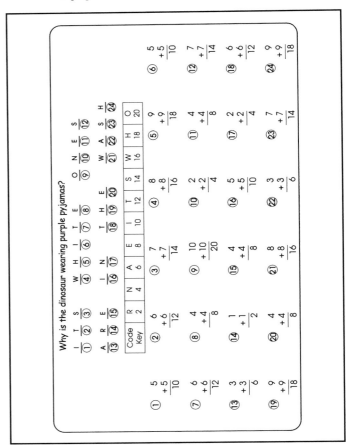

Lesson 3B, page 55

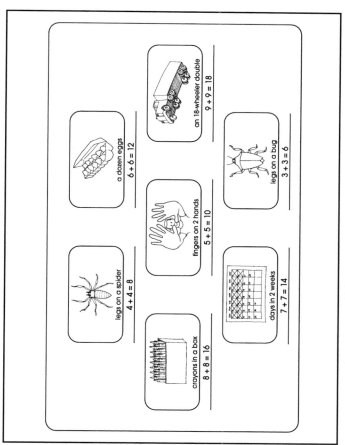

Lesson 3C, page 57

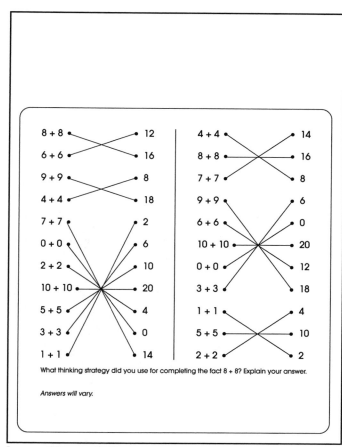

What thinking strategy did you use for completing the fact 8 + 8? Explain your answer.

Answers will vary.

Lesson 3D, page 59

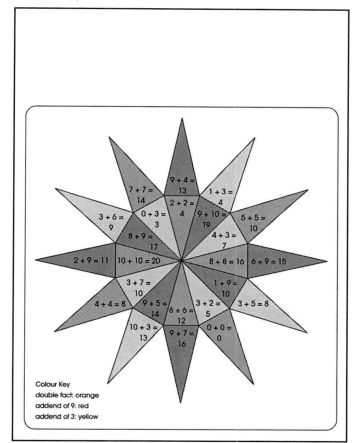

Lesson 3E, page 61

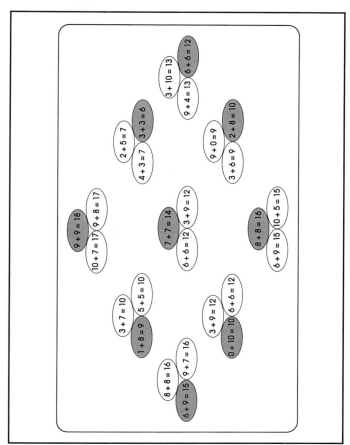

Lesson 3F, page 63

STUDENT ACTIVITY SHEETS

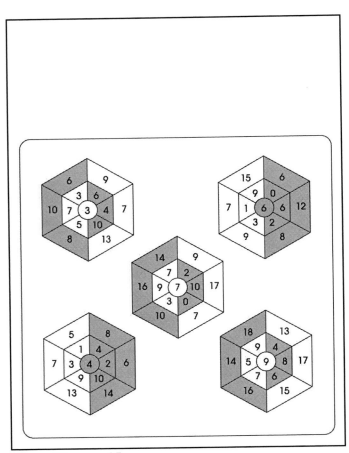

Lesson 3G, page 65

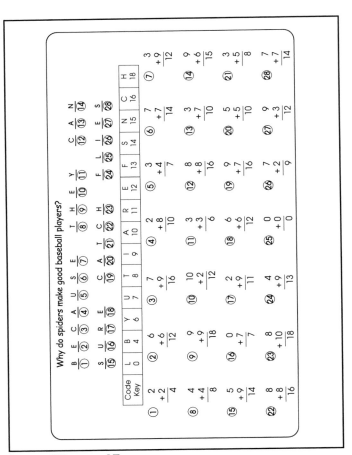

Lesson 3H, page 67

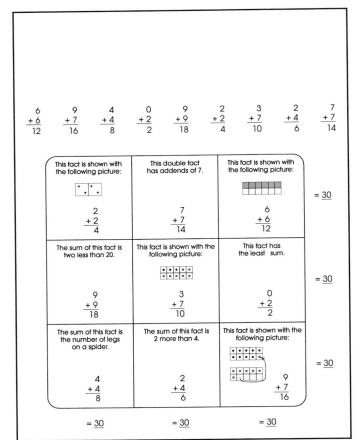

Lesson 3I, page 69

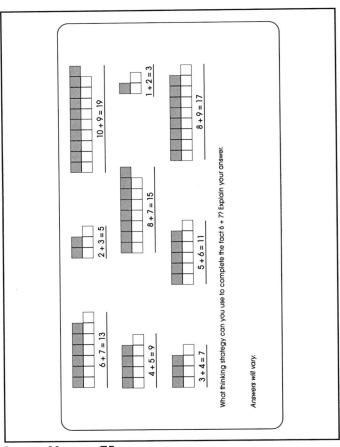

Lesson 4A, page 75

240

APPENDIX F

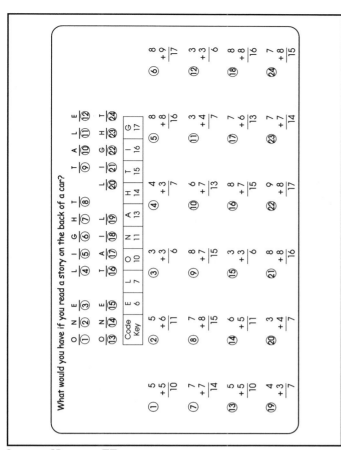

Lesson 4B, page 77

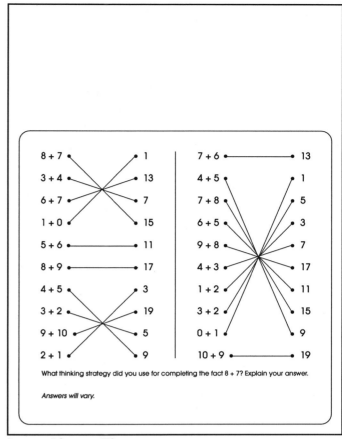

What thinking strategy did you use for completing the fact 8 + 7? Explain your answer.

Answers will vary.

Lesson 4C, page 79

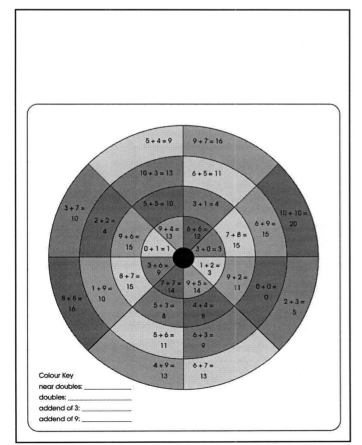

Colour Key
near doubles: _____
doubles: _____
addend of 3: _____
addend of 9: _____

Lesson 4D, page 81

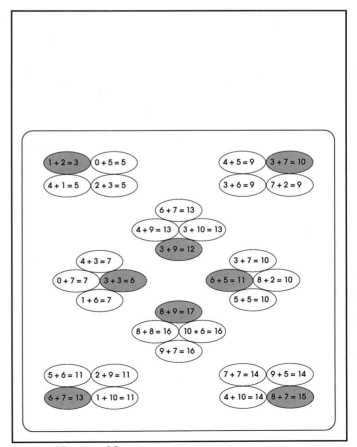

Lesson 4E, page 83

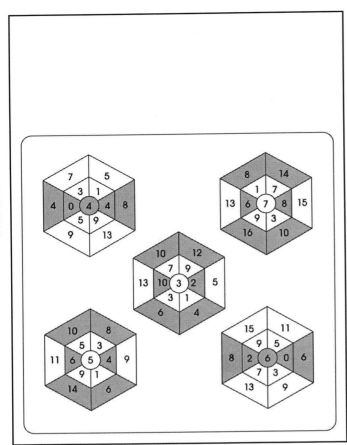

Lesson 4F, page 85

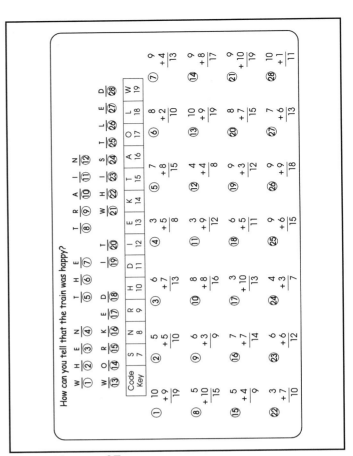

Lesson 4G, page 87

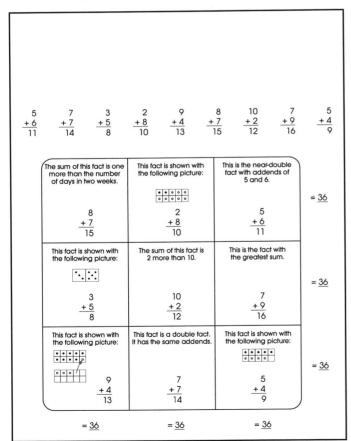

Lesson 4H, page 89

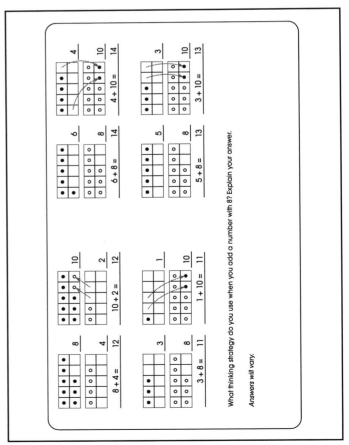

Lesson 5A, page 95

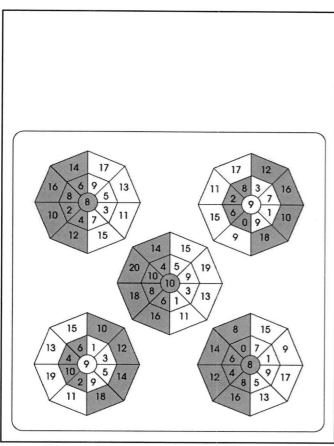

Lesson 5B, page 97

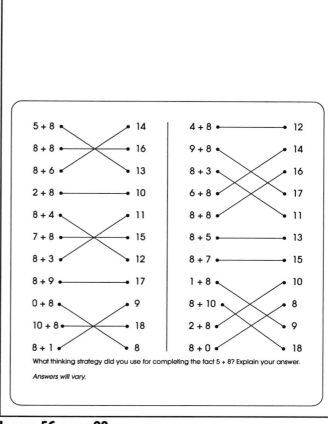

What thinking strategy did you use for completing the fact 5 + 8? Explain your answer.

Answers will vary.

Lesson 5C, page 99

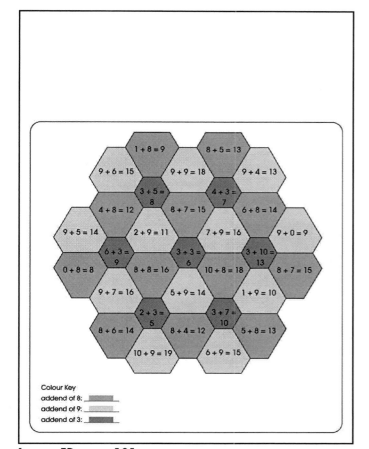

Lesson 5D, page 101

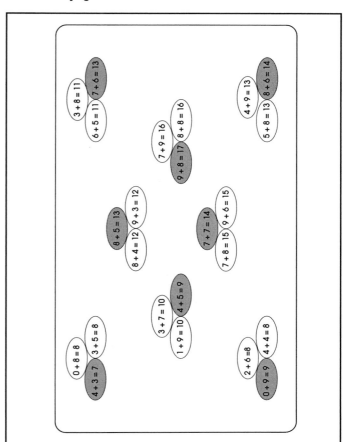

Lesson 5E, page 103

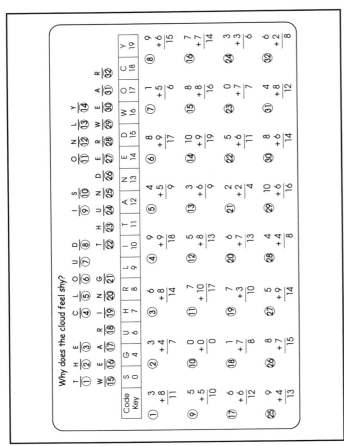

Lesson 5F, page 105

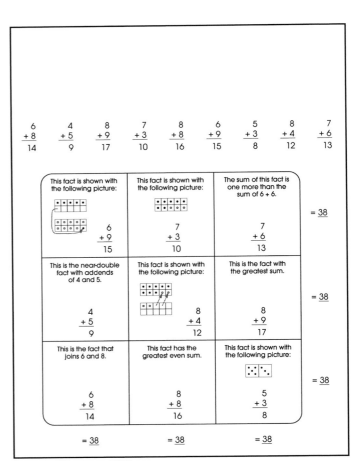

Lesson 5G, page 107

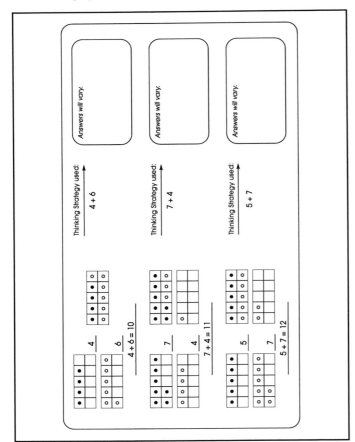

Lesson 6A, page 113

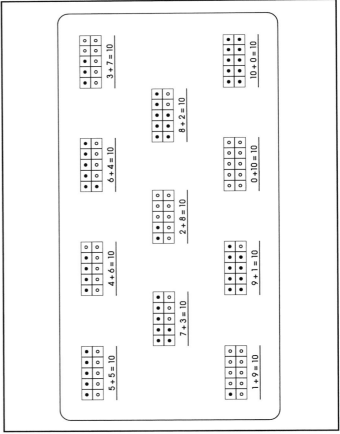

Lesson 6B, page 115

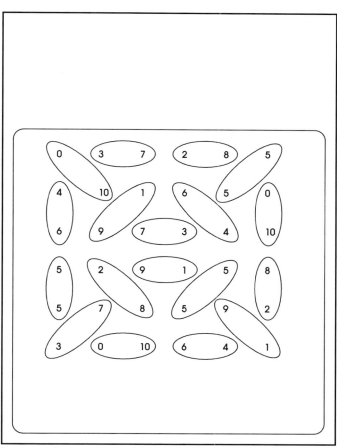

Lesson 6C, page 117

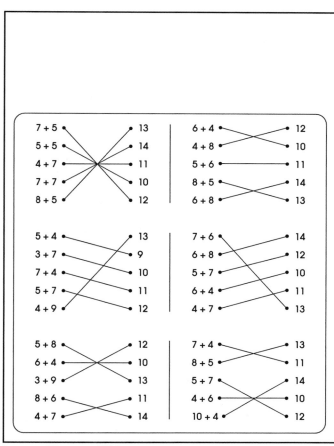

Lesson 6D, page 119

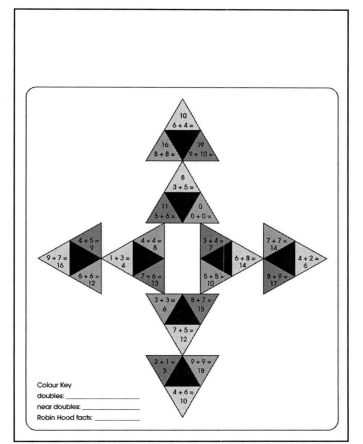

Lesson 6E, page 121

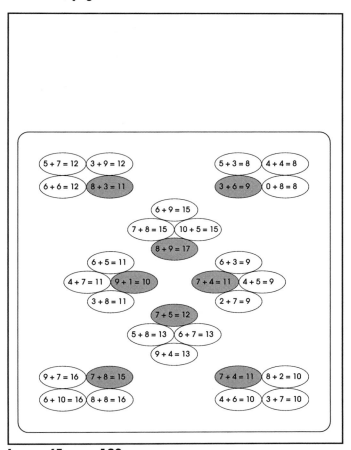

Lesson 6F, page 123

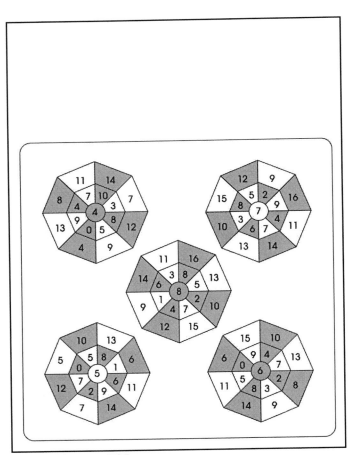

Lesson 6G, page 125

Why are the students wearing bathing suits to school?

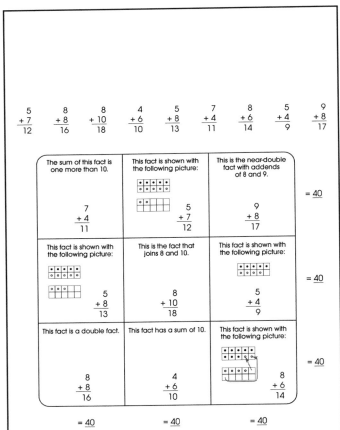

Lesson 6H, page 127

$$\begin{array}{cc} 5 \\ +7 \\ \hline 12 \end{array} \quad \begin{array}{c} 8 \\ +8 \\ \hline 16 \end{array} \quad \begin{array}{c} 8 \\ +10 \\ \hline 18 \end{array} \quad \begin{array}{c} 4 \\ +6 \\ \hline 10 \end{array} \quad \begin{array}{c} 5 \\ +8 \\ \hline 13 \end{array} \quad \begin{array}{c} 7 \\ +4 \\ \hline 11 \end{array} \quad \begin{array}{c} 8 \\ +6 \\ \hline 14 \end{array} \quad \begin{array}{c} 5 \\ +4 \\ \hline 9 \end{array} \quad \begin{array}{c} 9 \\ +8 \\ \hline 17 \end{array}$$

The sum of this fact is one more than 10. $\begin{array}{c}7\\+4\\\hline 11\end{array}$	This fact is shown with the following picture: $\begin{array}{c}5\\+7\\\hline 12\end{array}$	This is the near-double fact with addends of 8 and 9. $\begin{array}{c}9\\+8\\\hline 17\end{array}$
This fact is shown with the following picture: $\begin{array}{c}5\\+8\\\hline 13\end{array}$	This is the fact that joins 8 and 10. $\begin{array}{c}8\\+10\\\hline 18\end{array}$	This fact is shown with the following picture: $\begin{array}{c}5\\+4\\\hline 9\end{array}$
This fact is a double fact. $\begin{array}{c}8\\+8\\\hline 16\end{array}$	This fact has a sum of 10. $\begin{array}{c}4\\+6\\\hline 10\end{array}$	This fact is shown with the following picture: $\begin{array}{c}8\\+6\\\hline 14\end{array}$

= 40   = 40   = 40

Lesson 6I, page 129

PARTNER BINGO

1.   Partner #1: third row across

2.   Partner #2: diagonal from lower left corner

3.   Partner #1: third column down

4.   Partner #2: third column down

5.   Partner #1: first column down

6.   Partner #2: fourth row across

7.   Partner #1: second row across

8.   Partner #1: first column down

9.   Partner #2: second column down

10.   Partner #1: fifth column down

11.   Partner #2: fourth column down

12.   Partner #2: diagonal from upper left corner

13.   Partner #2: fourth row across

14.   Partner #1: fifth row across

15.   Partner #2: third row across

16.   Partner #2: fourth column down

17.   Partner #1: diagonal from upper left corner

18.   Partner #1: second column down

19.   Partner #2: second column down

20.   Partner #1: first row across

21.   Partner #2: first row across

22.   Partner #1: third column down

23.   Partner #2: second row across

24.   Partner #1: third column down

25.   Partner #1: fourth row across

26.   Partner #2: first column down

27.   Partner #2: third row across

28.   Partner #1: second row across

29.   Partner #2: fifth column down

30.   Partner #1: diagonal from lower left corner

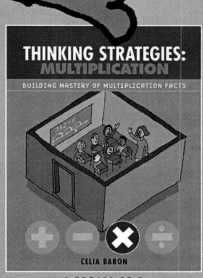
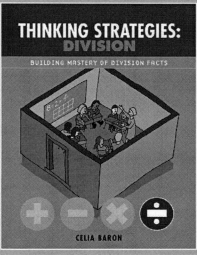

PROBLEM-SOLVING PUZZLES

A THINKING STRATEGIES RESOURCE

30 PUZZLES IN EACH PACKET

1-55379-073-1

1-55379-076-6

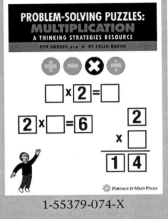

1-55379-074-X

1-55379-075-8

Problem-Solving Puzzles provide your students with additional practice for the basic facts.

These puzzles reinforce the skills taught in the Thinking Strategies resources by giving your students an opportunity to:

- practice selecting and using their thinking strategies
- develop their basic fact fluency
- practice their mental math skills

- improve their number sense skills
- use their problem-solving abilities
- self-correct their work

CHOOSE FROM FOUR EASY WAYS TO ORDER.

...hotocopy this form.

PORTAGE & MAIN PRESS

MAIL TO:
100 – 318 McDermot Avenue
Winnipeg, Manitoba, Canada R3A 0A2

CALL TOLL FREE: 1-800–667–9673
FAX TOLL FREE: 1-866-734-8477
ONLINE ORDER: www.portageandmainpress.com

NAME

ADDRESS

CITY   PROVINCE/STATE

POSTAL CODE/ZIP CODE   PHONE

METHOD OF PAYMENT

❏ Purchase Order Attached   ❏ Cheque or Money Order Enclosed   ❏ VISA ❏ MasterCard

CREDIT CARD #

SIGNATURE

EXPIRY DATE

Problem-Solving Puzzles: Addition_____copy(ies)
Problem-Solving Puzzles: Subtraction_____copy(ies)
Problem-Solving Puzzles: Multiplication_____copy(ies)
Problem-Solving Puzzles: Division_____copy(ies)
Total number of copy(ies)_____ @ $25 each

Shipping & Handling
$1 – $60 ....$8.50
$61 – over 10%
*shipping and prices
subject to change

Subtotal _____

Shipping & Handling _____

Add 7% GST/HST _____
(IN CANADA ONLY)
Total _____

www.portageandmainpress.com